XX CENTURY ARCHITECTURE

Matteo Siro Baborsky

XXCENTURY
ARCHITECTURE

WILEY-ACADEMY

Translation from Italian by
Jay Hyams

Published in Great Britain in 2003 by Wiley-Academy a division of
John Wiley & Sons, Ltd., The Atrium, Southern Gate, Chichester,
West Sussex, PO19 8SQ, England
National 01243 779777
International (+44) 1243 779777

E-mail (for orders and customer service enquiries): cs-books@wiley.co.uk

Visit our Home Page on www.wileyeurope.com or www.wiley.com

This publication is designed to provide accurate and authoritative information in regard to the
subject matter covered. It is sold with on the understanding that the Publisher is not engaged in
rendering professional services. If professional advice or other expert assistance is required, the
services of a competent professional should be sought.

Other Wiley Editorial Offices

John Wiley & Sons, Inc., 111 River Street, Hoboken, NJ 07030, USA

Jossey-Bass, 989 Market Street, San Francisco, CA 94103-1741, USA

Wiley-VCH Verlag GmbH, Boschstr. 12, D-69469 Weinheim, Germany

Jacaranda Wiley Ltd, 33 Park Road, Milton, Queensland 4064

John Wiley & Sons (Asia) Pte Ltd, 2 Clementi Loop #02-01, Jin Xing Distripark, Singapore 129809

John Wiley & Sons (Canada) Ltd, 22 Worcester Road, Etobicoke, Ontario, Canada, M9W 1L1

724.9 BAR

ISBN 04708587880

Printed and bound in Italy

A004690 1
£ 19.99
28 /11/06

Contents

Introduction

"To my parents and to their beautiful craft" (M.S.B.)

March 1, 1998, Forty-second Street in New York City: The considerable mass of the Empire Theater, mounted on steel rails, is relocated fifty meters to the west to reach Eighth Avenue, apparently dragged into position by a pair of nine-meter-tall balloons of Abbott and Costello. The operation, part of the large-scale program of urban renewal taking place in the area around Times Square with the aim of restoring the square's theatrical and commercial potential, included converting the "historic" building—it first opened its doors in 1912—into the atrium of the new AMC Theater, equipped with twenty-five screens and 31,000 square meters of space. Without going into the details of the complicated operation involved in the relocation, which was nothing new to the history of modern engineering and structural operations—there was, for example, the movement of the Egyptian temples of Abu Simbel—we can affirm, straying into the territory of analogy, that on March 1, 1998, in the heart of Manhattan, Abbott and Costello challenged Vitruvius. Given the time required for the various phases of the operation, the slicing off at the foundations of the Empire Theater obliterated the statute of *firmitas* ("soundness") which, along with those of *utilitas* ("utility") and *venustas* ("beauty"), form the so-called triad that is the basis of Vitruvius's treatise, which dates to the age of the Roman emperor Augustus, and in the pages of which, taken from successive editions, is written: "All these works should be executed so that they exhibit the principles of soundness, utility, and beauty. The principle of soundness will be observed if the foundations have been laid firmly." Therefore, the staggering distance of fifty meters, incredibly covered by a building that walks, can assume the status of metaphor for the

Frank Lloyd Wright, Fallingwater, Bear Run, Pennsylvania, 1934–1937

Aldo Rossi, Bonnefanten Museum, Maastricht, 1990–1994

indefatigable progress of the new architectonic science that, today more than ever, associates the decline in the notion of *firmitas* with a celebration of new and unsettling paradigms. The longed-for dynamicity in the architectonic space that has been prophesized by every avant-garde movement since the beginning of the twentieth century seems, in point of fact, to have reached the stage of complete feasibility thanks to developments in computers and digital design. Set free from all the right-angled, box-like configurations of the traditional past, walls, beams, columns, and roofs extend upwards and expand outwards in complete safety right up to the point of static paradox, generating a new "informatic landscape," magically unstable and dynamic, with the safety and price of each new structure verifiable by new models

Frank O. Gehry, Guggenheim Museum, Bilbao, 1991–1997

of mathematical calculation, based, if necessary, on the technology of aerospace simulations. Even so, in its drive for innovative reforms, which translates into an informal architectonic language, this new, informational avant-garde— exactly like the more radical avant-gardes of the early twentieth century—has established a relationship with the history of architecture that, as happened in the difficult birth of Modern architecture, oscillates between rejection and celebration of the past. Whether through negation or continuity, no architecture can avoid a relationship with history, and that relationship, with all its discontinuity, can be seen to form a thin red thread that unites the twentieth-century architects assembled in the pages of this book and arranged here alphabetically by name. Apparently unconvinced by the doctrines of the

Moving the Empire
Theater, New York, 1998
(first phase)

Moving the Empire
Theater, New York, 1998
(second phase)

Richard Rogers, Lloyd's of
London, London, 1978–1986

Modern movement, which, in the hope
of achieving the much desired liberation
from the academic stylistic codes of the past,
prophesized a new architectonic style in keeping
with the progress made in technology and
industrial production, history continued to make
its appearance as an instrument of architectonic
design throughout the twentieth century,
apparently as necessary to architecture as any
building material. From the classical stylistic
elements evoked and reworked in the earliest
manifestations of protorationalism and industrial
architecture to the structural conquests
of nineteenth-century engineering that led
to the twentieth-century use of new materials,
increasingly resistant yet incredibly flexible,
to the ostentatious display of classical tympana
and columns that is an aspect of contemporary
historicism, Modern architecture has maintained

its relationship with tradition, so much so that the evolutionary route towards the promised land of progress has been anything but linear.

The proving ground and acid test of this contradictory background to Modern architecture has been the modern city, in which the act of building now confronts social and cultural values and in which the architectonic phenomena must adapt to a plurality of meanings that have become increasingly difficult to foresee in the planning and design stages.

The buildings presented in this book would not fit the commodious but out-of-date definitions of masterpieces of the twentieth century. Rather, they are meant to reveal the internal contradictions in the birth of the Modern phenomenon in architecture, describing, as far as possible, the plurality of meanings that the creation of an architectonic organism involves.

Auguste Perret, house in rue Franklin, Paris, 1903–1904

Paul Bonatz, dam on
the Neckar River at
Rockenau, 1926–1936

The entries, with their illustrations, give
preference to individual buildings built anywhere
in the world over the course of the twentieth
century. Each entry is designed to be
independent, consultable separately from
the others that compose the volume.
A quotation, almost always from the architect
involved, opens each entry, giving the reader
an immediate sense of the building's ideological
and architectural background and introducing
the work within a gamut that runs from
the inheritance of Modern architecture
to the present day—with excuses on the part
of the author for the omission of favorites.
The book ends with biographies of the architects
of the illustrated works.

William S. Eames, Roth
& Study, water intake towers
on the Mississippi River,
St Louis, 1894 and 1915

Following page
Oswald M. Ungers,
Ungers House, Utscheid,
Eifel, 1986–1988

The works

Workers' Club, Jyväskylä, Finland
1924–1925

"Our ancestors will forever be our masters"(A.A.)

In 1924 the young Alvar Aalto was in Florence, an obligatory stop during a trip to Italy for any aspiring artist and in this case destined to prove decisive in the Finnish architect's career. It can also be seen as having been an important moment in that version of art history—a version by no means new to the culture of the Nordic countries—according to which the Mediterranean area was the cradle of classical architecture, perhaps even the birthplace of Western civilization. This concept was now to lead to a new form of classicism,

Nordic Classicism, a sensibility and a viewpoint based on an imaginary encounter between the Baltic Sea and the Mediterranean.

Looked at in this way, the Workers' Club building in Jyväskylä can be judged an excellent example of Italian culture transplanted to a Nordic city. Aalto treated the building, which was based on the architectural typology of the Italian Renaissance palace, as a total work of art,

unrelated to the surrounding urban context. He designed every aspect of it, down to the smallest detail, including the furnishings and illumination. The Workers' Club is located on an intersection, and each of its four façades is different, almost as though designed to be seen separately; they are connected one to another only by a Doric colonnade of slightly differing spans that runs along the ground floor of the building. Inside the building is a theater, with seating for 400, that is distinguished by the curving wall of the stage; there are also rooms for a café, maintenance facilities, services, and a restaurant. It is in the curve of the gallery wall in the area of the foyer that Aalto made his most explicit reference to what he had learned during his stay in Florence. There can be no doubt but that the two-color decoration that stands out along the curve of the wall is modeled on the Rucellai Chapel in San Pancrazio in Florence, designed by the architect Leon Battista Alberti between 1461 and 1467. In adapting this decoration to the large area of the curving wall, Aalto was forced to distort the original model, but even so he faithfully repeated the chapel's circular marble inlays set within polychrome squares. This youthful work by Aalto is thus clearly marked by an open dialogue with history; so much so, in fact, that the design for the Workers' Club represents a reinterpretation of a model from the past that succeeds in transforming itself into a new and unusual compositional theme.

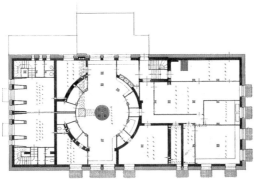

Alvar Aalto 1898–1976

Paimio Sanatorium, Paimio, Finland
1929–1933

"Truly functional architecture must be functional from the human point of view"(A.A.)

In distinguishing the linguistic canon of "organic" architecture from the stylistic features of rationalist architecture recourse is most often made to the use of contrasting terms, such as realism versus idealism, naturalism versus stylistic quirks, tradition versus innovation, regular forms versus those that are irregular, and closed, rigid geometry versus dynamic shapes in a state of continuous evolution. All of this to describe a stylistic approach distinguished by a strong preference for free forms that respond to the laws of nature and are created in an infinite variety using a wealth of materials.

It is common custom to divide the work of Alvar Aalto into two periods, the first Constructivist, the second organic. To the first period belong those works in which the typical Nordic Classicism is flanked by a technological sensibility inspired by the dictates of functionalism; the second period includes works in which the dialogue with nature and efforts to achieve harmony played a fundamental role in the genesis of each project. The Paimio Sanatorium falls along the thin line that separates the two periods in the architect's career. For many reasons the sanatorium can be said to meet to the requirements that are typical of functional

architecture (the correctness of its planimetric distribution, the use of natural and artificial illumination, the importance given to air circulation); at the same time, however, every technical aspect of the sanatorium reveals deep psychological reflection on the part of the architect. The three linear structures that compose the sanatorium, arranged across the landscape as distinct bodies, serve to divide the various departments of the sanatorium into separate wings, with one for the patients' rooms, one for the kitchen and dining rooms, and one for the staff offices and

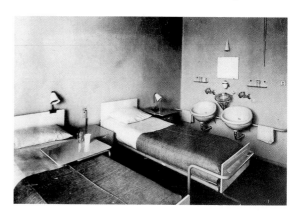

general services. The structures follow the slope of the ground and are positioned so as to exploit as much as possible the heat and light of the sun (the patients awaken in rooms warmed by the morning light, and in the afternoon, as the sun sets in the west, they are moved to a building facing in that direction). Aalto's design was not limited to the definition of the external shape of the volumes and instead extended

inward to the design of the furniture, the fixtures, every little detail, making clear even in the smallest dimension the goal of improving the quality of life of the patients.

During a conference in 1956, Aalto offered insight into some of the principles that he had followed for the project: "The building's main purpose is to function as a medical instrument . . . A primary requisite for healing people is offering them complete peace . . . The rooms were designed to accommodate the limited physical strength of the patients, lying in bed. The color of the ceiling was chosen to provide tranquility, the light sources are outside the field of vision of the patients, the heating is directed towards their feet, and the water runs in the wash basins without making any noise so that no one patient will disturb those in nearby beds."

Alvar Aalto 1898–1976

Civic Center, Säynätsalo, Finland
1948–1952

"I used the courtyard as the primary motif because in some mysterious way it awakens the social instinct" (A.A.)

Basic to the theory of environmentalism is the idea that a building should be in harmony with its surroundings. With the exception of some youthful works in which he demonstrates a close adhesion to the classical language, the relationship between architectonic form and natural landscape is such a constant aspect of the works created by Alvar Aalto that it can be taken as one of their distinguishing characteristics. In fact, the relationship with the site expressed in the form of a dialogue, the skillful use of local materials, and a sense of expressive freedom add up to rank Aalto's architecture among the most representative examples of the architectural style known as Scandinavian Neoempiricism, a movement that arose in northern Europe in 1930 and was a reaction against the functionalist dogma from central Europe. Rejecting functionalism's severity, it turned instead to a concern for the quality of life based on the recovery of certain psychological and human values.

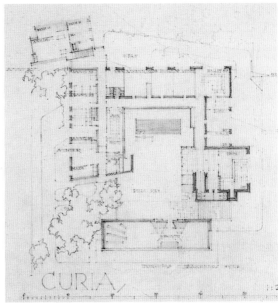

Among these values, a fundamental role was given the revival of various democratic ideals, taken as the bases for every collective and individual aspiration. Such ideals could be synthesized and manifested in the construction of a public building. Aalto, combining a close reading of the site with a revival of the typology of the courtyard house, gave the Säynätsalo Civic Center the sense of monumentality associated with the town halls of the past. The edifice has the form of a closed courtyard with lateral wings fitted to the slope of the surrounding landscape. The central area of the composition thus takes shape as an urban plaza, around which are a library and city offices. A long pathway leads from that plaza to the city hall. The pathway turns, rises, and falls as it follows the ups and downs of the hill on which the civic center stands, and the pathway has, as its final and unexpected conclusion, the entrance to the council chamber, which is 17 meters high and, like the rest of the complex, dressed in exposed brick. Because of the simplicity of the building materials used and the interrelationships among the volumes, the structure stands as one of the best syntheses between the adaptation of a natural landscape and the invention of an artificial one.

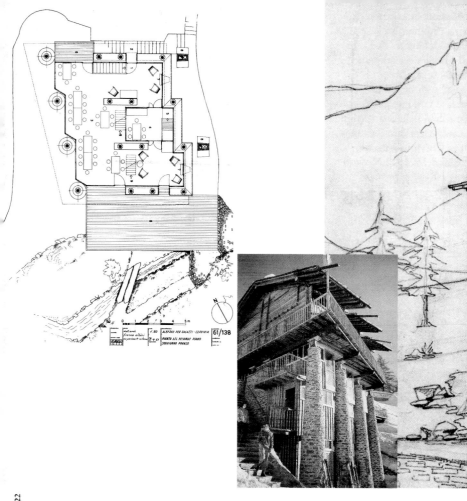

Rifugio Pirovano, Mountain Refuge, Cervinia, Italy

(with Luigi Colombini)
1948–1952

"All building methods are valid at all times provided they are logical and still efficient" (F.A.)

During the Fifth Triennale in Milan (1936), a photographic exhibition was held entitled "Rural Architecture in Italy," conceived by Giuseppe Pagano and assembled by Franco Albini, among others. Almost all of the photos had been taken by Pagano and had as their subject the large farmhouses, estates, suburban residences, cottages, and villas scattered over the Italian landscape. The myth of bright illumination, cleanliness, and functionalism typical of rationalist architecture was thus brought face to face with the innate values of anonymous, spontaneous structures with their simple, essential construction methods.

The Rifugio Pirovano can be considered the outstanding example of this renewed interest in rural architecture, an interest destined to influence several trends in contemporary international architecture. The layout of the mountain refuge follows the slope of the hill, with the individual internal units

arranged side by side or at an angle with respect of the line of the façade. The first three floors of the building are partially dug into the mountain, while the top floor and the attic below the roof stand well above the level of the terrain. The walls of the top two floors are made of horizontal wooden beams fitted together using the local *rascard* technique. The walls stand on long wooden beams held up by joints of local stone in a characteristic mushroom shape. These beam-supporting joints, as well as the projecting terrace with its panoramic view of the valley, are in turn supported by massive rustic columns that taper upward. Shops are located on the ground floor, and the second has the refuge's centralized services; the third floor, with long, narrow, ribbon windows, is taken up by a large living room. The last two floors, designed to resemble a true Alpine hut, have the "units for nocturnal repose," which are reached by way of steep wooden stairs.

The use of a standard unit type that is repeated on the various floors, the long, ribbon windows, and the strikingly panoramic orientation give the structure a vaguely Modernist sensibility, but its integration with the surrounding Alpine landscape is achieved through the application of time-tested local building methods.

La Rinascente Department Store,

Rome, Italy
(with Franca Helg)
1957–1961

"The structural orchestration of a building is a technical decision, but at the same time it is an architectonic decision in the sense that it divides the volume into quiet rhythms"(Franca Helg)

It is a well known fact of the professional practice of

architecture that the efficient solution to any given technical problem almost always requires the abandonment of the more expressive and formal architectonic values of the building. With the exception of the more high-tech trends in Modern architecture that have as their expressed goal the ostentation of the forms and structures related to scientific progress, technological adaptations rarely assume esthetic values

in keeping with the original design of a project.

In 1957 the professional studio of Franco Albini and Franca Helg received the commission for the new La Rinascente department store in Rome. The large store, with its closed, compact volume, was to occupy a corner lot between Piazza Fiume and Via Salaria, a very central area near the Aurelian Walls surrounded by residential housing dating to the late

nineteenth century. Presented as a large, multistoried container, the building has three underground floors and seven above ground. The underground floors, made of reinforced concrete, house the services and the physical plant. The seven above-ground floors are the store's salesrooms and offices. The floors are held within a visible steel frame composed of uprights, long longitudinal beams, and transverse girders. The

openings in this structure are filled with prefabricated panels of crushed granite and red marble with vertical folding pilasters. The interior space formed by these folds was used to hide the tubes and service ducts for the air conditioning and lighting. The steel frame creates a large iron cornice at the level of each floor, giving the façade of the building a natural, classical feel, and the part of the cornice that projects beyond

the eaves hides the track for the trolley used in the cleaning and maintenance of the façade. Albini and Helg thus skillfully turned the requirements presented by technological apparatuses into expressive strengths, so much so that the elements adopted by the project, with their allusions to the typology of the middle-class Roman palace, succeeded in establishing a dialogue between the new store and the surrounding urban scene.

Church of the Light, Ibaraki, Osaka, Japan
1987–1989

"Light is the origin of all things: When it strikes the surfaces of objects its delineates their profiles; by producing shadows behind objects it establishes their depth" (T.A.)

The lightning-swift transition from a patriarchal, feudal society to a modern industrial nation that began following Japan's opening to commerce with the West in 1868 left in its wake many problems of adaptation for Japan's national identity, many of which are still felt today. Caught between the precepts of the ancient East and the dictates of the modern West, the national spirit found itself forced to adapt rapidly to a double sensibility, imposed by the coexistence of modernity and tradition. From 1920 on, modern Japanese architecture has itself evolved along a complex route marked off by the rhythms of a dialogue between traditional building methods and ideas from the international avant-garde, the borderlines of which can become lost amid the lively exchange between Orient and Occident. For many European architects, a trip to the East has meant the unexpected discovery of the restrained and highly modern simplicity encountered in Shinto temples, Zen gardens, or teahouses; in much the same way, the first generation of modern Japanese architects was clearly influenced by the work of the European masters of the Modern movement. The critical revival of the construction principles tied to Japanese tradition, which in terms of international architectural theories is an example of what Kenneth Frampton first called Critical Regionalism, thus supports the combination of local traditions and functionalist Modernism. All of the work by Tadao Ando is directed at achieving the ancient and invaluable harmony between the artificial dimension and the natural dimension; Ando is the foremost contemporary exponent of a Japanese architectonic identity that is expressed using the techniques and components of the Modern language.

The Church of the Light, built between 1987 and 1989 in Ibaraki, a residential suburb of Osaka, stands as an extraordinary embodiment of the poetics of form and content that characterize every work by Ando. Conceived as a simple space surrounded by solid cement panels—the molds and frameworks for which, as by now has become customary in his works, were built by teams of highly skilled carpenters recruited by Ando himself— the Church of the Light is first of all a closed box isolated from the external world. It is "a construction of obscurity," intersected by a diaphragm wall that, breaking into the central volume at a 15-degree angle, separates the entry area from the space used for religious rites. As Ando explained, this is because "Light must be accompanied by darkness in order to be able to shine and demonstrate its power." Thus the interior of the church rests in profound darkness: "In this darkness an isolated cross of light floats, and there is nothing else. The external light, having been architecturally manipulated and rendered abstract by the opening made in the wall, introduces tension in the space and sanctifies it." The floor, covered by rough wooden planks, slopes down towards the altar; the pews, as would be suitable in the spare and antidecorative simplicity of a Shinto sanctuary, are also made with rough panels of wood, in fact recuperated from the scaffolding used on the worksite.

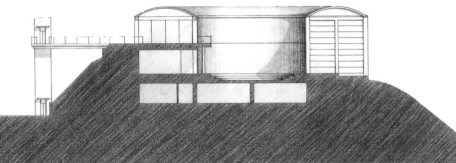

Museum of Culture, Gojyo, Nara, Japan
1993–1995

"To bring to light and make evident the invisible logic of nature, it must be contrasted with the logic of architecture" (T.A.)

For the design of an artificial and autonomous object to achieve symbiosis with nature, the object must not impose itself on the surrounding terrain but must, if possible, comply with it by way of a harmonious gesture in which the architectonic construction and the shape of the site ultimately coincide.

The traditional relationship between Japanese architecture and its environmental context, designed to achieve complete harmony between nature and art and directly related to the ancient respect for the *genius loci*—the spirit of the place—still represents the most passionate area of contention between contemporary Japanese architecture and its historical patrimony. It is in part against this background of contention—or perhaps it would be better to say of continuity—that Tadao Ando's plan for the Culture Museum of Gojyo should be viewed. Located atop a hill overlooking the ancient city of Gojyo, the museum, exploiting a panoramic setting "torn" from the surrounding forest, offers a spectacular view of the city

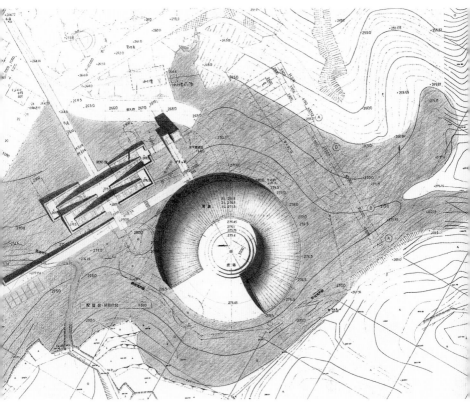

below. The perfectly circular shape of the construction contains the museum spaces, arranged in a ring around a central courtyard open to the sky. The ring is composed of two above-ground stories that are also partially underground so seem to rise from the hillside; neither does the ring close completely around its central nucleus, leaving an opening facing the valley that gives the central courtyard a view of Gojyo. A system of stairs and ramps covers the natural slope of the terrain and directs visitors to the various floors of the museum. The museum is made of reinforced concrete; its internal walls are of untreated concrete, while the external walls have been dressed in panels of galvanized steel since, as Ando said, "This material seems able to absorb both wind and light." Thus, in terms of the material used in its dressing, the Museum of Culture of Gojyo must be seen as a departure for Ando, who for many years now has shown a preference for bare concrete because of the stimulating effects it achieves as it ages. In this instance, that material has been replaced by materials destined to hold up over time while also helping to keep down maintenance costs.

City Library, Stockholm, Sweden

1918–1928
"Classical architecture blended, up to a certain point, exterior and interior in a single constructed form" (E.G.A.)

The architectonic lexicon of the Modern movement, inspired by the positivist themes of the Industrial Revolution and by new construction techniques made possible by modern building materials, was moderated by the so-called Swedish Modern Classicism in the countries of northern Europe. Originally developed in Denmark, this particular form of classicism owed its delayed assumption of the Modern language to a special, re-evaluated assessment of the classical Mediterranean legacy. Reactions to the Modern and International Style, identified by their new parameters of standardization, typification, and prefabrication, generated various classicist and regionalist revivals that had in common a general rediscovery of the classical as an art with universal application and widespread popular recognition. The various manifestations of this phenomenon can be traced to two distinct and recurring attitudes towards the historical material of architecture. The first encompasses those who take the material literally, mechanically reproducing its formal aspects; the second— which is the one that interests us here—involves those who study the classical example, but then treat it as only a departure point for various translations that are achieved through the progressive removal of its immutable values as a model. In this sense Gunnar Asplund's library, while inspired by the archaic forms of the classical world, is a modern building, a monument to invention; in fact, in the planimetric distribution of the library Asplund carries out the transgression of a building typology. Although the layout involves a U-shaped outer body (the side originally left open was closed off during a later enlargement of the structure) with a taller, drum-shaped construction containing a circular reading room at its center, the building cannot be related, as Carlos Martí Arís has pointed out, to the centrally planned type of layout. This is because the component parts of the library are not subordinate to the central volume of the cylinder, which stands as an autonomous component of the building except for the three points of tangency, which are the points of access, leading to the entrances to the library. Located slightly off the axis of the street corner formed by the crossing of Sveavägen and Odengatan streets, the library, with its compact, serious appearance, is endowed with a strong symbolic force that makes it stand out against the surrounding urban context. A high string course runs the full length of the outer bodies, dividing their volume into two parts and ending with a pseudo-Egyptian frieze presenting scenes of daily life. Simple cornices frame the large central cylinder; the curving walls of the elevated reading room inside the cylinder are covered to a certain height by shelves of books.

From the street level one enters the main hall from below by means of a steep ramp, the angle of which serves to increase the unexpected encounter with the upward surge of the central cylinder.

Erik Gunnar Asplund 1885–1940

Enlargement of Town Hall, Göteborg, Sweden
(final version)
1934–1937

"A building must respect its neighbors, which can enjoy far longer lives that one might expect. Respect, however, does not mean imitating style"(E.G.A.)

A principle of coherence runs through the continuous revisions and reworkings that, beginning in 1913, led Gunnar Asplund to work out the final version of the reconstruction of the town hall of Göteborg, a highly successful case of the coexistence between modern architecture and a building from the past. Going over the various steps and stages of the process involves in large part following the evolution of the architectonic debate that begins with the simple imitation of the stylistic repertoire of the past to arrive at a true critical revision of buildings or parts of buildings from the historical patrimony of our cities. In 1913 Asplund won first prize in the competition, which called for the partial reuse of the building designed in 1672 by the architect Nicodemus Tessin the Elder, which faced a canal to the south and today's Gustaf Adolf Square to the west. Asplund's winning design involved an autonomous and unitary building facing the canal, but this had to be adjusted when the decision was made to give preference to the side overlooking Gustaf Adolf Square. Asplund's later studies, beginning in 1920, thus had to make room to accommodate another building located in difficult proximity to the monumental, symmetrical structure built by Tessin. One of the first solutions to this problem involved a neutral zone between the two buildings, composed of three simple windows, followed by an autonomous building, narrower and more vertical than the pre-existing structure. This proposal was followed, in 1925, by a variant that, maintaining the neutral zone, aligned the floors of the new building to those of the old and also repeated that building's decorative stylistic elements.

In 1934 the two contrasting volumes, with the presence of two entrances, were replaced by a proposal that involved

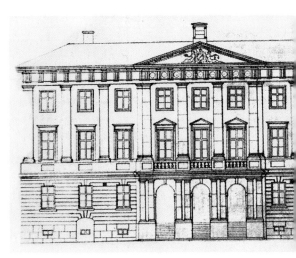

connecting the two bodies to form a single, continuous whole interrupted at their point of juncture by a simple offset.

Asplund preferred the idea of two autonomous structures but ultimately gave up on the idea of uniting them to form a single organism; in 1936 he reached the final solution, that of creating new architecture to add to the pre-existing body.

Although Asplund's new façade presents itself as a piece of openly modern architecture, including a narrow seam of bare cement used to mark divisions and asymmetrical openings, it nonetheless succeeds in deriving its composition from constructive logic and from the classical articulation of the adjacent building. Inside the enlargement is a covered space with windows overlooking the old courtyard. In this double-height space is the main entrance to the enlargement, including the large staircase whose single ramp moves from floor to floor and leads to a gallery facing the atrium of the new court of justice.

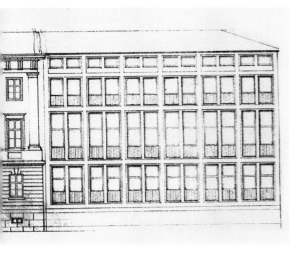

Monte Amiata Housing Complex, Gallaratese 2, Milan, Italy

(with Maurizio Aymonino, Giorgio Ciucci, Vittorio De Feo, Alessandro De Rossi, Mario Manieri-Elia, Sachin Messaré, and Aldo Rossi)
1967–1972

"Perhaps this is the basic truth of architecture: to make a part of a city formally finished so that it can endure over time, even when put to different uses" (C.A.)

The "piece by piece" theory of the city, which looked on the city as a place of study and planning, established that, in order for any one piece to qualify as a piece that was part of the whole, it must be formally complete, meaning architectonically recognizable. The theory, which was worked out during the last years of the 1960s, concentrated on separate urban elements, such as a building or a section of a city, thus differing from those urbanistic theories that, following abstract and formal reasoning, sought to modify the city in its totality.

In the work of Aldo Rossi, Giorgio Grassi, Carlo Aymonino, and many other Italian architects, pure design activity was therefore put in second place, with first place going to the careful urban analysis of the area or the building using the instruments of cartography, topography, and urban geography. Perhaps the most obvious result of this theory is the fact that the architectonic design of the city came to find itself closely connected, in a sort of work in progress, to urban analysis and planning. Urban renewal thus takes on a new architectonic quality, and one that is not derived from utopian models of an abstract ideal city but from the specific qualities of the actual place itself and of the buildings being taken into consideration.

The preferred field of action for urban analysis remains, however, the historical city, the city of the past, since outer areas simply do not offer the same wealth of precise attributes.

In his design for the Gallaratese 2 development, Aymonino responded to the typical absence of precise attributes by ignoring the site and its relationships with the surrounding area, a flat terrain with no outstanding features except for street intersections and a few isolated blocks of public housing. Deciding to emphasize this detachment from the surroundings, Aymonino created a large, compact construction for 2,400 inhabitants that recalls a different urban image and that uses an effective system of collective services to interact with the entire complex of the Gallaratese quarter, which is thus made "part" of the city of Milan. The general layout of the installation is based on the elementary geometric figure of two triangles, inside the projections of which are five bodies of different heights and depths.

The pedestrian connections among the various buildings, including ramps, galleries, and raised passageways, along with

34

the spaces made for recreation and casual gatherings, such as a three-quarter-circular outdoor theater and the plazas built over garages, create a system analogous to the public spaces of the city itself, giving the complex a genuine urban feel. In addition, the complex is composed of a variety of typologies of homes, ranging from one-room apartments to duplexes.

The center of the complex is the theater, from which the two main wings of the complex spread open.

Each of these compact, inclined bodies has eight stories broken down into the various sizes of apartment. The theater is also the starting point for two linear bodies that stretch towards the far ends of the property.

The lower of these is a white structure only three stories high with open-air corridors and a long collonade, Rossi's homage to the traditional Milanese typology in which several homes are located along a single *ballatoio*, or corridor.

San Cristóbal Stable and Folke Egerstrom House, Los Clubes, Mexico
(with Andrés Casillas)
1967–1968

"Any architecture that does not express serenity does not perform its spiritual mission. This is why it was a mistake to replace the shelter of walls with the storminess of stained glass"(L.B.)

On June 3, 1980, the jury of the Pritzker Prize, which ranks as a kind of Nobel for architecture, explained its official recognition of the Mexican engineer Luis Barragán in these words: "We are honoring Luis Barragán for his commitment to architecture as a sublime act of the poetic imagination. He has created gardens, plazas, and fountains of haunting beauty—metaphysical landscapes for meditation and companionship. A stoical acceptance of solitude as man's fate permeates Barragán's work. His solitude is cosmic, with Mexico as the temporal abode he lovingly accepts." The words of the jury provide an excellent synthesis of the activity of Barragán, who has often been referred to as a pioneer of Critical Regionalism, a term coined in 1983 by Kenneth Frampton to describe those architectonic movements that, without slipping into the folkloric, succeed in appearing

contemporary even while being designed with respect to local and regional traditions. Barragán is the undisputed leader of Mexican regionalism, which is based on Californian neocolonialism; he has elaborated themes from a personal, autobiographical vision, distinguished by solid constructions made of simple walls painted in intense limewash colors, "custodians" of silent gardens and melodious fountains. Based on the theme of a large central patio with a watering trough for horses, the San Cristóbal house and stable is perhaps the outstanding example of his mature work. In it, the most intimate themes of his poetics succeed in creating simple, clear spaces based on spare geometric forms, in which the areas for the horses receive special attention. Part of a larger allotment designed to create a residential area for horse lovers, the San Cristóbal stable is arranged around a central patio marked off by walls of various heights and colors. The watering trough is fed by a stream of water that cascades out of the rust-colored double wall that stands alongside the entrance to the stables. Horses are in fact the protagonists of these spaces, in which the forms of a modern and elementary geometry seem to be derived from symbols of popular Mexican culture.

Torre Velasca,
Milan, Italy
1950–1958

"It is clear that knowing history it not enough. One must meditate on it with precise goals, meditate in order to create new works, meaning authentic works"
(Ernesto Nathan Rogers)

Ernesto Nathan Rogers and his design theory of "environmental pre-existences" were behind the most substantial Italian postwar contribution to a new concept of tradition, translated in a new expressive effort that was highly attuned to the problems of setting and to the problems involved in inserting new architecture in historic centers. From the magazines *Domus* and *Casabella-continuità* and by means of his teaching activity at the Milan Polytechnic, Rogers established a delicate relationship between modernity in architecture and

innovative qualities that arise from the act of design.

The Torre Velasca, designed by the BBPR studio (Gianluigi Banfi, Ludovico Belgioioso, Enrico Peressutti, Ernesto Nathan Rogers) in 1950–1951 and constructed between 1956 and 1958, is a manifesto of this renewed dialogue between architectural design and urban context. The profile of the 99-meter-high tower, narrow in the lower part and wider in the upper, reflects the vertical arrangement of three functions: commercial on the street level, offices in the middle area, and apartments in the topmost area. This three-part functional scheme is based on that of the mercantile house and leads to a building typology of a tall building that, despite its 27 stories, does not resemble a skyscraper. Because of the verticality of its structure and the terminal portion, almost autonomous in the way it projects from the section below but joined to it by buttress-like supports, the tower makes allusions to several important elements of Milanese architecture, among them the city's cathedral and the tower of the Castello Sforzesco. Thus, the intentional repetition of traditional forms, further expressed in the sizing of the windows, the tonality of the prefabricated panels used in the dressing, and in the use of materials together create a modern and functional building typology with a vertical development that is capable, as its creators hoped, of "culturally summarizing the atmosphere of the city of Milan."

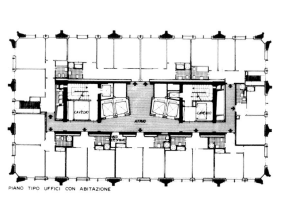

PIANO TIPO UFFICI CON ABITAZIONE

the universal value of history. In this way a new international method of architectonic design began to take shape in Italy. It involved the rejection of the artistic formalism related to the spontaneous inventions of certain masters of the Modern movement and arrived at a new form of environmentalism in which the historical and pre-existing values of a given site were blended with the necessarily

Delstern Crematorium, Hagen, Germany
1906–1908

"From history we see how the collaboration of a great technical skill and a deeply felt art have matured the style of an epoch" (P.B.)

It might seem surprising that when the architect Peter Behrens—judged Europe's foremost industrial designer on the basis of the work he did for AEG between 1907 and 1914—undertook the design for the crematorium in Hagen he made direct reference to several models of the past. In fact, in its planimetric distribution and in the treatment of its surfaces, the crematorium alludes to a certain kind of religious structure, the most outstanding example of which is the neo-Romanesque masterpiece that is Florence's San Miniato al Monte, although there are also traces of the façade of Santa Maria Novella and the Little Temple of the Holy Sepulcher in the Rucellai Chapel, these last two being works by Leon Battista Alberti that were made within the sphere of the mature Florentine Renaissance. It should not be surprising that Behrens, moved by the search for the fusion of art and technique in a single unity that he sought throughout his career and that represents the outstanding constant element of his work, should have turned to classical models from the past, in particular models from the early and late Renaissance in Italy, when working on this design. The passage from the sinuous,

floral forms of Art Nouveau to the classicist component that characterizes the protorationalist architecture of Germany at the beginning of the century and that celebrated its first technological triumphs, was filtered through a process of simplification of the architectonic language that, making appeal to the qualities of necessity, clarity, and economy, made the new form of classical art confront the new demands of Germany's social conditions.

So it was that Behrens, the leading exponent of German protorationalism, drew inspiration from the regularity of the classical canon and its archetypical typologies; he turned to the Italian Renaissance for its modern-seeming scientific vision and its geometric rationalization of nature and the visual world. For Behrens, Renaissance style became a possible means for achieving a new working coexistence between technique and style, since it was the Renaissance period, more than any other, that showed "in the clearest way the simultaneous flowering of technical skill and a new art," categories that are usually difficult to reconcile and that Behrens would succeed in integrating in a coherently unified process only later, in the creation of his industrial buildings.

The crematorium was part of a vast program of cultural renewal for the city of Hagen that was promoted by the benefactor Karl Ernst Osthaus between 1898 and 1920. It is raised on a solid base of rustic stone, the floor of which is

reached by means of a monumental semicircular stairway that leads to the main entrance. The façade, created using a bare geometric reductionism that makes it resemble some of the most recent historicist currents of contemporary architectural culture, is composed of simple, elementary geometric figures: a triangular tympanum with the sloping sides of the pitched roof, a bare and solid trabeation supported by six squared columns, past which is an entry vestibule. The original decorative covering, irreparably destroyed by deterioration and replaced by the layer of plaster that today covers the crematorium, was entrusted to heavy marble slabs, on the surfaces of which Behrens had applied a linear geometric decoration inspired by the polychromatic fields of color of Renaissance Florence. The funeral rites for which the building was made are suitably provided for in the decoration of the interior, where black decorations on white alternate with white on black, creating a dramatic sense of pure geometry.

AEG Turbine Factory, Berlin, Germany
1908–1909

"Our most pressing task is therefore that of giving an artistic quality to the advanced technique so as to create . . . by way of technique, great works of artistic inspiration"(P.B.)

In 1907, Emil Rathenau, founder of AEG (Allgemeine Elektrizitäts-Gesellschaft; the German General Electric Co.), named Peter Behrens design consultant for the company. In that position, which he held until 1914, the Hamburg architect oversaw the design of factory buildings, furnishings and fixtures, advertizing art and letterheads, as well as lamps, radiators, and every other

product bearing the AEG mark.

In October of the same year, in Munich, the Deutscher Werkbund was founded, an association of architects, artists, artisans, and industrialists united in the desire to coordinate the patrimony of artisan techniques with the demands of industrial production. The coincidence of the two dates is emphasized not only because the Deutscher Werkbund

numbered Peter Behrens among its many members but most of all because the figurative principles that Behrens followed in all of his industrial designs can be seen to arise from the ideal fusion of art and technology in a new unity that was promoted by the more progressive faction of the Deutscher Werkbund, for whom the creation of a new, impersonal style, suitable to industrial, assembly-line production, was less important than the renunciation of the individualist aspects of expressive acts.

This renunciation was also behind the simplification of architectonic language sought by protorationalism in Germany at the beginning of the century, a simplification to be achieved through the revival of the categories of symmetry, balance, and order that had always belonged to the classical canons of architecture.

Behrens made use of these same values when he faced the new technical and constructive factors involved in industrial building. The AEG turbine factory is inspired by a monumental esthetic that makes it the prototype of all modern industrial architecture, and Behrens achieved this end by following the architectonic principle of "concentrate the metal masses and do not spread them out, as is usually done in lattice-beam constructions."

The industrial complex is composed of a large industrial shed, the Turbinenhalle, 123 meters long and more than 40 meters wide, and a smaller body beside it. The long side

of the Turbinenhalle, facing Berlichingerstrasse, is a glass wall with fourteen steel columns that taper towards the ground and rest on exposed hinges. These appear to carry out the basic role of supporting the iron beam that runs down the long sides of the building. In reality, however, the steel frame of the structure is supported by a complex system of trussed girders located behind the glass surfaces, between the

columns and set back from the surfaces of the columns. The main hall is topped by a stately gable with a jointed outline, beneath which are a pair of massive masonry pylons that seem to serve a bearing function but in fact do not.

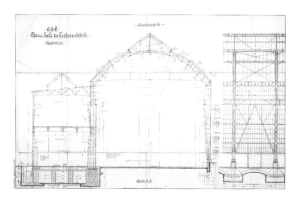

Stock Exchange, Amsterdam, Netherlands
1896–1903

"At the beginning of every artistic period the right architectural principle prevails: it is the principle of good and genuine construction" (H.P.B.)

With the advent of the twentieth century, architectonic culture began to achieve liberation from the eclectic and historicist forms that had marked the close of the nineteenth century. This movement aspired to the category of esthetic morality. A morality of content, first of all, as indicated by its programs of artistic reform directed at ongoing social progress; and also a morality of forms, meaning those generated by an impersonal and objective technique of composition capable of giving life to what Hendrik Petrus Berlage called a "new style." The dogmatic formal contamination with which various styles of the past found their most fitting application in pre-established architectonic typologies left room for a slow process of revision that eventually led to the birth of Modern architecture. The Amsterdam Stock Exchange stands out within this process as a true turning point. Impressive symbol of the most modern middle-class commercialism, the neo-Romanesque-style

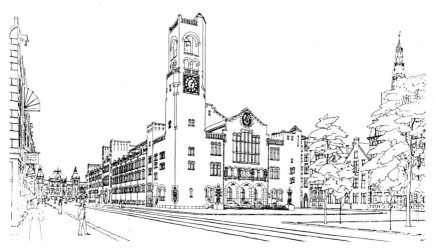

building stands in the seventeenth-century heart of the city of Amsterdam. What keeps the building from being just one more example of an eclectic revivalism is the way in which Berlage "addressed" the neo-Romanesque: "The Romanesque is consistent with basic modern concepts because of its simplicity, its structural disposition of masses, and the role given to decoration. There is the danger, however, of being snared in this style." Located on an elongated trapezoidal lot, the building's components are arranged in a clear and elementary fashion: there are the Commodities Exchange, which has the main façade with its arched entry and corner tower; the Grain Exchange; and the Stock Exchange. These three spaces are marked off by bare brick walls beyond which stand the high corner tower and the blocks over the stairways.

Berlage achieves a critical rereading of the historical model of the Roman basilica, as seems particularly evident in the central hall of the Commodities Exchange. Here an ample hall, flanked by a double row of galleries, forms a kind of large urban square with shelter from poor weather provided by reticulated iron trusses that support a transparent covering made of glass and hammered iron.

Les Espaces d'Abraxas, Marnee-la-Vallée,
Paris, France
1978–1983

"The Marne-la-Vallée project was conceived as a monument. The symbol is the gate to the city"
(R.B.)

Ricardo Bofill believes that the homes of the working class can be endowed with serious and socially representative architecture by applying forms and models of historical inspiration to the construction of large-scale blocks of public housing. Doing so would relocate to the peripheral areas of large European cities some of the spirit of collective urban awareness that seems to have been lost. The models of urbanization advocated by the rationalist and Modern culture are usually based on growth by functional zones; Bofill and the firm Taller de Arquitectura, founded in 1963, oppose such models, presenting in their place plans inspired by models of historical cities that are based on the proven value of the pair of urban categories of the plaza and the street. The suburbs of large metropolitan areas would thus be enriched by new high-density neighborhoods in which the traffic schemes and architectonic forms would not be limited to evocations of stylistic morphologies of the past, as much of Postmodern culture would like, but instead would offer a concrete alternative to the periphery as a place without qualities. Bofill has experimented with historical typologies in an eclectic range that extends from the baroque patrimony to

stylistic elements of the neo-nineteenth century, but all his work has had to contend with the strict financial restrictions that regulate the creation of public housing, forcing him to adjust the exuberance of the repertory of historical forms to the assembly of a few repeated prefabricated elements produced by the industrialization of the building industry. Much of Postmodern architecture has sought the evocation of traditional values by way of a revival of craft techniques; Bofill, however, has replaced this with acceptance of the standard components that result from the prefabrication of reinforced

concrete, thus adjusting his mannerist architecture to the economic processes that make it possible.

The housing complex of Les Espaces d'Abraxas, which stands on the outskirts of Paris, is composed of three separate bodies arranged in accordance with a typically baroque spatial model. The first of these is *Le Palacio*, whose U-shaped form hosts 441 apartments on 18 floors. Then there is *Le Théâtre*, a building with a semicircular layout housing 130 apartments on 9 floors. Two of its facades face the internal courtyard, and these are decorated with areas of glass walls shaped like

46

the shafts of columns. Facing out to the surrounding plain the convex front of the semicircle becomes more monumental. The last of the three bodies is *L'Arc,* which stands between the other two bodies at the center of the courtyard and is a true triumphal arch; despite its appearance, it is in fact another housing unit, with 20 apartments arranged on 10 floors.

Stylistic elements derived from the historical patrimony and applied to these structures give the great complex in Marne-la-Vallée a striking character, both monumental and symbolic.

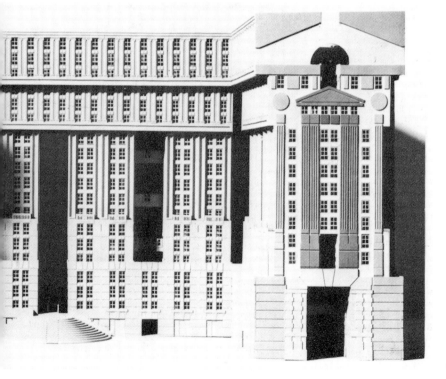

Ricardo Bofill 1939

Canalization of the Neckar River, dam at Rockenau, Germany
1926–1936

"The fundamental problem was to give a clear expression to the necessary elements . . . and at the same time to emphasize function by way of form" (P.B.)

The perfect harmony of technical form with artistic form is a striking aspect of several large, successful works that are best described using the generic term *infrastructure*. In such works, the building elements compete with technical advances often to rival the physical laws of nature. These constructions were the basis for a new style that originated in Germany during the first decade of the twentieth century. From the first forms of protorationalism it flowed into the stylistic canons of the Neues Bauen ("new building") and of Maschinenstil ("machine style"), which were spread internationally by the Modern movement. A program marked by the principle of the highest economy and simplicity, together with the widespread use of reinforced concrete, led to a revival of classical components inspired by the values of symmetry and balance. These are the values in the great infrastructures designed by Paul Bonatz, which perform technical

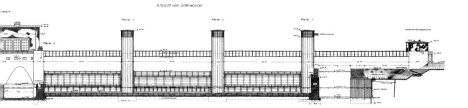

Ansicht vom Oberwasser

Ansicht vom Unterwasser

functions of environmental control and planning while at the same time re-establishing the relationship between landscape and architecture. "What is pleasing in these constructions is the objectivity, the sincerity, therefore the absence of a false presence," said Bonatz, explaining the characteristics of his technical constructions, inspired by the new architectonic language he called *Arbeitsstil* ("work style"), fated to coincide with the ideals representative of the Third Reich, for which Bonatz redesigned the entire German road network.

The ten dams on the Neckar River between Stuttgart and Mannheim that Bonatz and the engineer Otto Konz made in the decade between 1926 and 1936 are composed of a series of simple constructive elements that are repeated each time and kept clearly distinct thanks to the use of different materials adopted to achieve the proper insertion of the new technological structures in the traditional landscape. The primary constructive elements of which each dam is composed include the step-dam, the hydroelectric plant, and the piers of the dam, connected by service walkways made of colored iron. Set up with the regular cadence characteristic of antique watchtowers, these are capable of performing a new kind of environmental control.

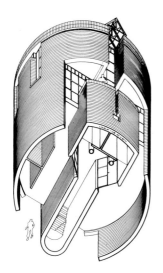 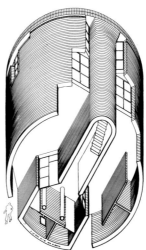

Casa Rotonda,
Stabio, Ticino, Switzerland
1980

"My intention was to subtract the building from comparison and contrast with the surrounding constructions and to establish instead a spatial relationship with the landscape and the distant horizon" (M.B.)

The reduction of architecture to a limited repertory of simple geometric forms and elements can be taken as the distinctive characteristic of the simplified architectonic language that Mario Botta has been using since the 1970s. It is a style that also involves the revival of various morphological elements drawn from the historical patrimony of architecture. This single-family home in Stabio, known as the *casa rotonda* ("round house") because of its shape, stands on the outskirts of a village within an environmental context in which the division of the fields into agricultural lots has been replaced, over time, by a parceling out of the territory into anonymous residential installations.

On one hand, the geometric shape of the home is derived from a return to the typology of the central layout, based the primary figure of the cylinder and skillfully adapted to the needs of a modern home; on the other hand,

the villa, setting itself apart
from the mediocrity of the
surrounding structures, opens
the compactness of its volume
in a profound dialogue with
the primary elements of
nature: the earth and the sky.
Architecture and landscape,
in their most basic, primary
forms, thus achieve an ideal
symbiosis through the
construction of a building
that, as Botta has said, "finds
its justification in the space it
occupies between the earth

(to which its perimeter is
anchored) and the sky (to
which it is vertically open by
way of the skylight").
With a circular layout about
12 meters in diameter, the
house extends over four
levels; the internal spaces
of the building are arranged
along a north-south axis that
is the true fulcrum
of the entire composition.
The stairs that connect
the various levels run along
this axis, as does the fissure

that "crosses" the top of
the cylinder by means
of a skylight in the form
of a tympanum and thus
brings in light along the
central axis of the building.
In the overall configuration
of the house Botta has
willfully rejected the very idea
of windows, and the interior
rooms receive their natural
illumination from a series
of cuts and fissures that seem
dug out of the original mass
of the architectonic volume.

Museum of Modern Art, San Francisco, USA
1989–1995

"I think that to be 'universal' and to face external reality in its own context, it is important to be profoundly 'local'" (M.B.)

One of the most lively debates within the panorama of contemporary architecture concerns the international aspect attributed to many of the most recent products of architecture, an aspect that is thought to result not only from the ongoing globalization of modernization but also from the acceptance and consequent ascendance of an international architectonic language that is opposed to the values of permanence and tradition associated with local specificity.

The international circuit of architectonic production is fueled by new forms of sponsorship and is increasingly tied to large-scale political programs, in some cases undertaking to reconfigure entire areas of cities. There is also the aspect of the current "market" for architecture created by international competitions. Within this new situation is a movement that has focused its efforts on the coexistence of vernacular and international dimensions in an attempt to achieve what Franco Purini has called the "poetics of difference."
The San Francisco Museum of Modern Art occupies a special position with regard to this debate, since in it the constants of the architectonic language of the Swiss architect Mario Botta have been adapted

to the requests of the sponsors, who selected him not by way of a true international competition but because they believed he was the architect most qualified to create "well proportioned spaces, sober, illuminated in large part by natural light, and respectful of the works of art they are to hold."
Inserted in the context of the downtown tourist district between the theater designed by James Stewart Polshek and the new Center for the Arts by Fumihiko Maki, the Museum of Modern Art, with its monumental volume in brick cladding, rises as the dominant feature against the profile of the surrounding buildings. The recurrent themes in Botta's poetics, identified by critics as the "wall," the "opening," and the "light," show up in this, his first creation in the United States. Indeed, in this museum organism it can be said that natural light was treated as a building material, fully equal to the bricks and granite that dress the building. Adjusted to the strict earthquake and fire codes that regulate construction in San Francisco, the classic brick surface is superimposed over prefabricated concrete panels secured to the steel framework that forms the bearing structure of the building. The entrance atrium, which leads to the stairway and the various galleries of the museum, has a polychrome covering that gives it the unexpected sense of a cathedral interior. It is illuminated by a shaft of natural light from the large skylight in the central tower.

Flatiron (Fuller) Building, New York, USA
1901–1903

"The great city is projected into its future as practically a huge, continuous, fifty-floored conspiracy against the very idea of the ancient graces" (Henry James)

The first trial runs at creating what eventually would become the typology of the skyscraper took place at the end of the nineteenth century and were located, at least primarily, in Chicago. Curiously enough, these structures resulted from the "dilation" of a typology from classical architecture, that of the Renaissance palace, the sharp vertical and horizontal divisions of which conferred a sense of verticality. Still restrained in terms of height and designed in accordance with the classical tripartite sections of base, shaft, and capital, this typology was put to vast use in Chicago in the construction of the warehouses and commercial buildings that were built in enormous numbers during the reconstruction of the city, which had been nearly totally destroyed by the terrible fire of 1871. The first tall buildings with metal frameworks were usually limited to a maximum of fifteen stories. The so-called Chicago School came into being on the basis of the formal and structural variations of this type, leading, as a result of certain eclectic trends within the school itself, to the application of "fragments" of Beaux-Arts models of European derivation to commercial architecture. These, in the guise of classical

style, soon merged with the technical and functional needs of the modern American skyscraper.

New York, however, was the city destined to celebrate the verticality of building, and in that city the formal references to the Renaissance palace were replaced by a revival of the typology of the tower, and this, while still connected to eclectic and late Gothic references, soon rose to become the symbol of the large corporations and holding companies that had taken their place within the business world of the city. Given the high cost of building at ground level, such companies had good reason to want taller buildings, leading to a kind of frantic competition in which being the highest came to have a certain symbolic importance.

The Flatiron Building owes its originality as an intermediary between the typologies of the palace and the tower to the anomaly of the block it stands on. Facing onto Madison Square, the building follows the triangular outline of a lot that narrows to form a sharp angle towards the open space of the square. Twenty-two stories high (86 meters), the skyscraper is divided into the classical tripartition, such that it seems to follow the typology of a tall classical palace when viewed from the sides facing Broadway or Fifth Avenue, but when seen from the narrow end pointed at Madison Square it evokes more the image of a column or tower, classically divided into base, shaft, and capital. The multiplicity of readings that the building invites found

their most fortunate expression in the many images made using the technique of photography, which by the beginning of the century was already coming to assume its role as the ideal artistic form for grasping the complexity of the changing New York skyline.

Daniel Hudson Burnham 1846–1912

TGV Rhone Alps Station, Lyons-Satolas, France
1989–1994

"Honestly, I do not go in search of metaphors. I never once thought of a bird. Mine was rather a search in the direction of what I am at times presumptuous enough to call sculpture"(S.C.)

Santiago Calatrava's double training boasts a degree in architecture from the university of Valencia (1974) and a graduate thesis in engineering from the Federal Institute of Technology of Zurich (1981), followed by a doctoral thesis on the "foldability" of load-bearing structures. Calatrava is today recognized as an outstanding figure in the field of contemporary architecture and engineering, but since the early years of his training he has demonstrated how the integration between the figure of the engineer and that of the architect is not only feasible but desirable, since it offers the opportunity to give life to new forms of artistic expression.

Calatrava's work makes use of the important patrimony of twentieth-century engineering, but he succeeds in applying this learning with a new level of freedom such that the figure of the engineer, freed from the a priori rules and regulations of mathematical calculus, succeeds in "awakening new emotions." This integration, ideal in terms of the discipline, is a rare phenomenon in the history of modern and contemporary architecture, encountered in a very few figures gifted with a double training and usually isolated from architectural criticism. These figures, among them Pier Luigi Nervi, Riccardo Morandi, Eduardo Torroja, Felix Candela, Frei Otto, and Ove Arup, carrying out border crossings between the disciplines, succeed in transferring to the field of engineering questions that are usually left within the formal language of architectonic research and the history of inventions. In a parallel development, beginning around 1950, as a result of the new expressive possibilities offered by the use of reinforced concrete, various architects began including a strong sense of structure in their formal repertories. This sense of structure was made apparent not only in the direct systems of support skeletons and frameworks but as the underlying raison d'être of architecture itself.

Calatrava, who operates as confidently in the field of urbanistics as he does in that of structural calculus, seeks the essence of his architectural creations in the dynamic tension of structures, in the kinetic values of building. The structural compositions he creates are thus quite often comparable to sculpture. They are prepared using experimental test models and pictorial sketches that use the cross-section as their primary point of reference since, for Calatrava, "architecture is made from the inside out." Often compared to the image of a bird in flight or the carcass of a prehistoric animal, the TGV terminal of Lyons-Satolas, made for the French rail line (SNCF), with the purpose of connecting the network of high-speed trains to the Lyons airport of Satolas, stands out sharply, highly visible on the landscape. It is composed of three distinct elements: the main body with the services, the area of the tracks, and the elevated gallery for connections to the airport. The station has six tracks, the central two of which are enclosed in a body of reinforced concrete calculated to withstand the shockwaves caused by the TGV trains. The central, triangular body occupies two levels connected by escalators; on the lower floor are the station services and the check-in area for the airport, while the upper level has a refreshment area spread across two cantilevered corbels. The structure of the main triangular hall rests on a series of reticulated arches about 100 meters wide, attached to the tops of the triangle by means of cement blocks. The high glass-and-steel walls are covered by the overhang of the roof, made of aluminum sheets and up to 40 meters high. It is the silhouette of this roof that reminds some people of a bird in flight.

Santiago Calatrava 1951

Competition for the Cathedral of St John the Divine, New York, USA
1991

"I am only an architect, not an artist or someone trying to foment a revolution"(S.C.)

Over the course of the history of architecture, ribbing, a motif derived from the natural form of the tree as well as from the anatomic ribbing of a skeleton, has acquired increasingly expressive and symbolic values that have come to be freed, at least in part, from the original function served by this architectural element, which was that of structural reinforcement. The interweaving of ribs employed in late Gothic European architecture demonstrates how complex structures, geometric and ramified, slowly gave way to a logical building system based on the repetition of bays spanned by cross vaults, which originated from the crossing of the ribs on supporting pylons. This system, including its more experimental digressions (as for example in the case of the system of star vaults), takes the very complexity of nature as its point of reference. A passage from Hegel's *Aesthetics* applies here: "Enter the interior of a medieval cathedral, and you are reminded less of the firmness and mechanical appropriateness of load-bearing pillars and a vault resting on them than of the vaultings of a forest where in lines of trees the branches incline to one another and quickly meet." These lines

place us directly in the middle of the complex relationship between architecture and decoration, and more precisely in the coincidence between decorative structure and static structure, a coincidence that, freeing the architectonic forms from the presumed correspondences with the forms of construction, frees architecture to assume new and unexpected meanings. This is the case with certain experiments related to the use

of reinforced concrete, in which the ribbing network that serves as the static support for the covering is translated into an architectonic element distinguished by the formal aspects of the covering itself. In this sense a marked Gothic-like and symbolic osteology characterized the design by Santiago Calatrava for the transept of the cathedral of St John the Divine, winner of the invitational competition but,

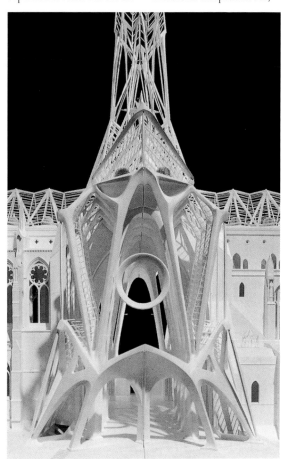

unfortunately, never built, because of a lack of funds. The neo-Gothic cathedral of St John, located on the northern end of Manhattan, on the border of the borough of the Bronx, was built in 1892 as a replica of a Romanesque-Byzantine basilica and later, in 1911, was Gothicized by the architect Ralph Adams Cram. To this layout Calatrava's design added a new southern transept and a hanging garden, located at 55 meters from the ground and created in the attic of the central nave along the longitudinal axis of the new transept. Symbolically inspired by Eden, the hanging garden would have filtered natural light into the cathedral without changing the layout. The new transept, based on the sacred symbol of the Tree of Life, was presented as an organic system composed of vertical supports in steel, granite, and calcareous stone, thanks to which Calatrava, aside from supporting the hanging garden, would have "brought back to life the Gothic impulse and transmitted its energy, making full use of the materials."

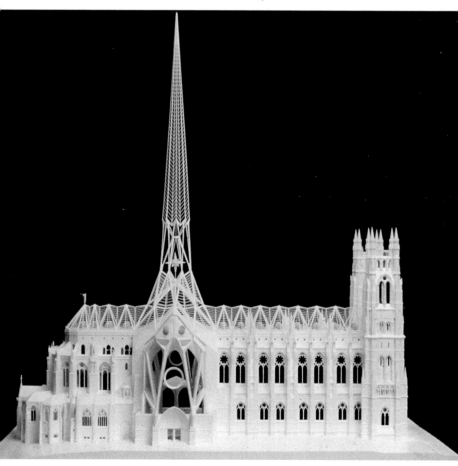

The Analogical City
1973, oil on canvas,
200 × 700 cm
Civica Raccolta d'Arte, Milan

"It is a question of method, for which the transmission of one's own work or thinking takes place through the reduction of one's margin of liberty in favor of the clarity of what one wants to say"
(A.C.)

Exhibited at the Fifteenth Triennale in Milan (1973), this canvas presents an architectonic landscape that is above all theoretical. Inspired by the "capriccio" genre views of the seventeenth and eighteenth centuries, the painting by Arduino Cantafora has an illustrious precedent, the famous capriccio in which Canaletto created a virtual, or at least a non-existent, city by placing in Venice three buildings based on Palladian designs, two of which were in fact in Vicenza and one of which had never been built anywhere. Canaletto's painting, like Cantafora's, brings us face to face with the delicate question inherent in the phenomenon of painted architecture and of its relationships with built architecture: the architecture by Palladio and the monuments assembled by Cantafora unequivocally represent architectural ideas for a city. The debate became more heated in 1976 when Aldo

Rossi presented his theory of the analogical city. In doing so, he took his cue from Canaletto's painting: "The three monuments, of which one is only a project, constitute an analogue of the real Venice composed of definite elements related to both the history of architecture and to that of the city itself. The geographical transposition of the two existing monuments to the site of the intended bridge forms a city recognizably constructed as a locus of purely architectonic values." In this way, a city in the form of a painting gave shape to a new theory of design, focused on the relationship between construction and urban context and destined to become, although not without misunderstandings, the principal theoretical concern for an entire generation of architects. Across a vast, almost limitless surface, Cantafora has assembled various references to the city of the present and the city of the past. The result is a sort of urban catalog in which monuments of the past and endless apartment buildings alternate and converge towards the center of the composition, which is dominated by the monumental spiral-staired tower, perhaps the origin of every figurative civilization. This is painted architecture with a strong sense of place, which is thus the sense of the city.

Church of Atlántida, Uruguay
1957–1958

"No distraction and waste: only thus can one achieve the conquest of that which we call 'economy in the cosmic sense,' which supposes a harmony with the ineffable mystery of the universe"(E.D.)

People usually attribute the twisting, unpredictable forms of the most recent informal architecture to advances made in computer simulations. Roofs, walls, beams, and columns, apparently set loose at last from the classical shapes of rigid skeletons, are made the subjects of mathematical models, derived from the technology of aerospace simulations, that safely "push" and expand them to levels that challenge the materials of which they are made. The new science finds its most daring and experimental point of application in the design of the roof (central theme of every structuralist exercise), often made as an autonomous piece and detached from the body beneath. Thus, a broad repertory of forms, derived from the biological world or inspired by static collapse, takes the requirement of lightness that is inherent in every roofing system and makes it assume the shape of a cloud, for example, of perhaps that of a wave. Closer analysis, however, reveals that the history of modern architecture includes many experimental works whose construction preceded the spread of modern models of virtual simulations and whose hardly orthodox forms must be attributed either to isolated currents within the

field of architecture or, more often, to the highly original creativity of their designers. The term *creativity*, abused and distorted by critics, has ended up being seen as a celebration of the personal vanity of the artist to the loss of the social and cultural qualities of the architectonic profession. It is these very qualities, however, that have been uppermost in the mind of the engineer Eladio Dieste, while always directed towards true creativity, which in practice results from proper responses to the true requirements of an architectonic program. There should be nothing amazing about the great economy of means that Dieste has applied in the creation of audacious and dynamic forms, for he has been active in Uruguay, where the creativity of any artist must come to terms with the realities of limited resources and artisan methods of construction.

The church of Atlántida stands out among Dieste's works as the most striking example of a synthesis between economy of means and creativity of forms. Made entirely in reinforced ceramic (a mixture of brick, cement, and iron rods), the layout of the church forms a rectangle of 16 × 30 meters. The perimeter walls, 30 centimeters thick and 7 meters high, literally seem to move in a waving sequence of concave–convex folds; the eaves of the roof extend a few centimeters over the outer edge of these wave walls. The roof itself is based on a system of undulating vaults made of brick, mortar, and iron; these are dressed in light porous brick that covers spans of up

18.8 meters. Thus, because of its strength and lightness, brick became the instrument with which Dieste kept building costs to a minimum while doing the same to the thicknesses of the walls and the vaults, thereby obtaining that desired "cosmic economy" that is not only financial economy but is also the fruit of a harmony between the real conditions of the world and the laws of static, dynamic equilibrium.

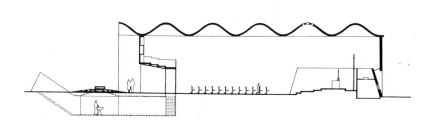

Eladio Dieste 1917

Karl Marx-Hof, Vienna, Austria
1926–1930

"When the city administration of Vienna made the decision to build on the Heiligenstädterstrasse, it found itself facing a far more difficult undertaking than had been realized until then" (Vienna City Council)

The socialist municipal authority of Vienna that came to power following the elections of 1920 launched a program of political reform designed to fill the glaring lack of housing for working-class people, a lack that had become serious even before World War I. Along with tracking down existing housing, the social democratic politicians promoted a drastic reduction of the minimum rents, which would thus weigh less heavily on the salaries of workers, assisting and containing the costs of industrial production. The financing of this new housing policy came about through the construction of new *Höfe*, large housing projects with an internal courtyard (*Hof*), a typology historically tied to the growth of the working-class quarters in Austrian and German cities (*Mietkesernenhaüser*). The efforts of the Viennese authorities were thus translated into a series of high-density housing complexes composed of blocks of five or six stories, with collective services, such as laundries, infirmaries, and nursery schools, arranged around large internal courtyards that were somewhat like public plazas. It is quite clear that the Viennese authorities hoped to make complexes whose form would reflect that of the existing city, in that sense avoiding the route taken by the Germans in their *Siedlungen*, experimental self-sufficient city neighborhoods with low-density populations inserted into the green outskirts of urban centers.

More than one kilometer long, the Karl Marx-Hof is a clear and symbolic emblem of the working class located in the historic center of the middle-class city. The layout of the installation is divided into three large courtyards, the central one of which, opening on the Heiligenstädterstrasse, hosts the large central plaza. Being the center of the installation, the plaza is crossed by two streets, large enough for vehicles, that cross the installation by way of two monumental arches.

The four main arches of the central body, each topped by a symbolic entrance tower, lead to the pedestrian connections between the plaza and the Boschstrasse. The outer body of the installation follows the shape of the lot, with set-back areas that enliven the long facades; this façade is four stories high for its entire length except for the area above the entrance arches to the central plaza, which is six stories high. Built to house 1,500 families for a total of 5,000 inhabitants, the complex is designed using the repetition of a single building unit served by three stairways and is composed of a vast range of apartment types, running from 21 to 60 square meters. A system of essential services composed of centralized laundries, indoor swimming pools, showers, nursery schools, infirmaries, clinics, and stores provides the collective facilities needed by the neighborhood community. Stronghold of the working class, a sort of modern and functioning phalanstery, the Karl Marx-Hof was damaged by artillery shells in February 1934, during the course of armed clashes between the social democrats who had taken shelter in the area and the soldiers of the reactionary Austrian government.

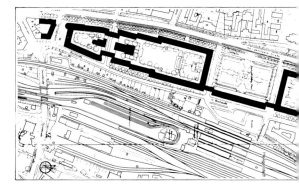

Karl Ehn 1884–1957

Karl Ehn 1884–1957

House I, Princeton, New Jersey, USA
1967–1968

"Architecture will have to be capable of discussing both its traditional mode of expressing meaning and its way of resolving the problem of function" (P.E.)

"Cardboard architecture": between 1967 and 1983, Peter Eisenman designed a series of ten houses, numbering them with Roman numerals I to X. He referred to them as cardboard architecture by way of synthesizing the process of dematerialization and abstraction that he had

followed in creating them. Despite the sense of ephemerality in Eisenman's definition, House I can be taken as the first concrete manifestation of Eisenman's theories, which were destined to change the development of contemporary architecture. More precisely, Eisenman's plans for House I can be seen to date to the period when he was a member of the group of architects that came to be known as the New York Five.

In 1969, a show was held at the Museum of Modern Art in New York at which Kenneth Frampton presented the works of Eisenman, Michael Graves, John Hejduk, Richard Meier, and Charles Gwathmey to the public. The five architects were recognized as a group only in 1972; what their styles had in common was the search for a conceptual architecture that, rejecting all mannerist expressions, took a polemical stand in favor of the pure and abstract forms of classical modernity and took Le Corbusier and the De Stijl movement as their principal sources of inspiration. Made for particularly sophisticated clients, the group's experiments, highly original operations of decomposition and deconstruction of the architectural object, came under attack from critics for being extraneous to the American landscape and—with particular reference to Eisenman's houses—for presenting architecture possessed of only scarce functionality. But it is precisely that refusal to accept functional demands as matrices and guidelines that serves as the starting point for Eisenman's daring designs. Applied to the construction of houses, these audacious ideas create objects with all the qualities of true experiments. With the approval of the buyer, the geometric arrangement of the house may undergo sudden 90-degree rotations, columns do not reach the ground, stairs do not necessarily lead to another floor, and the volumes of a house become stratified

through the overlapping and sliding of the geometric masses used as basic shapes. House I resulted from the ambitious goal of creating a new spatial model and was the response to a hardly traditional request from the buyers. In fact, the house was conceived as a toy museum, an annex to the nearby residence of a couple of Princeton professionals. With its unusual L shape, the house is an attempt to create a relationship between two very different dimensions by way of a superimposition and stratification of the floors: there is the dimension of the toys, with its reduced scale, and there is the dimension of normal human activity. The result is a series of spaces that, with leaps in scale from the normal to the very small, is designed to make the visitor concentrate on the size of the toys. Despite its experimental program of spatial deconstruction, the house remains tied to a certain formal rigidity that is typically Modernist.

Peter Eisenman 1932

Aronoff Center for Design and Art, University of Cincinnati, Ohio, USA
1988–1996

"What all of that alludes to is the overcoming of the classical concept of composition in favor of that of transformation, synonymous with the process protracted in time"
(P.E.)

The term *deconstructivism* loomed large in the field of architecture during the summer of 1988, most of all

Peter Eisenman, Zaha M. Hadid, Coop Himmelblau, and Bernard Tschumi, architects having in common the use of computerized design and elaboration in their efforts to create new spatial structures. It was the French philosopher Jacques Derrida who provided a clear definition of the term *deconstruction* and, thanks to his cross-disciplinary learning, applied it to the field of architecture: "When I discovered what is today known as deconstructivist architecture,I was interested

with the other media and other arts so as to contaminate architecture." What Derrida theorized found concrete application in 1988 in Peter Eisenman's design for the Aronoff Center for Design and Art in Cincinnati.
The electronic and digital control of the design allowed this creation by Eisenman to confront a new, complex spatiality, becoming a sort of three-dimensional synthesis of every twentieth-century avant-garde experiment in the dynamics of space and the non-linearity of figures and thereby contaminating architectural procedures with influences from a variety of other fields, first among them that of the deformability and fluidity of structures. Every traditional approach to the discipline of architecture was replaced by a system based on geometric diagrams (functional, reading of the context, deformation, torsion, superimposition, movement), the elaboration of which resulted in the final decomposition of the building. Eisenman replaced the traditional naturalistic or environmental references with an electronic diagram of the pre-existing structures, following which the shape of the Aronoff Center was modeled on the directrixes of the contours of the site, adapting itself, by way of continuous rotations and movements, to the primary axes of a pre-existing building. The resulting structure looks like a dynamic arrangement of superimposed boxes, and it seems to derive its segmentation in layout and in elevation from an ongoing

as a result of an exhibition at the Museum of Modern Art in New York organized by Philip Johnson and Mark Wigley entitled "Deconstructivist Architecture." As the event's two creators emphasized, the exhibition was not intended as an effort to attribute a new style to contemporary architecture but was designed to assemble the works of Frank Gehry, Daniel Libeskind, Rem Koolhaas,

in the fact that these architects deconstructed the essential aspects of tradition and criticized anything that subordinated architecture to something else; as, for example, the value of being useful, or pretty, or inhabitable. And not so as to build things that were useless, ugly, or uninhabitable, but to free architecture from all such external objectives . . . and to put architecture in relationship

structural deformation, whose complex elaboration and visual presentation would not be feasible by way of traditional systems of graphic design.

Peter Eisenman 1932

The Market Place

قرية الـ...

Rural village of New Gourna, Luxor, Egypt
1948–1953

"When an architect has a clear and sharp tradition, such as a village built by peasants, he has no right to destroy it with his personal fantasies" (H.F.)

New concerns of an environmentalist nature have brought the most recent expressions of contemporary architecture into a close rapport with the values typical of a given landscape and with the problems of adjusting to and also preserving local and regional ecosystems. Such new concerns are partially responsible for the contemporary reappraisal of traditional and regional styles of architecture.
The village of New Gourna, designed and built by Hassan Fathy between 1948 and 1953, represents the attempt to reintroduce an ancient building method that involves, as a primary first step, the use of low-cost traditional technologies, in particular handmade mud bricks dried in the sun.
Even more, however, the undertaking meant the return to urban layouts and building designs based on traditional Islamic architecture.
The need for the new village arose from the need to relocate the community

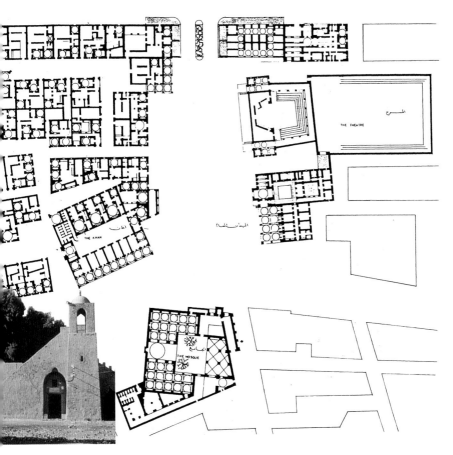

of workers involved in the archeological excavations at nearby Luxor.

The new village has a compact layout composed of the dense pattern of the residential fabric, which includes large open spaces surrounded by public buildings.

The mosque, the market, and the artisan center are the fulcrums of the new village, with the public life of the village taking place around these sites.

The residential system, on the other hand, displays a great deal of variety, with a wide gamut of possibilities, all of which, however, have in common a recurrent building type with an open central court, the *sahn*. Around this space, site of encounters among members of the various family units, the domestic life of the village takes place. These areas include the typical double-height central area, topped by a dome and

surrounded by the many *iwans*, vaulted portals opening into the dome itself.

A system of paths and narrow passages connects the main streets of the village with the semi-private internal courtyards located within the domestic walls, for, as Fathy himself stated, "The sensation of moving from a public to a private space should not be traumatic but instead should be something special for the person who experiences it."

Museum of the Glaciers, Fjærland, Norway
1989–1991

"Try to speak to stone and you will hear a mystical resonance. Speak to a chain of mountains, and it will resound like a mirror. Listen to a forest buried in snow, and you will hear silence"(S.F.)

Perhaps the grand, antique dream of scientific collectionism, that of assembling within a single physical space, a *Kunstkammer*, all the evolution of the cosmos arranged in a hierarchical series of objects, moving from the works of nature up to the artistic creations of humans, could be fulfilled (excluding here every typological reference to the *Kunstkammern*) by the Museum of the Glaciers in Fjærland, if by work of art it is permissible to include the design of the museum itself, the work of the Norwegian architect Sverre Fehn. Located in a deep fjord at the foot of the vast Jostedal glacier, the museum, visited by excursionists on their way towards the peaks of the glaciers, hosts a collection of glacier-related finds and paleontological fragments recording the geological evolution of the land on which the museum itself stands. An expression of the ongoing extension of the architectonic typology of the museum, which today, as Aldo Rossi has

noted, ranges from the cemetery (first historical form of the museum, involving the collection of human bodies) to the missile museum of NASA, the Museum of the Glaciers in Fjærland seems to have derived its forms from the shape of the place itself, against the climatic rigors that it is destined to resist over time, much like the geological fragments it preserves, which have escaped centuries of erosion. Composed of a central, elongated volume that is the bearing axis of the composition, the museum is composed of distinct building elements annexed to its central body.

The cantilevered wooden roof of the entryway leads visitors to the main entrance and then continues upward, flanked by two exterior stairways that lead to a belvedere on the roof of the museum. The central body of the building, the museum's gallery, is illuminated by a series of vertical skylights. To one side of this is the cylindrical volume of the auditorium; to the other is a triangular body occupied by the restaurant, whose walls, made of slanting panes of glass, contrast with the cement solidity of the museum's exterior.

Enlargement of the Olivetti Factory
Ivrea, Italy
1939–1940

"The new architecture, the true architecture, must result from a close adherence to logic and rationality. A rigid constructivism must dictate the rules"(Gruppo 7)

The "new spirit" of architecture that was predicted and then brought into being by the architectonic avant-gardes of European rationalism found its most effective instrument of promotion in Italy in the writings and works of the members of Gruppo 7, an

types, arrived at by the esthetic value of necessity. In solid terms, Gruppo 7 aimed at spreading the expressive potentials of new building methods, such as frameworks in reinforced concrete and large glass surfaces, whose "surface values" and rhythms could give the new architecture monumental and esthetic values not unlike those of classical architecture. Among those few fundamental building types was the industrial factory, always a preferred field for modern architecture because of its outward celebration of

technological innovations were the fruit not only of the experiments of the two architects, who were without doubt influenced by the international lexicon of rationalist architecture, but also of the innovations introduced by the entrepreneurial drive of Adriano Olivetti, whose frequent contact with the United States inspired him to arrange his vast production apparatus in accordance with a scientific organization of work.
Among the various enlargements, the one that, between 1939 and 1940,

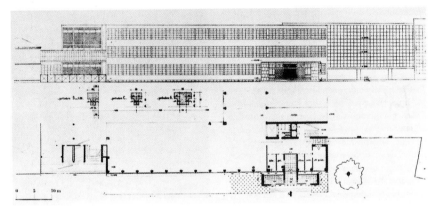

association of seven young architects founded at the Milan Polytechnic in 1926. Keeping their distance from the innovative furor of the Futurist avant-garde, the members of Gruppo 7 sought a more cautious renewal of Italian architecture, one that would involve the rejection of individualism and originality, a goal that could be achieved by limiting the practice of architecture to the use of a few fundamental building

progress. One of the most exceptional and successful examples of this type in Italy was the series of enlargements that the architects Luigi Figini and Gino Pollini, who had been highly active members of Gruppo 7, by then extinct, made for the Olivetti factory in Ivrea between 1934 and 1957.
Expressions of a refined internationalism in architectonic forms, the enlargements and their

turned the factory's façade on via Jervis into a single, uninterrupted glass surface based its profiles on the use of a curtain-wall system of building. However, the double windows that uninterruptedly cover the grid of pillars (4 × 13 meters) give the surface a highly original value.

Figini–Pollini

Garrison Church,
Ulm, Germany
1906–1910

"The needs of the Protestant church, whose fundamental objective is a unitary space with good acoustics, leads to the use of the new large-span supporting structures"(T.F.)

The first president of the Deutscher Werkbund, the famous association of artists, artisans, and industrialists

founded in Munich in 1907, Theodor Fischer made, between 1908 and 1910, the first religious building in Germany with a supporting structure of exposed reinforced concrete. The Protestant church was created to meet the needs of the many soldiers garrisoned in Ulm. Fischer was called on to create a space capable of holding, as required by the competition, more than 2,000 soldiers, and to do so without competing

with the symbolic supremacy held by that city's Gothic cathedral.

The exceptional modernity of the religious layout Fischer created results only partially from the reinforced-concrete framework, which can be schematized as a series of arcing trusses left visible and resting, on the exterior, on an equal number of buttresses made of bush-hammered cement, thanks to which the vault rises to cover an open

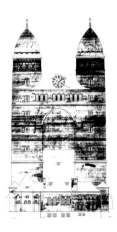

span of 28 meters without intermediate supports. Most of all, the sense of modernity results from the new process of typological trespassing with which Fischer revisits the Romanesque typology of the church with a single apse and a façade of two towers. The revolutionary technique of reinforced concrete permitted him to create a compact and unitary interior space, somewhat comparable to the typology of a single-nave church, but at the same time Fischer overturned the classical layout followed by the Catholic religion, according to which the light and the sequence of the space should converge on the main altar. The distortion of the historical model, expressed in the location of the entrance to the church in the tower placed in the area of the apse and in the location of the body of the towers, the traditional Westwerk, towards the east behind the altar, is reflected in the internal space, which, following the Protestant liturgy, concentrates the faithful as close as possible to the bare walls of the pulpit and the altar. In this way every scenographic and dramatic element is held in abeyance until the moment of leaving the church, when the faithful turn their backs to the east.

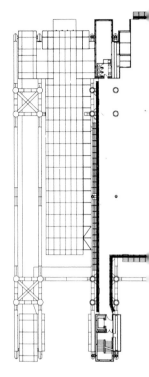

Hong Kong and Shanghai Bank, Hong Kong, China
1979–1986

"The project makes it possible to reconcile the artistic aspects of the construction with the problems of cost, time, and quality control" (N.F.)

The development of Modern architecture is historically related to parallel developments in technology. The definition of the architectonic image as an unrestrained reflection of the technological prestige of its constructive elements is associated with a certain trend within contemporary architecture, attributable to the most recent high-tech style; at the same time, however, the idea boasts deep roots that can be traced back to the nineteenth century and the innovations that the practice of structural engineering then began bringing to the language of architecture, loading it with new techno-formal requirements.

Without doubt the most recurrent of these innovations is the one in which architects reveal the bearing structure of a building, along with the elements of its physical plant, in the façade of the building, thus obtaining the highest degree of flexibility in terms of the internal spaces. The style, attributable to a generalized celebration of the esthetics of

progress, has come to the fore thanks to the widespread use of reinforced concrete and steel. It has found its preferred field of application in the typology of the skyscraper. With a height of 180 meters, the new central office of the Hong Kong and Shanghai Bank stands in the heart of the business quarter of Hong Kong. Having cost an estimated US$600 million, it is believed to be the most expensive building of the modern era. Its structure revolutionized the classical typology of the skyscraper as a compact column. Indeed, it presents a revolutionary steel structure composed of four enormous pilasters that, repeated in double series on each of the three faces that divide the building, bear giant strutted beams from which the floors of the company offices are literally suspended by way of steel cables.

These are set at different heights on each of the three faces, ranging from a minimum of 28 to a maximum of 47 floors. The structural system, highly visible from outside the building, is revealed in all its skeletal apparatus in the central volume of the building, which, 59 meters high, uses a system of natural lighting regulated by a series of mirrors "capable" of filtering light thanks to computerized mechanisms set to follow the solar calendar.

Carré d'Art, Nîmes, France
1984–1993

"No diagonal in the structure must have an industrial appearance" (N.F.)

The structural gigantism that characterizes the most spectacular creations of high-tech architecture finds its corresponding dimensional reduction in the Carré d'Art, a building that Norman Foster inserted in the special historical site of the ancient Roman forum of Nîmes, measuring himself against the pre-existing environmental and monumental setting. Far from the overworked structural estheticism of high tech, Foster's undertaking is concentrated on several principles of ancient architecture, even if he clearly detaches himself from classical architecture in the formal and figurative senses. The indifference to contextual setting that often isolates the products of technological invention from the surrounding urban setting is transformed by Foster into an encounter between the ancient and the new, a contrast achieved through the construction of a cultural complex (the Carré d'Art) directly opposite the Maison Carrée (a Roman temple dating to the third century AD).

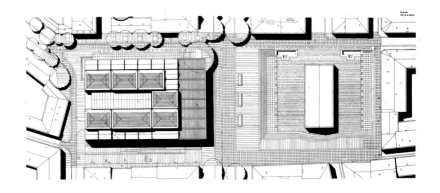

Standing on the edge of a lot occupied by a theater that was destroyed by fire in 1952, the Carré d'Art is a technological cubic envelope that hosts a media center and a museum of contemporary art within its shiny and regular panels, shielded by *brise-soleil*.
Raised on a solid base dressed in white stone, the center includes a system of pathways that leads by way of three parallel stairways from the raised floor of the covered plaza to the art galleries, located on the upper floors and illuminated by a system of skylights, or to the underground floors occupied by libraries, media centers, a cinema, and storerooms.
The side of the new building that faces the plaza and the side of the Roman temple is shaded by a full-height portico supported by thin steel pillars that give it a sense of classical austerity. In this way the new, hypertechnological volume of the Carré d'Art presents itself as a pure expression of the spirit of our time rather than a manifestation of the personal artistry of its creator, and seeks to create a dialogue with the eternal and impersonal form of the Maison Carré.

Maison des Artes, Michel de Montaigne University, Bordeaux, France
1992–1995

"Architecture understood as a discipline, like writing, is of no interest to me at all; architecture interests me when it is not architecture" (M.F.)

The recent urbanistic investigations into the sense of discontinuity and the fragmentary nature of urban phenomena have led to a new kind of relationship in the field of designbetween architectonic product and urban structure.

that perhaps only certain modern films succeed in analyzing with scientific clarity. In this regard various statements from Massimiliano Fuksas on the future of architecture seem apt: "The ideal place for architecture to exist is where there is an interruption, an accident, a moment of suspension in the urban metabolism"; "Types do not exist because buildings only rarely maintain the same function; usually transformations are the only way for an architecture to continue to exist as itself." A consequence of this instability and absence of sense of place

articulation of functions that has always been associated with the complexity of the urban scene.

The Maison des Artes in Bordeaux hides behind its elegant copper film a theater, an exhibition gallery, studio-laboratories, a projection room, and administrative offices. The building's layout, a narrow, elongated rectangle, is composed of a series of three blocks. The first is the large auditorium; on top of it, and set down so as to project markedly beyond its façade, is a glass parallelepiped protected by a sun guard. A slightly inclined ramp, covered by a light roof, connects this area to the level of the roof of the building. The hermetic volume of the façades is broken only by a horizontal strip that runs along the entire perimeter of the building and by two vertical cuts in the longer sides that are furnished with glass doors that permit the visitor to make out the purpose of the building. Oxidation of the material of the covering will maintain the provisional and mutable character of the building through the passing of time.

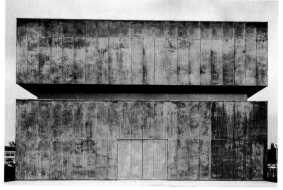

The traditional readings of the city, based as they were on typological and morphological research, with reference to the temporal conformation and stratification of the parts of the city, left room for a new discipline that, banishing the traditional urbanistic tools, seeks to make its way into the most indecipherable folds of the suburban discontinuity, the places and spaces that are exposed to that loss of meaning and representability

is the tendency found in certain contemporary architecture to apply sculptural modeling to volumes that are closed and isolated with respect to the surrounding environment. The building and its "sculpted" shape are thus made into bearers of the urban and artistic values that are physically absent, values that our collective imagination still identifies and concentrates in the shape of its outlines, the

Massimiliano Fuksas 1944

La Bottega d'Erasmo, Turin, Italy
1953–1956

"We have never proposed ourselves a typology, unrepeatable, not even by us; we would want every act to be conclusive in and of itself, born from the fecundation of its own hypotheses, formed from remote suggestions" (G. – I.)

When it was first presented in the pages of the magazine *Casabella-continuità* in 1957, this building, designed to house an antiquarian bookshop and apartments, was considered scandalous. Today, its façade seems at the most original, but at the time it was immediately seen as a symbol of the thoroughly Italian style that took the name of neo-Liberty, and it set off a heated international debate, in which the revival of the values of tradition proposed by a group of young Italian architects was misunderstood by the authoritative English critic Reyner Banham, who saw it as "the Italian withdrawal from modern architecture," guilty of "regressing," according to the historian, towards certain stylistic elements typical of the Jugendstil, of Art Nouveau, or of the Vienna Secession.

Looked at more closely, La Bottega d'Erasmo ("The Workshop of Erasmus"), designed by Roberto Gabetti and Aimaro Oreglia d'Isola,

can be seen to have been a courageous gesture that, within the sphere of a general rejection of an evolutionistic model of modernity, inaugurated an attitude of critical revision of the linguistic canons of the Modern movementand the International Style. Neo-Liberty opposed these by enriching the architectonic lexicon with various forms from the historical tradition and by returning to the artisan dimension within architectonic design; attention to the constructive detail and the pre-existing context thus replaced the values of standardization and indifference to place proposed by Modern architecture. Designed, therefore, to inaugurate a new and still-active period of design, the building by Gabetti and Isola evokes a plurality of historical references and of time-tested building methods that have their roots in the Turin building tradition. More specifically, with curtain walls in exposed brick and projecting bow windows supported by decorative brackets that taper downward, the building revived "remote suggestions" derived not so much from any style of the past as from a certain decorative and plastic symbolism abolished by the culture of Modern architecture.

Casa alle Zattere, Cicogna Condominium, Venice, Italy
1953–1958

"If a construction does not have a certain quality of adhering to use, clearly it is located outside the possibilities of being architecture. . . . However, this adherence to use is not sufficient if it does not possess an emotional charge that makes it become architecture, and not construction" (I.G.)

The problematic coexistence of the new and the antique, a situation whose conditions are amplified by the values of the historical and environmental patrimony of the city of Venice, finds a point of balance in the construction of the Cicogna Condominium, which Ignazio Gardella skillfully inserted beside the church of the Spirito Santo on the Giudecca canal. The prohibition of any local or regional characteristic, and the need to adjust the architecture to repeated and universal constructive principles, made Gardella pay close attention to the setting in order to initiate a highly intense dialogue between architecture and setting. Attributable to the principles of environmentalism included in the theory of "environmental pre-existences" elaborated by Ernesto Nathan Rogers and experimented with in the Torre Velasco in Milan during this same period, the

Casa alle Zattere is full of the contextual and typological allusions that Gardella used to proportion and revisit the geometric and dimensional matrices that underlie the construction of a functional and modern condominium typology. The house stands on a corner lot between the fondamenta della Zattere, on the Giudecca canal, and the calle dello Zucchero, and occupies the base of a pre-existing building except on the side where it touches the church of the Santo Spirito, where it is indented in order to leave the corner pilaster visible.

The house has five floors; on the front facing the canal the fourth floor is recessed slightly from the line of the façade, while the last floor on the front facing the canal is recessed all around to make room for a terrace whose parapet closes off the entire composition.

Gardella fitted the new building to the pre-existing setting along the Giudecca canal not only by using traditional building materials in the modern structure (plaster made with crushed brick, windowsills, parapets, and wainscoting in "Vicenza limestone," and "Venetian-style" windows), but also by basing the geometric modulations of the partitions of the new façade on the adjacent Renaissance façade.

Casa Milá, Barcelona, Spain
1906–1910

"The projecting elements must be put together with those that are recessed in such a way that each convex element, which is located in full light, is contrasted by a concave element, meaning one that is in shadow"(A.G.)

The international language of Art Nouveau, which arose from the generic rejection of the historical styles of the past, which it replaced with new symbolic forms inspired directly by nature, led to various regional variations, including one that developed in Barcelona during the last decades of the nineteenth century and came to be known as Catalan Modernism. Although similar to other contemporary European reactions to nineteenth-century eclecticism, Catalan Modernism stood apart from such movements because of its thoroughly indigenous character, which, against the backdrop of a more widespread cultural rebirth of the Catalan tradition, joined progressive tendencies towards a renewal of classical values based on both the Mediterranean culture and the more traditional forms of Spain's Islamic patrimony. The transfiguration of this stylistic repertory, along with a version of naturalism that was inspired not so much by predetermined forms drawn from the "great book of nature" as by a process of metamorphosis innate in the patrimony of living forms, found its most successful manifestation in the work of Antoni Gaudí, a highly original exponent of Catalan Modernism.

Often compared to the waves of the sea or to the roundness of the rocks of Monserrat because of its wavy outline, the Casa Milá is a unique architectural compendium of technological innovations and natural and symbolic forms. Based on an aggregation of mutable basic units, the distribution of the six floors that compose the building is centered on two internal patios, one circular and one semi-oval. The four large apartments located on each floor are arranged around and between these patios and are served by two elevators and three stairways, along with

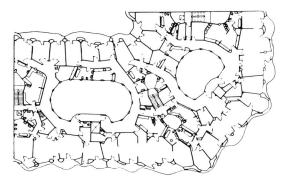

winding hallways of variable width. The exceptional dynamism of this arrangement is achieved by way ofaninnovative method of construction, thanks to which Gaudí prefigures the revolutionary typology of the free, or open, interior plan. The absence of bearing walls is achieved by a system of columns made in brick and concrete or, in the lower floors, of stone that, together with a network of iron girders, rise along the floors, without any vertical continuity, each one supporting a different concentric load.

The concave – convex sinuosity of the profile of the façade was obtained by "hanging" the exterior covering from a framework of iron beams, while a system of parabolic arches permitted Gaudí to configure the cornice of the building as an undulating body of varying height.

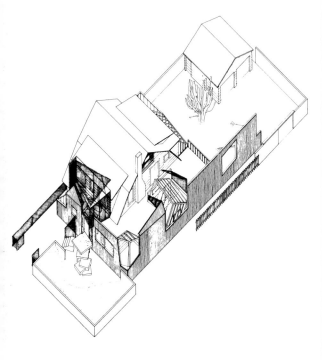

Gehry House,
Santa Monica,
California, USA
1977–1979

*"The appearance and then
disappearance of people that pass
behind the antique windows, today
inside, between the living room
and kitchen, has an almost unreal
theatricality" (F.G.)*

It was the reworking of a small
house located in a modest
residential neighborhood of

Santa Monica that thrust Frank
Gehry into the center of
public and critical
attention. The house was his
own, and he performed this
operation of amplification in
1977. In effect Gehry
subverted the changeless
familiarity of an ordinary two-
story Dutch colonial style
house by emptying out the
interior of the building and
then wrapping it in a new
"film" made up of a collage of
chain-link fencing, corrugated

metal siding, and safety glass,
the simple, mundane materials
with which Gehry went on to
create his popular and
collective poetry of the
"cheapscape," destined to
reappear with increasing
frequency in his later works.
The result of the enlargement
was a new, U-shaped body,
covering three sides of the
original house and leaving the
fourth side unchanged, thus
making it still possible to
recognize the outline and

volume of the original. The added volume projects from the façade of the original home. On the ground floor it includes an entryway vestibule, with access to the house provided by a series of uneven, recessed steps, and the area of the kitchen, where Gehry's experimentalism inserted a large skylight positioned at a slanting angle to the house and an exterior wall, where a layer of asphalt, in an ideal continuity with the sidewalk alongside the house, acts as pavement.

Gehry seems to have turned to the avant-garde experiments of the early twentieth century for much of the inspiration of his radical innovations. The first that comes to mind is the technique of the ready-mades with which Marcel Duchamp took quite ordinary objects and managed to load them with symbolic values and double meanings. In the same way, the original house, left intact with all its domestic connotations and only partially concealed by the anonymous corrugated-metal shed, achieves the status of an *objet retrouvé*, the first cause of the intended sense of disorientation that the house today transmits to its visitors.

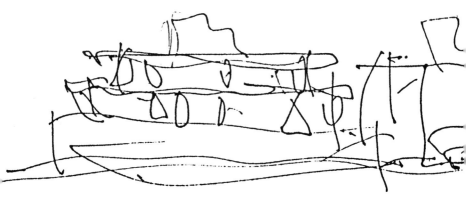

Chiat/Day/Mojo Advertizing Agency, Venice, California, USA
1985–1991

"Even if our cities have a horrible appearance, they are expressions of our politics, which are not authoritarian" (F.G.)

The relationship between Frank Gehry's eccentric constructions and the language of pop art is in plain view in the building he made

in Los Angeles to serve as the headquarters of Chiat/Day/Mojo. A true paradigm of revisited pop architecture, it is a building that could not find a more ideal setting than Venice, California, a protected suburb in a chaotic Los Angeles where the experimental efforts of a new and emerging generation of artists began to make themselves felt in the 1980s. The populist spirit that characterizes the informal

approach of much of contemporary American pop architecture originated in experiments performed in the 1930s, parallel to developments on the film sets of Hollywood, that charged certain architectural typologies with new iconic and symbolic values. Among the most entrancing of the techniques that Morris Lapidus has called the "architecture of persuasion" is the leap in scale, meaning the

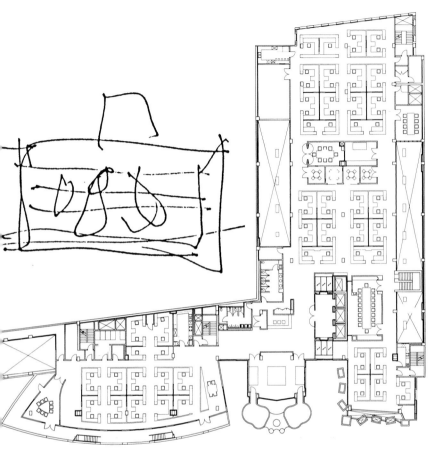

enlargement of objects drawn from daily life and then applied to experimental architecture or that themselves become architectural volumes. Generated in part by a strategy designed to attract the attention of car drivers— people moving along the endless roadways of Los Angeles while making use of the only means capable of offering them freedom of movement—these pieces,

most often produced by local artists, were giving artistic and sculptural bodies to buildings as early as the 1930s, freeing the structures from every traditional construction procedure.
Developed on three floors, with a total surface area of about 7,000 square meters, the new headquarters of Chiat/Day/Mojo faces Main Street with three different architectonic "episodes." Located between an

unbroken, curving façade dressed in stucco and marked off by regular openings and a body dressed in copper that ends in an "earthquaked" section of beams and girders is an outsized pair of binoculars designed by Oldenburg and van Bruggen that, apart from functioning as an exceptional addition to the agency's image, serves as the main entrance to the building and hosts offices and meeting rooms on its two floors.

Guggenheim Museum, Bilbao, Spain
1991–1997

"My sketches are gestures: how to have them built? I have succeeded thanks to the computer; otherwise I would never have tried" (F.G.)

The dynamic city envisioned by the futurist avant-garde; the vital energy with which Cubist painting fragmented three-dimensional space, presenting it from multiple points of view; the dematerialization of architectonic structures performed by the plastic, curvilinear forms of architectural Expressionism; and, finally, the most recent fluid deformations of architectonic objects—all of these seem to flow together in the virtual "living organism" that is the Guggenheim Museum in Bilbao, Spain. With its exhibition spaces spread across a total area of 24,000 square meters, the museum has prompted the conversion of the postindustrial area in which it stands into a stronghold of the services sector, coming to involve the Basque city in a more widespread program of social restructuring. Looking out over the Nervión River and scenically extended beneath the Puente de la Salve, which crosses it, the museum hosts an auditorium for 300 people, shops, restaurants, and exhibition

spaces for temporary and permanent shows distributed in the central multifloor gallery—which rises at its highest point to 50 meters above the level of the river—as well as the several elongated galleries that open off it. Gehry's preliminary studies, of a Neoexpressionist matrix, were translated into the flowing, "informal" shapes that characterize the outline of the museum by means of a complex program of digital elaboration. The artistic and gestural forms that Gehry produced, and which hardly seemed feasible to build, were first geometrically re-created in three-dimensional digital models. These were then reworked by way of graphic reproductions and scale models, with each step of the final construction subject to such detailed cost controls that in the end the creation of the curvilinear structure was made financially competitive.

Built on a ground plan that resembled twenty-sevenpetals twisted around the central nucleus of the entryway, the museum's shiny titanium cladding hides a supporting structural complex of galvanized steel. The thrilling fluidity of the architectural object reveals further qualities during days of strong wind. At such times the thin titanium plates (0.38 mm) vibrate, in some places expanding in surface area under the force of the wind.

Frank O. Gehry 1929

Restoration and rehabilitation of the Roman theater of Sagunto, Valencia, Spain
1985–1993

"Working on constructions that are in a ruinous state almost always means working on things that still seem, for some reason, incomplete, that have not yet exhausted their responses . . . such constructions still seem like ongoing projects" (G.G.)

The debate on the theory of architectural restoration has taken different forms over the course of history in response to continuous changes in terms of the limits that should

be placed on such undertakings. The theory of philological restoration, based, at least in principle, on solid documentary support and on granting the restorer only the mostrestricted faculties of initiative, has been replaced by a discipline in which the limits of the operation established to separate the field of architectonic design from that of restoration tend to be annulled or at least reduced. Leaving aside the lively debate

that has taken shape around the specific qualities that should belong to the techniques involved in the preservation, restoration, or reuse of the existing patrimony, we will refer to a practice of disciplinary trespassing that can be defined by the term "critical restoration."

In essence, it is a discipline characterized by two contrasting attitudes: respect for the work that is the object of the operation, taken in its actual state, and the actions taken tochange that state with the goal of bringing the symbolic value and the constructive logic of the structure back to life. Thus "critical restoration" is not an expression of the desire for an undefined autonomy of the creative act over the conservationist act, but rather is the point of arrival of a slow internal process within the discipline of restoration that, in contrast to purely stylistic restoration, gives life to the new technique. Applied to the preservation of a structure, this technique succeeds in restituting the constructive logic of the forms and does so through recourse to changes and additions.

Within the most recent trends that contrast careful and rigorous preservation of ancient structures with new interventions carried out using the technique of comparing and contrasting, the work of Giorgio Grassi represents a different and exemplary case, played out along the vague borderline in which the supremacy of the new over the old alternates with the novelties that the old (the

ancient structure) can unexpectedly succeed in exhibiting in a project.

The restoration and "architectonic restitution," of the Roman theater of Sagunto followed the scrupulous and precise program laid out by the architect.

The initial necessary consolidations and completions of the existing structure were followed, in respect to the archaeological remains, by the reconstruction of pieces and portions of the theater aimed at restituting a clear and recognizable reading of the "architectonic space" to the Roman theater of Sagunto. The phase of cleaning and restoration was followed by the architectonic resolution of the structure that Grassi adopted to resolve the reconstruction of the parascenium of the theater. Aware of the impossibility of restoring the ancient splendor, Grassi went against the canonical configuration of the parascenium and instead made visible the wall of the postscenium (the back of the parascenium, traditionally hidden from the view of the public). This wall,covered by large decorative and archeological elements that had been housed in a small museum earlier located at the foot of one of the two towers of the postscenium, performs the eminently theatrical role of the traditional parascenium, synthesized by Grassi with monumental wainscoting and stairs in the lower area, traditionally resting on the proscenium.

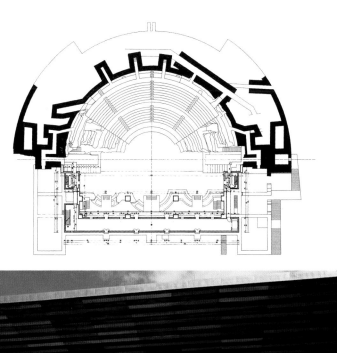

University Library, Valencia, Spain
1996–1998

"We must almost always recognize that monumentality in architecture is grandness obtained with a minimum of means. It is the grandness of simplicity and of the ordinary that never ceases to amaze us"(G.G.)

Giorgio Grassi's most recent works, whether involving the reconstruction of an ancient building or the creation of new structural volumes, have been grouped in a collection that their author called *Progetto per la città antica*. This is intended to make immediately clear that each of his creations, even if immersed in the reality of the contemporary city, takes the ancient city as its model, and not only in the material sense but also in the wider meaning that includes the customs and habits of the city of the past. The object, as Grassi lucidly explained, is to take action in the city not by means of personal poetics but rather on the basis of plans that seem to have always belonged to the city, "as though they had been included, even before their appearance, in the expressive horizon of the city as it has always been."

It is only logical that such a design methodology would evoke the category of mediocrity, which is often and

necessarily cited by Grassi to describe his works. It is mediocrity that implies clarity in the intention of a design obtained, under the formal profile, by means of recourse to the values of schematics, banality, repetition, and normalcy, accompanied by an instinctual renouncement of all personal inventiveness. The university library in Valencia evokes all the categories cited above, to which it is permissible to add that of monumentality, which for Grassi is synonymous with good architecture. It is a modern, scientific library, meaning fully functioning. In terms of itsphysical arrangement, it has a central layout, being arranged around a large full-height atrium, around the perimeter of which are shelves of books on several floors, accessible by way of galleries. Beyond the perimeter walls of the central atrium are the true stacks, in turn directly connected to the reading rooms located on three floors. The library, dressed entirely in brick, stands apart from the surrounding buildings thanks to the rustic stone base on which it is raised and which extends around its full perimeter. It is an element that serves to detach the library from its context and to isolate it; it also serves to house the main technical services and a large covered parking area.

Humana Building, Louisville, Kentucky, USA
1982

"The main interest of the language of architecture is the metaphorical representation of man and the landscape"(M.G.)

The movement known as Postmodernism began with a strong objection to the Modern, which was seen as a period dominated by the ideal of progress and by the promotion of the new and the untried. In terms of architecture, first in America and later in Europe, the 1960s saw a renewed relationship with traditional and vernacular building methods, to which was added a widespread return of the styles of the past. An immediate consequence of this contemporary historicism was the revival of the symbolic and decorative values that the rationalistic and homologizing language of the Modern movement had silenced. The new symbolic paradigm and the plurality of signifiers which it can recall in the field of Postmodern architecture have been synthesized by the critic Charles Jencks in the concept of the "double code." "A Postmodern building is a building that, to put it briefly, communicates on at least two levels at the same time: to other architects and to the minority that understands the specific meanings of architecture, and to a more vast public or to the inhabitants of the place that think about other problems, such as comfort, traditional construction, style of life. Thus Postmodern architecture looks like a hybrid . . . this discontinuity of taste

and culture is the theoretical base of the 'double code' of Postmodernism."

Looking at the Humana Building by Michael Graves from this point of view, one must admit that it is one of the most successful works of Postmodern culture. Not only because of the outstanding skill its creator demonstrated in rejecting the compositional system presented by the textual citation—the principal cause of Postmodern failures— in favor of a design technique inspired by the reworking and reforming of architectonic elements from the past, but most of all because this building possesses urban qualities with which every citizen can identify.

A result of the rejection of the inexpressiveness that characterizes the contemporary typology of the skyscraper, the Humana Building is a modern office building that, with its 27 stories of height, is loaded with symbolic and monumental values that can be perceived by the public at large. Based on a shaft–pyramid shape and composed following the classical tripartite division (base, shaft, capital), the building stands in a row of low Renaissance-style buildings and a tall anonymous skyscraper in iron and steel. The base, which extends to sidewalk,is in the form of a portico, with high, narrow openings that,creating an open connection to the street, lead to an internal plaza at the center of which is a spectacular fountain. The tower, set back from the base, rises through an uninterrupted series of floors to end at a convex, projecting body that acts as a cornice.

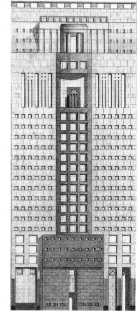

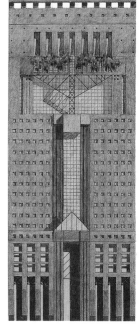

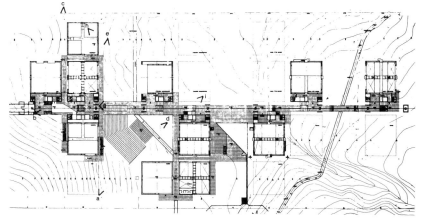

The New Campus University of Calabria, Cosenza, Italy

(with Emilio Battisti, Hiromichi Matsui, Pierluigi Nicolin, Franco Purini, Carlo Rusconi Clerici, Bruno Viganò)
1973–1984

"To build the project one must first of all establish a rule . . . what gives truth and architectonic solidity to the rule is its encounter with the site: only experience of the site can generate the

exceptions that will open and shape the architecture"(V.G.)

Beginning with an evolutionistic point of view that sees as the origin of architecture not the first homes set up in those mythic caves, and much less the establishment of the structural guidelines behind the primitive hut, but instead the taking possession of a certain piece of land and its subsequent modification at the

hands of human beings so as to set it apart from the undefined remainder of the surface of the earth, Vittorio Gregotti has traced the coordinates for a method of architectonic design that, while making no attempt to imitate the environmental setting, creates model installations suitable to the complexity of the pre-existing geographical conditions. The topography of the site thus becomes a new parameter of measurement to

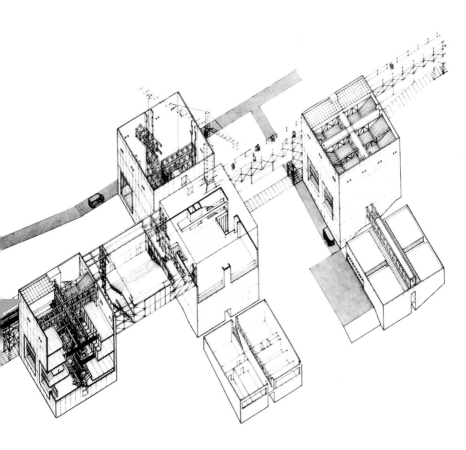

which the architect can refer in determining the relationship between architecture and landscape, adapting, for large-scale undertakings, the necessary "typology" of the megastructure or the infrastructure, to determine the impact of the architecture on the site. The design for the University of Calabria adjusts to the altimetric unevenness of the hilly region of the valley of the Crati River by means of the linear structure of a metal bridge supported by pylons of reinforced cement that, extending 3,200 meters across the valley, connects the various pavilions and the services that compose the university, in all 21 different buildings. Aligned at the constant height of the bridge, the various teaching facilities built as pavilions follow the variations in height of the site and are joined to the large infrastructure on three levels (pedestrian, technical services, automobiles) by means of thin vertical technical volumes.

The university services are located at the points where the metal bridge crosses the streets that serve the various hills. These are also the sites of a system of plazas that connects the residential units located above with the university system in a more general cohesion between site and architectonic installation.

ENEA Research Center alla Casaccia, Rome, Italy
1985

"The use of historical material in design has become increasingly frequent; it has gone from ideological to stylistic to evocative to demonstrative to the rejection not of what is new but of what is contemporary"(V.G.)

Vittorio Gregotti expressed his rejection of the obsessive relationship that certain contemporary architecture establishes with history and with the architectonic forms of the past by way of an appeal to the values inherent in the correct professional practice of architecture, which, following the line of rational thought, arrives at the principle of "not artisticity." Architectonic forms that are almost depersonalized and that have been purified of every symbolic formalism imposed a priori or inherited from the historical patrimony end up re-establishing a direct relationship with contemporary reality, restituting to architecture its lost integrity. The creations of the Gregotti and Associates studio fall into esthetic categories that refer to principles of regularity, symmetry, simplicity, and objectivity. In these works, the elaboration of the exterior form is often given less weight in the design than the complexity of the spatial and functional interrelations to which the program of a modern building, public or private, must respond.

One such "merely" programmed building is the new research center of Italy's ENEA (Ente Nazionale di Energie Alternative; the national institute for alternative energy). The closed and almost hermetic form of its volume is directly related to the functional and technical requirements of the scientific laboratories located within its walls. Built to house laboratories for the performance of reliability tests along with spaces for computer research, the building is laid out around two large full-height main laboratories for the performance of mechanical tests. These are separated from each other by a glassed-in corridor from which all the phases of the work can be overseen.

The offices are located off a series of halls running along the outer walls of the building on all four floors. They are illuminated by the 160 × 160 centimeter windows that give the façade of the building its regular pattern. The window frames are set back from the façade of the building, exposing the 70 centimeters of distance between the exterior dressing of iron gray prefabricated panels and the interior perimeter of the building, which shows up on the façade in the electric blue of the trimming and is strategically exploited in the housings for the technical implants necessary for the offices and laboratories.

104

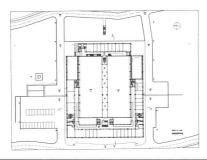

Vittorio Gregotti 1927

Fagus Works, Alfeld-an-der-Leine, Germany
(with Adolf Meyer)
1911–1914

"One sensed that this building had been conceived to make the work done by people and machines easier for both of them. For the workers, light and air; for the machines, space and order" (W.G.)

Between 1908 and 1910, Walter Gropius worked as an apprentice in the Berlin office of Peter Behrens, who was busy during that period on the important worksite of the AEG turbine factory. For Gropius, those were years of a certain monumentality matched by a sense of the classical, rare aspects of his work that show up in the building he designed for the offices of the Fagus shoe-last factory, a building that stands as his masterpiece, distinguished for its surprisingly mature and revolutionary rationalist language. The result of efforts to achieve an architectural language that would incorporate the conquests of industrial and technological progress in a way that would confer the sense of "machine" to the design of a building, the Fagus Works complex is arranged to serve the needs of mechanical processes and assembly-line production, its spaces, rhythms, and overall layout corresponding to those criteria.

An accurate reflection of the organization that determines and regulates the rational division of labor, the factory presents its most successful encounter between the architectural culture and industrial civilization in the glass body of the offices, the L-shape of which surrounds the lower volumes of the factory and laboratories. Stripped bare of the noble classicism with which Behrens had turned the AEG factory into a new cathedral of work, the language used by Gropius owes its originality to items of industrial production that he managed to adapt to the scale of the building. Thus the enormous glass surfaces and the thin steel skeleton, which for the first time in a building supports the outer shell of the building but is not visible, are nothing but unaltered objects of industrial production that have been enlarged to make the factory building itself into an oversized industrial product. The transparency of the glass shell, exceptionally maintained, evenat the corners of the structure, where the glass sheets turn without upright supports (and clearly reveal the interior floors and the stairways, which seem to "float" freely), is counterpointed by the monumentality of the main entrance hall, clad in brick and off center with respect to the longitudinal axis of the main building.

Bauhaus, Dessau, Germany
1925–1926

"The Bauhaus wants to make its contribution to the progress of the contemporary problem of housing, from the simplest domestic utensil to the dwelling itself, designed in all its details"(W.G.)

The state-financed school of art and architecture known as the Bauhaus was founded in

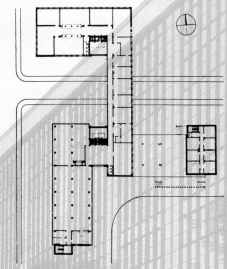

Weimar, Germany, in 1919 with the objective of teaching arts and crafts in a way that produced objects that, unlike those created in traditional schools of the applied arts, would exploit the advances made in industrial technology to become models or prototypes for mass production. The Modern movement divides the history of the school into three periods based on the school's changing locations: Weimar

(1919–1924), Dessau (1925–1930), and Berlin-Steglitz (1930–1933); in a similar fashion, the history of the school experienced alternating periods of support or rejection according to the political climate in Germany and the character of the school's director: Walter Gropius (1919–1928), Hannes Meyer (1928–1930), and Ludwig Mies van der Rohe (1930–1933).

In 1933 the school was definitely closed by the Nazi regime.
Aside from the establishment of the school's underlying philosophy, the years of Gropius's direction were the period in which the various contributions of the European avant-garde, which converged on the school in a confused creative swirl, were directed in an operational method that had as its final goal a realistic encounter between creative

work and mass production. This was achieved in terms of the designed object as well as in terms of the architectural structure by means of a rational process that, freed of any historical or formal preconceptions, broke down the object or structure into elementary parts that served determined functions; these were then reassembled following a more generic combinatorial procedure. This analytical procedure can easily be recognized in the design for the school's new headquarters, made by Gropius in Dessau between 1925 and 1926 and recognized as an unrivaled manifesto of German and European rationalism. The complex of buildings is pervaded by a marked dynamism, perceptible in the arrangement of the structures and further emphasized by the use of different surface treatments for the various façades. The ground floor of the main rectangular building was taken up by the classrooms and workshops; a second, L-shaped building housed the teaching laboratories, auditorium and stage, and a dining hall with kitchen. A bridge suspended over the road between the two buildings added further communication between them and distributed the administrative offices on two floors.
The juncture of the various bodies of different heights gave the complex a dynamic G shape; away from this stood the five-story building with the students' rooms, each with a small balcony projecting from the cubic mass of the building.

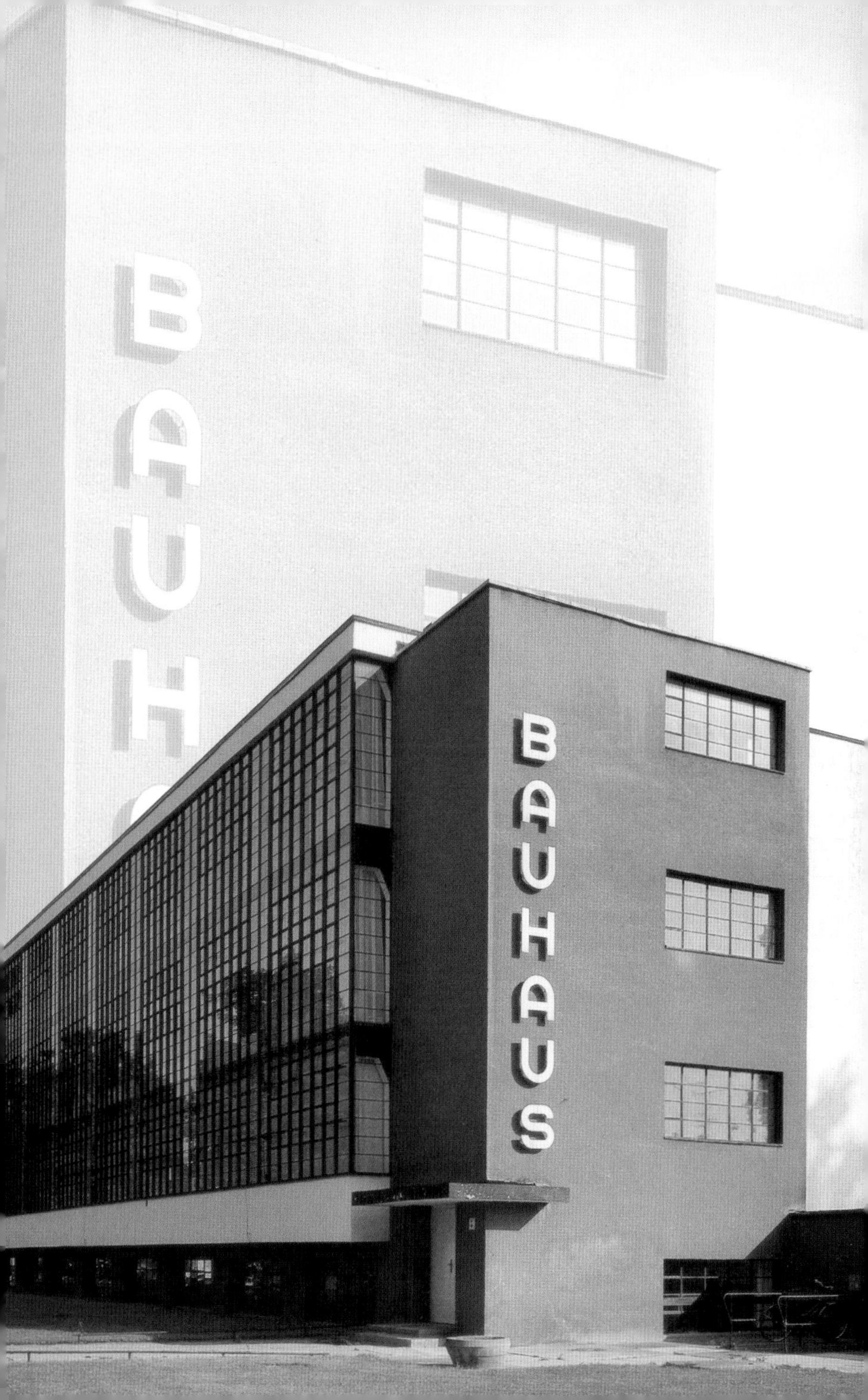
BAUHAUS

Pan Am Building, New York, USA

(with TAC)
1958–1963

"I've been attacked for having contributed to placing a massive building in the middle of an overcrowded area" (W.G.)

The exodus of artists from Germany following the National Socialist takeover in 1933 included the most illustrious members of the Bauhaus. Not even Walter Gropius was spared. Defamed as a "bolshevist of architecture," he moved first to London, where he spent the years 1932 to 1937 in an unsuccessful attempt to continue his experiments within an "English Bauhaus." In 1937 he crossed the Atlantic, having been made a teacher at Harvard University in Massachusetts. In 1945, together with six young colleagues, he founded TAC (The Architects' Collaborative), a modern architectural studio active on a world scale.

The Pan American Airways skyscraper, which was to have become the largest building in the world, located at the center of Park Avenue in New York, was produced by the collaboration of Gropius with the members of TAC. Thus Gropius's artistic decisions, shaped as always to serve the physiological and

psychological needs of humans, had to come to terms with such new concerns as property taxes and, of course, the massive flow of pedestrian and vehicular traffic in the heart of Midtown Manhattan. The resulting building stands over Grand Central Station, a strategic point of confluence of rail and subway lines that is crossed by about 400,000 people each day on its ground floor, which is connected to the station below. The offices of the airline company were spread along the floors of the high tower, which stands on an octagonal base and is supported by a steel framework holding a grid of prestressed concrete.

The Pan American Airways skyscraper creates a visual barrier that blocks the view down Park Avenue, leading some critics to rank it among the worst urban follies of the 1960s.

LF One Pavilion, Weil am Rhein, Germany
1996–1999

"As architects we must respect the habits of people, but at the same time we must design forms of life that are stimulating" (Z.M.H.)

A new relationship between the architectonic object and its setting seems to be giving way to an "informatics landscape" in which, thanks to the most recent applications of computer technology (or IT, Information Technology), the artificiality of architecture can be made to coincide with the true construction of a place. Put in relationship with the essential, cosmic, and natural forces of a site, architecture is transformed into a "natural and topographic solidification" of the land to the point of becoming a kind of Land art. As Charles Jencks has observed, following this artistic process the building becomes a form of the territory; in synthesis, the architecture becomes an articulation of the landscape, a "landform" building. What makes this new relationship between the fluid spatiality of architecture and the natural formations of the landscape possible is geometry, which with the assistance of today's computers can be used to codify natural processes and present them in graphic images.

The LF One Pavilion in Weil am Rhein is a fine example of this new relationship between artifice and nature. A site for rest and entertainment within the Landesgartenschau, the international gardening exhibition in Weil am Rhein, the pavilion is an integral part of a vast garden with a varying topography.

The composition of the building is based entirely on the routes of the garden walkways, three of which, in crossing one another, create

the building's layout.

The first route runs along the southern flank of the pavilion; the second, following the gentle slope of a ramp, leads to the pavilion's roof; the third, making a deep double curve, crosses the pavilion's shortest side. The distribution of the pavilion's inner spaces, which are partially joined one to the next, results from this crossing of directrices.

An exhibition hall and cafeteria are located along the outer walls of the building so as to enjoy natural lighting as well as views of the surrounding nature. The inner nucleus of the building is taken up by offices and secondary rooms; a footpath leads to the terrace and from there to the roof of a small environmental research center located to the north of the exhibition hall and partially underground. The path then continues its way across the garden. Zaha M. Hadid thus transforms the latent and hidden suggestions of the site into architectonic forms and planimetric distributions capable of creating a new, artificial landscape.

112

Zaha M. Hadid 1950

**Model Farm
Gut Garkau, Lübeck,
Germany**
1924–1925

"If we want to recover a form that is free from preconceived notions, if we want to reach a configuration without a priori means, we must put ourselves in harmony with nature, acting not against it, but from within it"(H.H.)

The most authentic roots of organic architecture, and perhaps also of the more recent ecological architecture, can be traced back to the few,

In place of the predetermination of geometric forms, which the rationalist lexicon used abstractly to serve certain determinant functions, Häring proposed an architectonic procedure that, by perfectly adjusting a construction to the purpose it was to serve, derived its form not from a geometric code determined a priori but from a mutable natural order based on the vital needs of humans in their labors on the land. The classical difference between formal work (*Gestaltwerk*) and functional

spaces. Developed on two floors, the oval shape of its outline reflects the perimeter of the animal pen that wraps around the stall's central feed trough. In turn a long passageway wraps around the perimeter of the pen, giving access to the animals for care and cleaning. The upper floor is the hay loft, its floor open at the center to allow feed to drop directly into the central feed trough. The curves of this section of the structure are repeated in the semicircular volume located on the northern side of the stall, in

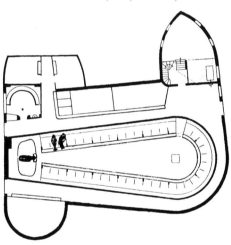

sporadic constructions and the theoretical works of Hugo Häring, an isolated and forgotten leader of Modern architecture. The significance of his practical and theoretical legacy can be attributed to the concept of *organhaftes Bauen* ("organoid construction") by means of which Häring sought to establish an alternative route to the "mechanization" of the world proposed by rationalism and by German functionalist architecture.

work finds a new equilibrium in the "organic creation of form," to achieve which Häring abolished every trace of artistic individuality, replacing it with the universality of his design method.
The stable of the Gut Garkau farm, part of a vast agricultural installation that was only partially completed, follows Häring's method: its architectonic form is based on the organization of its internal

which the absence of sharp
angles serves the direct
purpose of avoiding injury to
the young calves that were
often grouped in this area of
the building, while the body
shaped like a pointed arch that
extends from the southern
side is the site of a hay silo
and, beneath it, a grain bin.

Heinz Galinski School,
Berlin, Germany
1990–1995

*"The school is a city within a city.
Its streets meet at squares and the
squares become courtyards."(Z.H.)*

Several twentieth-century
avant-garde movements share
the rejection of compositional
parts based on the geometric
principle of the right angle
along with those based on the
traditional trilithic structure.

These movements included
one that, drawing its
inspiration from the organic,
natural world, arrived at the
creation of fluid, dynamic
forms. Known today as
Neoexpressionism, this trend
applied the same ideas to the
field of urbanistics, opposing
the artificial, modular city
proposed by the Modern
movement with studies and
analyses of urban expansion
based on the processes
of biological growth. The

Heinz Galinski School in Berlin
is based on a series of
metaphors drawn from nature.
Its layout can be seen as a long
vortex along the helicoidal
whirl of which the bodies of
the school are arranged—as if
they were the florets in the
head of a sunflower. The
buildings are joined one to the
next by halls as twisting and
sinuous as snakes and by flights
of stairs similar in shape to
mountain slopes. The spiral, its
design based on the centripetal

structure of the sunflower, creates a strong pull towards to the fulcrum of the school, which, with its central emptiness, represents the point of convergence of the various buildings that together compose the scholastic structure. Zvi Hecker controlled the exceptional spatial dynamicity of the architectonic organism through recourse to the mathematical laws of the spiral and concentric circles.

Commissioned by the Jewish community and the Berlin Senate, the Heinz Galinski school is the first Hebrew elementary school built in Germany since Nazism. Located in Charlottenburg, on the northern edge of the Grunewald forest, the school complex is composed of a series of buildings, including a hall with seats for 500 people that can also be used as a synagogue, a cafeteria, two kitchens, and forty classrooms.

The sunflower form begins in the entryway courtyard, with its trees; the tops of the bodies of the buildings, overlapping, converge on that central space. The spaces that the helicoidal progress of the spiral creates between the buildings are occupied by courtyards and public spaces. The overall dynamics are so clearly perceptible that Hecker was moved to compare the organism of the school complex to a pod of friendly whales.

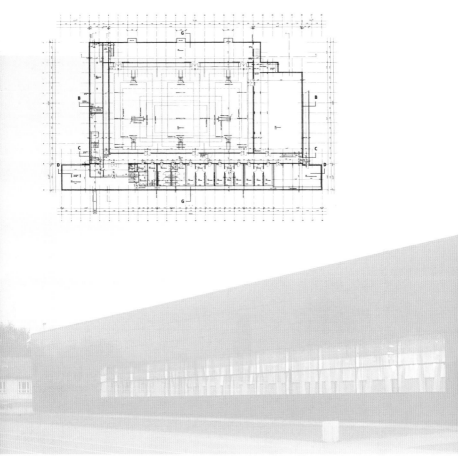

Pfaffenholz Sports Center, St Louis, Haut-Rhin, France
1989–1993

"This culture carries on earlier forms of behavior and construction more in terms of their appearance than in their original coherent form" (H.–de M.)

A certain indifference to the environmental context, taken in the historical sense of *genius loci*, can be taken as characteristic of much of the recent minimalist trend within contemporary architecture. Affected by the artistic avant-gardes of Arte Povera ("impoverished art"), Land art, and conceptual art, minimalist art reduces the architectonic patrimony to a repertory of a few primordial and archetypical elements, such as the wall, the partition, the volume, and its envelope, to then concentrate on the complexity of the "states of the material" of which these are composed. The result is architecture in which the envelope, taken as an outer film, implies a clear division between artifice and nature on one hand, but on another implies a break in the relationship between internal and external. As Pierluigi Nicolin has observed, in so doing it makes architectonic design approach the techniques of packaging, in the most successful cases

conferring the dignity of typology on the shape of a container.

The only outward indications that the glass parallelepiped designed by Jacques Herzog and Pierre de Meuron in St Louis, northeastern France, contains a sports center are an outdoor running track and three nearby soccer fields. Hidden behind the hermetic envelope of the main building is a large central hall that can be divided off to create three small gyms, a gymnastics room, and areas that can provide seating for the public. Built into the side of this building is a second, lower structure with a cantilevered projecting roof that serves as the main entrance while also housing locker rooms, showers, and other services for sports activities. The main parallelepiped is dressed in plates of green glass, on the surface of which is serigraphed the mesh of the fibers that compose the thermal insulation located behind the panels, which filters daylight into the main hall. The partitions that make up the low building with the dressing rooms, along with the underside of the slab that forms that building's projecting roof, are in sheets of prefabricated concrete, the surfaces of which have a chiaroscuro photographic effect achieved by a chemical procedure.

Tate Modern, London, UK
1994–2000

"The relation with the pre-existing architectural and structural form is inevitable and important. Architecture never comes into being from nothing. But there is no longer a mediating tradition" (H.–de M.)

More and more often these days, the creation of a new museum, an exhibition space,

or, in the most general sense, of any new site for culture means dealing with pre-existing buildings and therefore involves the discipline of restoration or, to put it more accurately, of reuse.

Those undertakings that, within the sphere of restoration, gave old buildings new functions by radically reworking their original structure have given way to operations of reuse in which

the new use of the building, including the services related to exhibition activity, are fitted into the body of the building and take on the appearance of "functional complements" to the pre-existing structure. This flexible, discreet attitude guided the project of Jacques Herzog and Pierre de Meuron, winners of the competition published in 1994 by the Tate for the conversion of the Bankside Power Station to a new, permanent home for

the Tate Modern. With its 9,200 square meters, the power station offered a large enough space to house the permanent and temporary exhibitions of the Tate Modern, and with its 99-meter-high smokestack, the site was immediately seen as not only ideal for the future expansion of the Tate but as symbolic of a larger urban change, one that, together with the rebirth of Shakespeare's Globe Theatre, would renovate the entire borough of Southwark, long cut off from the economic development in the nearby City. Herzog and de Meuron's design includes an access ramp located on the western end of the building that, apart from connecting the Tate to the surrounding neighborhood, leads into the former turbine hall, the heart of the industrial building, now converted into an exhibition space and a meeting room with a ceiling more than 30 meters high. A bridge at the height of the second floor leads from the former turbine hall to a system of galleries to the north, towards the river, and to the back of the building to the south. The top two stories of the galleries, the fifth and sixth level, consist of a skylight roof added by Herzog and de Meuron that extends the entire length of the building and floods the galleries with natural light.

Herzog-de Meuron

Palais Stoclet, Brussels, Belgium
1905–1911

"Stoclet wanted to create a large but highly refined house; he loved art very much, and gave us absolute artistic freedom. The shape of the layout corresponds exactly to the needs of comfort that he presented and to the ideas that were set out beforehand" (J.H.)

The symbolic and ornamental value of the dynamic line

based loosely on a plant tendril that, schematically, came to characterize much of the universal language of Art Nouveau was expressed in its Austrian version by a particular geometric and formal adaptation known as the Vienna Secession. Indeed, in Austria, the ornamental elaborations of natural and organic forms with which the various expressions of the international lexicon of Art Nouveau made their definitive

break with the repertory of nineteenth-century eclecticism went through a process of symbolic schematization tied to the personalities of Otto Wagner, Joseph Maria Olbrich, and Josef Hoffmann. Especially in the works of Hoffmann, this process led to abstract architectural configurations based on a few elementary geometric figures. This movement towards abstraction, which critics have seen as a foreshadowing of

protorationalist trends, had its greatest architectural manifestation in the Palais Stoclet, which Hoffmann built in Brussels for the rich Belgian industrialist and art connoisseur Adolphe Stoclet. Both private home and at the same time "gallery" of the Stoclet collection, the palace presents itself as a total work of art, a singular episode tied to the intellectual elite that represented the unique and ideal clients for the members

of the Vienna Secession in their efforts to achieve the total reworking of art. The rooms are arranged in accordance with a continuous spatial sequence, the fulcrum of which is the central two-story-high salon, around which the rooms of the palace are arranged, free of any symmetrical ties, including the dining room, which stands out from the others because of its ornamental mosaics made by Gustav Klimt. The shape of the

volumes is entrusted to the stylistic severity of the line, the geometric force of which is emphasized by a decorative molding of gilt copper that, projecting slightly from the surface of the walls, frames the surfaces of the volumes of the palace, which are dressed in silky white Turli marble from Norway.

Façade for the Strada Novissima, "The Presence of the Past" exhibit, Venice Biennale, Italy
1980

"It is a structural element that has become absolute architecture" (H.H.)

According to the basic precepts that govern the architectonic discipline, when a column is unburdened, meaning when it is not performing a structural role, it is classified as a decorative element, for which reason this architectonic element, with no changes made to its formal appearance but freed from all functional requirements, can stand as a symbol of architecture itself.

This work of temporary architecture by Hans Hollein, a multicolored and provocative review of the classical theme of the column, served an eminently representative and decorative role. It was part of the urban stage setting of twenty façades that composed the Strada Novissima, an ephemeral representation of an urban theme orchestrated by Paolo Portoghesi at the 1980 Venice Biennale. The theme of the Strada Novissima alluded to the space of the antique city, whose streets and plazas were reconsidered by way of the programmatic evocation, as proposed by Portoghesi, of the relationship between the urban scale and the architectonic scale that modern culture has dissolved. World-famous architects along with a group of beginners were invited to set up false building fronts inside the ancient structure of the Corderie (rope works) of the Arsenal of Venice, the industrial space of which was divided off into three areas by two rows of Tuscan columns supporting lateral intermediate floors.

For the show, the central hall, about 70 meters long and enclosed between the two rows of columns, was transformed into the Strada Novissima, decorated by ten façades on each side, each one fitted into the space between two columns and limited, according to the rules of the competition, to a height varying from a minimum of 7.20 meters to a maximum of 9.50 meters. Beyond the surfaces of the façades, a space 1.60 meters deep was set up to house a small personal show by the author. Although confined to the field of ephemeral architecture—from which Postmodern culture can be said to take its origins—Hollein's façade was the most striking of the lot because it drew its inspiration from the reality of the context in which it was inserted.

The series of variations on the theme of the column designed by Hollein begins and ends with the two Tuscan columns that mark off the space set aside for the Viennese architect's installation. The area between the columns is taken up by thematic variations of the column, a form of symbolic metamorphosis to which Hollein subjects the columns of the Arsenal itself. Thus, the space between the pre-existing columns is animated, in rhythmic sequence, by a trunk-column from which tree branches are beginning to emerge, symbolic of the tree that is the origin of the column itself; by the column as building, in this case a model of Adolf Loos's beautiful design for the Chicago Tribune Tower (see pages 162-3); by a broken column that performs the static paradox of hanging from the structure it is supposed to support and that by doing so creates the opening to the space behind; and finally the plant column, a vertical trunk of a tree, the structure that itself harbors the idea of the column.

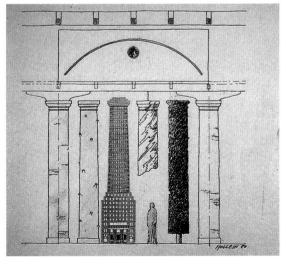

Hans Hollein 1934

Maison du Peuple, Brussels, Belgium
1895–1899

"To build a palace that will not be a palace but a 'home' where the air and the light will be the luxury so long excluded from the hovels of workers"(V.H.)

Between the last decade of the nineteenth century and the first years of the twentieth, a new artistic movement began making itself felt, first in the French-speaking regions of Europe and soon throughout Europe. This movement, which involved a reworking of the artistic language, came to be known as Art Nouveau and aspired to the creation of a

has led every period to produce its own architectonic style, represented the spirit of modernity. The overcoming of the stylistic elements of the past was thus predicated on a stylistic code that, having become international in a short period of time, replaced the elements of the past with a repertory of forms derived in part from new pieces, from components furnished by the steel industry, and in part from the symbolic forms of nature, whose organicity came to influence the general architectonic configuration of buildings as much as that of their individual parts. The reforms that Art Nouveau hoped to achieve by way of the

Because of the complexity of the building materials with which it was built and because of the many functions its interior was designed to serve, the Maison du Peuple prefigures the modern typology of a polyfunctional center.

Located on an irregularly shaped lot, the Maison du Peuple faced the curving side of the Place Emile Vandervelde with a concave façade and had obliquely angled façades that followed the direction of the side streets.

The fluidity of the facades, in which stone, brick, mountings, and iron beams were left visible, was repeated in the organization of the internal spaces. The ground floor housed a coffee room, entrance vestibule, and various shops and storerooms. The second floor was occupied by storerooms and offices, the third by offices and a small reception room, and the fourth had the main hall, 60 meters long and 11.6 wide, with seats for 1,500 people. Destroyed in 1964, the Maison du Peuple showed off its innovative structural system of mountings and iron beams, and these elements appeared where the sinuous lines of Art Nouveau were usually applied to the standard profile, almost as though the parts serving to support the building could themselves be transformed into a new form of decoration.

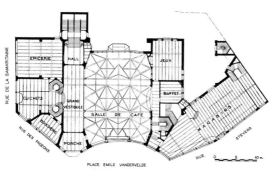

126

"new art," one that would be in keeping with the advances made in science and technology and with the revolutionary implications that the progress made at the beginning of the century promised to bring to all levels of society. In place of the stereotyped historicism characterized by the unquestioning repetition of the great styles of the past, Art Nouveau proposed a new style that, following the logic that

abolition of the hierarchical distinction between "minor" and "major" arts, which would be perfectly blended in the total work of art, found a rare physical manifestation in the Maison du Peuple that Victor Horta built in Brussels, the city that was the birthplace of the Art Nouveau movement. The commission for the work came from the Socialist Party of Belgium and was for the offices of the workers' cooperative of Brussels.

**Exhibition pavilion
for Japanese art
and technology,
Krakow, Poland**
1990–1994

*"Today an architect basically
has to decide whether he wants
to work in one single place
and always with the same
basic layout or if he would
prefer to work throughout
the world, creating
something absolutely unique"*
(A.I.)

Within the contemporary
architectonic debate the
propensity towards that which
is absolutely unique has shifted
the terms of the architectonic
composition in favor of
original geometric forms,
most often supported by
audacious technological
inventions. Arata Isozaki often
uses the term *mannerism* to
describe his designs, referring
to a style that, celebrating the
ease of execution of the
artistic gesture, reaches

geometric dissonances and
deformations, pushing
building materials to the limits
of static equilibrium. The
products of this "mannerist"
approach end up opposing
every theory of environmental
contextualization. Isozaki has
confirmed this himself: "My
buildings place themselves
programmatically in contrast
with the context in which
they are located—a town hall
may look like a spaceship
floating over a quiet village,

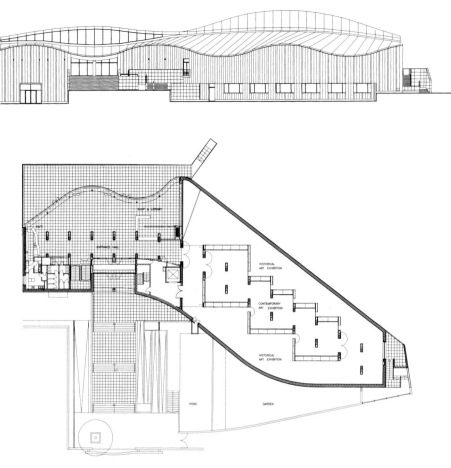

another construction resembles a beached whale at the base of a castle, or a sailboat run aground—and each of them is meant to shake up the surrounding environment."

The daringly wonderful shape of the roof of the pavilion Isozaki designed in Krakow does in fact recall the metaphor of the beached whale at the base of a castle, in this case the castle of Krakow. The pavilion occupies a triangular lot on the banks of the Vistula River beneath the castle. Set up as an exhibition pavilion for both temporary shows and permanent collections, the shape of the building may well refer to the bends in the nearby river, as Isozaki has stated, but its forms seem more like the result of a conflict with the surrounding context resolved with geometric and structural deformations. The wavy walls are dressed in pink-color local stone, while solid-brick stiffening walls constitute the support framework located along the central axis of the building and on which the roof rests.

The roof is composed of a complex structure of wooden beams that must have been pushed to the limits of their resistance to permit the opening of the two large skylights along the central beam that gives the building its unusual backbone.

Glass House, New Canaan, Connecticut, USA
1947–1949

"I consider my own house not so much as a home (though it is that to me) as a clearing house of ideas which can filter down later, through my own work or that of others" (P. J.)

The consecration of the European architecture produced between the 1920s and 1930s by the avant-garde groups of the Modern movement as a true international style took place in America. That it took place on that side of the Atlantic Ocean was no accident, being

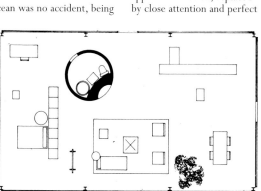

in large part due to the intuition of Philip Johnson and the learning of the historian Henry-Russell Hitchcock, who together prepared the text *The International Style: Architecture since 1922,* published in association with the exhibition "Modern Architecture: International Exhibition" held at the Museum of Modern Art in New York in 1932. This recognized the clamorous success of the architectural

styles of several European masters of the Modern movement. The text, pulling together Modern works from Europe made between 1922 and 1932 and decontextualizing the works of architectural rationalism from the social and political contexts that had produced them, identified three controlling principles of the new International Style. The three principles, all purely stylistic, were architecture conceived as volume, and not as mass; regularity as the primary rule to give form to architectural design; and the avoidance of applied decoration, replaced by close attention and perfect

execution of architectural detail.
The famous text, symbolically taken as an ideal "bridge" between Europe and America, succeeded in celebrating the "birth" of a new style that, claiming the same dignity as those of the past, aspired to the status of international esthetic canon, purified, however, of all less artistic aspects, meaning the functional ones.
Thus came into being a

"postfunctionalist" movement, and with Johnson's famous Glass House it laid the basis for a new language in which borrowings from the historical patrimony of architecture were not prohibited. The private home of the architect and unrivaled centerpiece of the enclosed "theme park" of his property, where the architectural theme of the pavilion found an extensive gamut of experimentation, the Glass House is a simple glass prism resting on a brick base 9.75 meters by 17.96 meters set atop a panoramic hill. The absolute transparency of the volume, obtained by using glass panes framed on all four sides by a thin steel frame, contrasts with the cylindrical masonry mass that houses the bathrooms and is the only space cut off from the surrounding nature.
Inspired by Farnsworth House, designed by Mies van der Rohe in 1945 and built in 1950, and also—as Johnson himself emphasized—by the architecture of Ledoux and Schinkel, the Glass House is, in its essential being, an archetype of the modern house, proving, as Johnson said, "that the modern house can be beautiful, beauty being the aim of everything."

Philip Johnson 1906

AT&T Building, New York, USA

(with John Burgee)
1979–1984

"I'm not Postmodern, in the sense that I always consider the basic principles of functionalism, I always begin a skyscraper on the basis of the distance between the elevator and the windows; the starting place is the nucleus of the elevators" (P.J.)

A new generation of skyscrapers appeared in the 1980s that was distinguished, in general, by an architectural language inspired by stylistic elements of the past and by the creation of public spaces that were located inside the buildings at street level but that were nonetheless more like true city plazas and galleries than enclosed spaces. These were eminently symbolic buildings of a style that rejected the image of the skyscraper as an anonymous glass box for offices, and they were usually associated with the formal categories produced by Postmodern culture.

Inspired by various classical forms and thus, in keeping with the company strategy of AT&T, recognizable by a vast public (much like the first Beaux-Arts skyscrapers of the Chicago School), the AT&T Building has been called the "principal monument of Postmodernism."

Located on Madison Avenue in the center of Manhattan and created to represent what was the largest company in the world, American Telephone and Telegraph, the skyscraper (today the Sony Building) entrusts its evocative monumentality to a classical tripartite division of base, shaft, and capital. As though to prove that the skyscraper was not to be confused with the passé formalism of certain creations of Postmodern culture, Johnson skillfully made the base of the building into a filter between the street and the building, creating a

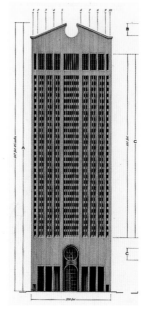

loggia 18 meters high with a central portal with a neo-Renaissance round arch flanked by rhythmic horizontal openings. This entry leads to the public atrium, which is the location of the elevators and a large covered plaza bound on the upper floor by a commercial gallery and the lobby.

The shaft, dressed like the rest of the building in "noble" pink granite from Connecticut, has traditional windows marked off by narrow pilaster strips that make the body soar upward towards its crown, composed of a loggia surmounted by a tympanum, a historical citation whose circular opening "releases" the force of the building, emphasizing its symbolic charge.

Johnson called the AT&T Building "a witness to changing times," and within the architect's long career it represents the most successful change of direction towards the codes of Postmodern culture, within a wider route made of sudden but strategic alterations in direction that have reached beyond the consolidated lexicon of the International Style to touch on more appealing and persuasive deconstructive formulas.

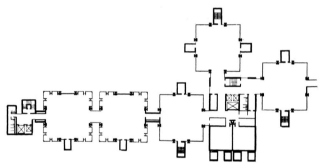

Richards Medical Center, University of Pennsylvania, Philadelphia, USA
1957–1964

"The Medical Research Building... is conceived in recognition of the realization that science laboratories are studios and that the air to breathe should be away from the air to throw away"(L.I.K.)

Between the 1950s and the 1960s, a movement within

Modern architecture, seeking to overcome the linguistic codes of the Modern movement and functionalist architecture, looked to the forms of architecture of the near and distant past for the sources of a renewal of the architectonic discipline. Thus a renewed relationship between history and design became an outstanding trait of the movement, which was destined to flow into contemporary historicism.

The architect who gave the movement its international dimension was Louis I. Kahn. He is credited with creating a new architectonic "look" that, turning to the most distant works of the past, succeeded, as Vincent Scully noted, in "seeing the buildings of the past as friends, rather than enemies; friends from whom one expected . . . to receive generous gifts." Kahn's outstanding merit was to keep this "drawing" of elements and

typologies from the patrimony of history from being translated into yet another version of eclectic formalism. Instead, it generated new and modern architectonic organisms. The towers that rise eight meters over the roofs of the pavilions of the Richards Medical Center are often compared to the medieval towers of the Tuscan city of San Gimignano, which in fact Kahn has depicted in a series of watercolors. This formal reference disguises the functional and scientific heart of the building, which Kahn's sense of history succeeds in giving an exceptionally monumental value. In keeping with Kahn's distinction between "servant spaces" and "served spaces," the medical research laboratories are arranged in four blocks (to which two were later added); the central block, to which each of the other blocks is connected by means of covered hallways, contains stairs, elevators, and service rooms. Each block has its own stairways and ventilation system to expel stale air and take in fresh air. These are enclosed in bodies that project from the roofs of the buildings— the service towers—and are dressed in brick, "transforming" simple technical structures into architectonic elements.

Kimbell Museum of Art, Fort Worth, Texas, USA
1966–1972

"The influence of the Roman vault, the dome, the arch, has etched itself in deep furrows across the pages of architectural history … They will continue to reappear but with added powers made possible by our technology and engineering skill" (L.I.K.)

Louis I. Kahn's statement about the values of architectural history should not be understood merely to mean the repetition of bits and pieces of buildings lifted from history books and applied to new structures. As proof is the fact that in much of his architecture, when Kahn has made use of such elements, he has used them within their original constructive systems, making them correspond to the principles of tectonics, which is the ancient art of correct building. So it is that the historical reference to the barrel vault and its constructive system becomes the regulating principle behind the Kimbell Museum of Art, Kahn's masterpiece, in which the principle of the free plan and its flexibility adds up to an effective system of natural lighting that is integrated within the logic of the structural system itself. The director of the museum (Richard Brown) wanted the museum to evoke the image of a villa rather than a palace, and as designed by Kahn the buildings rest on a robust base and follow an apparently simple constructive scheme. A succession of cycloid vaults, extending along a single span of 45.72 meters in length by 6.09 meters in width, rest on sturdy cement piers, thus creating a flexible system of galleries to host the works of art and the museum services. The use of independent structural elements made the system highly flexible: by removing the roof vaults in certain areas, Kahn created small open-air courtyards, as well as the large central court, around which the museum is arranged in a C shape. The simplicity of the constructive system is abundantly clear along the length of the main entrance, which, freed of its perimeter walls, performs the function of portico. The openings in the peaks of the vaults that bring natural light into the galleries reveal that the structural system of the roofing is not composed of authentic barrel vaults but of a curvilinear shell that acts like a reinforced truss, in the lateral stays of which Kahn skillfully hid the technical services necessary for the functioning of the museum.

Eigen Haard Housing Project, Amsterdam, Netherlands
1913–1921

"We are astonished by the sumptuousness of these people's houses"(Amsterdam City Council)

It might seem highly improbable that the field of application of the so-called Amsterdam school, an association of young architects that distinguished itself in the Netherlands between 1910 and 1925 for the creation of an imaginative and highly expressive language, turned out to be that of popular housing. Inspired by the teachings of Hendrik Petrus Berlage, who can be taken as their common master, and held together by the avant-garde magazine *Wendingen*, the members of the Amsterdam school succeeded in applying their Expressionist lexicon, based on criteria of highly pronounced individualism and artistic effects, not only to individual buildings but to entire blocks of popular housing, in so doing reconfiguring the appearance of several sections of the city of Amsterdam.

In the years before the 1930s spread of European architectural rationalism, the Netherlands were fertile soil for renewed social-democratic politics that led, with the approval of the housing laws of 1902 (the Woningwest), to the creation of "beautiful homes for workers, monuments to the struggle of the working classes." Thus came into being the close association between the policies implemented by the SDAP (Social Democratic Workers' Party) and the architectural ideas put forward by the Amsterdam school in order to give workers' homes the value of cultural objects with a new esthetic dignity, freed in part by the simple requirements of the economic laws. In 1905, the city of Amsterdam adopted the first building laws that established standards for illumination and for adequate ventilation, at the same time requiring that apartments be served by adequate stairs and be located at a maximum height of four floors plus an attic. Fate had it that some of the members of the *Schoonheidscommissie*—the "esthetics commission," whose principal activity, beginning in 1915, was the approval of the façades for all new buildings to make certain they harmonized with the surrounding setting—were active members of the Amsterdam school. In this way it became possible for a true artist like Michel de Klerk to make monuments for the working class, and the Eigen Haard Housing Project stands as a rare example of the application of expressive architecture to a structure usually considered only rational and functional.

The residential block, which because of the shape of its lot is in the form of an isosceles triangle, has 102 apartments divided into 19 types, all in keeping with the building codes in force at the time. At the tip of the triangle, facing the plaza, is a post office; within the triangular inner courtyard is a small, separate building used for condominium meetings, its scaled roof in the shape of an upside-down hull and its brick walls recalling certain aspects of rural Dutch architecture. The widespread use of decorations and colored bricks, together with wooden door- and windowframes in a variety of sizes, distance the building from the rigid designs of most popular housing and

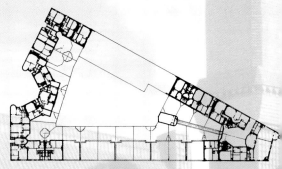

give the Eigen Haard Housing Project a powerful symbolic value, and in the corner that gives onto the Hembrugstraat, with its tall spire, the complex presents all the variety of an urban scene.

Michel de Klerk 1884–1923

Euralille Congrexpo, Lille, France
1991–1996

"Where there is only nothing, anything is possible.Where there is architecture, nothing else is possible"(R.K.)

To see nothing as the ideal setting for architectonic activity means giving the crisis in the culture of places a strategic role within the movement to redirect the analyses that regulate and direct contemporary urbanistics. Such themes as discontinuity, precariousness, and fragmentariness, always synonymous with the crisis of the contemporary city and grown out of all proportion in peripheral areas, clearly without control or precise meanings, portray the scene in which, for good or for ill, the practice of urbanistics must act today and from which, according to Rem Koolhaas, the practice of architecture can still wrest its redemption. Koolhaas's theoretical analyses of New York City and its skyscrapers revealed a "culture of congestion," emblematic of the exploitation of density and understood as the inevitable product of twentieth-century culture. This view became one of the guiding concepts for the later experiments of the OMA (Office for Metropolitan Architecture), founded in 1975 with offices in London and New York. A new paradigm for the contemporary city seems to take shape from this different point of view, which no longer sees the periphery as an incomplete or unfinished fragment of the city but rather as a dynamic field characterized by a plurality and a superabundance of the same rules that planned the city. Thus Koolhaas applied a new sense of space to what he himself called "bigness," seeing it as the only way to conceive a new type of city, since, according to him, "Bigness is a theoretical domain at this fin de siècle: in a landscape of disarray, disassembly, dissociation, disclamation, the attraction of Bigness is its potential to reconstruct the Whole, resurrect the Real, reinvent the collective, reclaim maximum possibility."

Spread over an area of about 70 acres of land, Euralille is a new center of commercial, cultural, and expository activity that arose in the immediate vicinity of the TGV station, the high-velocity trains that, stopping at Lille, make it a strategic point in the triangle London–Paris–Brussels. The urbanistic plan, coordinated by Koolhaas, is designed to make Euralille functionally and symbolically autonomous, with an infrastructure into which new individual buildings will later be inserted, connecting them to the underground system of junctions and networks so that they too will interact as autonomous, independent parts. Entrusting the rest of the design to leading contemporary French architects, Koolhaas himself designed the Grand Palais, the "big envelope," with its elliptical shape. The building was the result of putting together three smaller volumes, each of which had been made to serve a specific function. More than 300 meters long, the Grand Palais hosts a concert hall for 5,500 people, an exhibition space of 20,000 square meters, and a convention center composed of three halls. Accessible by means of underground paths, the flattened oval of the Grand Palais stands alone, separated from the surrounding context. It is thus in keeping with the fifth point in Koolhaas's theory of bigness, which holds that a building should be a self-sufficient island and should not integrate with its surroundings but at the most coexist with them.

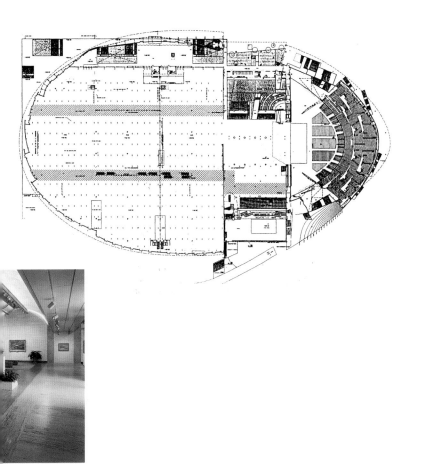

Krier House, Seaside, Florida, USA

1985–1987

"I work in architecture since I do not build.""I do not build because I am an architect" (L.K.)

Léon Krier is a self-declared classical architect since, as he has said, "The term classical denotes the best, it refers to the highest quality and is part of intellectual culture. The term *industrial* denotes the necessary, it has to do with the quantity required to make a profit and belongs to material culture." This should make perfectly clear the importance Krier attributes to the

classical. He applies this attitude not only in the architectonic field, drawing on the formal repertory of antiquity and traditional hand crafts, but also, and most of all, in the field of urbanistics. According to Krier, the reconstruction of the European city, devastated after World War I by the models of urban growth perpetuated by Modernist culture, should be based on the categorical abolition of zoning. Krier blames zoning, meaning the division of a territory into different zones according to specialized functions, for the destruction of the social and physical health of the preindustrial urban community. The alternative to zoning is included in the recomposition of the city that Krier proposes, in which the city is divided into complex and polyfunctional spatial entities, creating a "federation of autonomous neighborhoods," true cities within the city, served by a system of public spaces based on the age-old combination of street and plaza. The city block, restructured following the traditional morphologies of the European city, is the favorite subject of Krier's paintings and also of his design research, in which the classical values of architecture are reviewed with the details and stylistic elements of the classical and premodern patrimony, such as the truss, most often enlarged to an urban scale, the arch, the obelisk, and the column. Krier's refusal to build, understood as a general rejection of modern architecture and of all productive, technological, and consumerist values, puts him in the circle of the architects who paint. In that field, his greatest contribution is his classical-romantic vision of the city. The few, small constructions he has made are manifestoes for a return to the hand-crafted vernacular culture, attainable, according to Krier, by returning to the values of humility and collective sensibility that are common to the discipline of every applied art.

Thus, the home that Krier built for himself in Seaside, Florida, between 1985 and 1987, is a product of the art of building "understood as manual, artisan building, based on the logic of tectonics." Built using the technique of carpentry, the home reproduces the model of a tower villa from the classical language, on the top of which stands an additional volume in the shape of a prostyle temple. Made in keeping with the urban code of Seaside, Florida, which calls for the use of vernacular and classical styles in new buildings so as to maintain a sense of community, the house stands as a rare three-dimensional expression of Krier's architectonic and urbanistic theories, most of them the result of his deep reservations concerning modern industrial society.

Léon Krier 1946

Parisian Cabaret, Budapest, Hungary
1907–1909

"I went overseas with the intention of never coming back . . . I came back promising myself to dedicate my life to the ideal of making architecture Hungarian" (B.L.)

The above declaration from the architect Béla Lajta and its connection to the rebirth of a national Hungarian identity should not mislead. Lajta was in fact a pioneer of Modern architecture, not only in Hungary but more generally within the entire panorama of Europe at the beginning of the twentieth century.

The rapid process of modernization in Hungary that followed the 1867 compromise with Austria led, in the field of architecture, to a slow and difficult break with

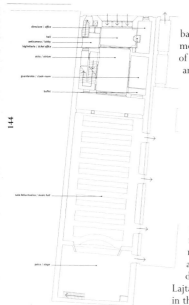

the spirit and practice of the reigning historicist eclecticism. Lajta's teacher and colleague Odön Lechner was a pioneer of the Hungarian national style but was in no sense involved in this break. His formal language, inspired by an ideal fusion of the ornamental patrimony of popular Hungarian art with the decorative wealth of the Orient, exhausted itself in endless replicas of the eclectic lexicon. The drive to overcome the more contaminated blends of historical styles that began in the early years of the twentieth century seems to have resulted from the rediscovery of rural and vernacular Hungarian architecture, which was highly esteemed for its strikingly national qualities and for its modern style. The isolated figure of Lajta stands out against this background of the slow movement towards the birth of a modern art. In his architecture he proved himself capable of blending the apparently irreconcilable values of rationality and ornamentation. His Parisian Cabaret, which miraculously escaped the devastations of World War II and was recently restored to its original state, is a masterpiece of his style, making fully clear the modernity of a new relationship between architecture and decoration.

Lajta applied decorative notes in the form of fragments and unexpected citations to a bare, stone surface composed of smooth slabs of Carrara marble. These decorative touches had the power to unite cultures and traditions that were far distant from one another in time, and also they were able to form a unitary and inseparable organism. The entrance to the small theater is by way of three richly carved silver-color doors framed and set back from the façade by an embrasure.

As a cornice piece to the bareness of the façade, reminiscent of the antidecorative work of Adolf Loos, ten copper angels, created by the sculptor Géza Maróti, occupy the roofline of the building. The vertiginous "dance" of their square wings alternates with the frivolity of the blue majolica tiles bearing the letters of the name of the cabaret, pushing the decorative apparatus towards a playful unreality, in which the invitation to enter the cabaret blends with the symbolic forms of Magyar and Transylvanian tradition, as well as with the abstract and geometric forms of Mittel-European modernism. The interior of the cabaret, now known as the Arany János Theater, is directly accessible down a small hall leading to the ticket window, followed by the atrium and the coat room. A flight of stairs leads to a small bare room on an intermediate floor. Just past the atrium is the music hall, whose narrow elongated shape (circa 12 × 15 meters) is as high as the street façade. Its short side is taken up by a small stage for performances.

144

Béla Lajta 1873–1920

Villa Savoye, Poissy, France
1928–1931

"The house is a box suspended in the air in the fields over an orchard"(L.C.)

The distinctive characteristic of rationalist architecture is directly related to the axiom according to which the form of a building should be based on the function that it will serve. This theoretical proposition was also the basis of the

architectural ideas that Le Corbusier presented in a series of articles that appeared, beginning on October 15, 1920, on the pages of the magazine *Esprit Nouveau*; these articles were later collected in the book *Vers une Architecture*, published in 1923.
The new approach to architecture that emerges from these works is one in which structural volumes were to be reduced to an abstract combination of planes and

surfaces. Le Corbusier meant for this new synthesis of technique and art to be applied to the most traditional of all building typologies, the home, which Le Corbusier radically defined as "a machine for living in."
"Our homes are not worthy of the age we live in. They are neither practical nor beautiful." In 1927, to make up for the missing functional characteristic and to adjust architecture to the new

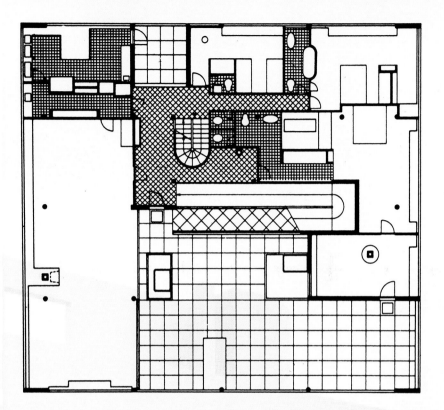

civilization of the machine, Le Corbusier delineated his "Five Points of a New Architecture," which architects were to bear in mind for the design of any type of building. Made universally possible thanks to the modern technology of reinforced concrete, the five points were: use of the *pilotis* (column or stilt), to lift the structure off the ground; the roof garden; the free, or open, interior plan; the use of long, ribbon windows; and the free façade. Le Corbusier applied these points in several single-family homes that he built, of which the Villa Savoye can be taken as an outstanding example. The villa stands in the middle of a garden, suspended off the ground by means of a system of *pilotis* arranged in a square and spaced about 4.50 meters apart. The rooms on each floor enjoy a functional freedom since their walls are unrelated to the load-bearing columns that form the structural grid, and they are served by a stairway and by a ramp that serve as the central fulcrum of the entire composition. The ramp leads to a large terrace on the second floor." The purified external volume has been reduced to a simple parallelepiped standing on thin columns, its facades, freed of every support element, perfectly suitable for the luminous strips of the ribbon windows.

Villa Le Sextant,
Les Mathes, France
1935

"Architecture is in the great buildings, in the difficult, reverberating works handed down over time, but it is also in the small hut, in the boundary wall, in everything sublime or modest that contains sufficient geometry to establish a mathematical relationship"(L.C.)

A classical ideal, dedicated to architecture understood as a "pure creation of the mind," accompanied the entire career of the most celebrated master of the Modern movement, until evolving, in 1930, into a search for the universal and eternal principles of architecture.

Contained in the pages of the text *Le Voyage d'Orient,* the impressions collected by Le Corbusier in the course of a journey in 1911, are the themes destined to be translated in a rereading of the universal idiom that architecture had based on the Mediterranean style and the patrimony of the vernacular tradition. The radical innovations of the purist avant-garde inaugurated by Le Corbusier throughout the course of the 1920s forced architecture towards a modern spirit dominated by the advances made in industrial production and the esthetics of the "machine," but some of the constructions Le Corbusier made after the 1930s show signs of a knowing detachment from modern, technological requirements in favor of the "spirit of order" preserved in every classical and traditional code. Inspired by the necessary and spontaneous forms of local rural architecture, the Villa Le Sextant presents a main structure made with rough stone walls in *opus incertum* (rough masonry) and a secondary structure composed of works of carpentry separate from the main wall. Prefabricated glass panels, plywood, and asbestos cement were used for the finishing, applied following a unitary

principle of construction, dictated in part by a work program designed to keep costs to a minimum. The local, traditional materials that give the villa the sense of a local farm structure were skillfully used by Le Corbusier in a planimetric distribution of two floors in an L shape, reminiscent of his purist experiments on the theme of layout. The exterior surfaces of the villa include a system of porticos and loggias, the openings of which contrast with the solidity of the stones of the perimeter walls. In this way a modest theme is transformed into an architectonic question since, as the great master of architecture recalled, "You employ stone, wood, and concrete, and with these materials you build houses and palaces. That is construction. Ingenuity is at work."

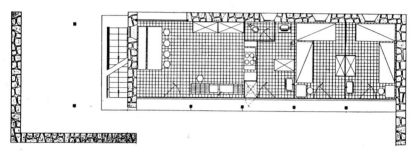

Unité d'Habitation, Marseilles, France
1947–1952

"Even a home can rise to the splendors of architecture"(L.C.)

The Unité d'Habitation of Marseilles, an enormous urban structure capable of housing 1,600 people in its 337 apartments, is an isolated experiment of the broad system of "macroarchitecture" on which Le Corbusier based his modern urbanistic plans for the contemporary city. The basic principles of modern urbanistics that Le Corbusier brought to bear on the cities devastated by the world war date back to the utopian proposals contained in his 1922 plans for "A Contemporary City of Three Million Inhabitants" and his 1930 plans for a "Ville

Radieuse." Le Corbusier proposed new satellite cities, to be laid out on the basis of the historical city, the morphology of which Le Corbusier's extreme modernism spared only the principal monuments. These cities were to take shape through the division of land into lots. These spaces would then be used for the building typologies of the "Immeubles-Villas" and the "Redent." Five or six stories high and

liberated from the nineteenth-century typology of an internal courtyard, the residential structures had double faces on parks and on the immense green spaces that were to divide the residential units from the new city. In this way, under the aegis of a rationalist utopia, the constituent elements of the historical city—the city block fronting a street—were swept away, replaced by a circulation system restricted to mechanical transport, the basic parameter for every future urban development. From the history of the city, Le Corbusier took the dwelling unit that uses the least amount of urban frontage, the Gothic house, with its narrow, elongated form and the vertical stacking of its internal spaces. The vertical repetition of such modules is the basis for the aggregation of dwelling units that compose the "great building" of the Unité d'Habitation of Marseilles. Inspired by the concept of "individual liberty in a collective organization," which Le Corbusier had encountered in certain monastic settings, the 23 different types of apartments present a recurrent typology, generated by the fitting together of two complementary cells occupying three successive floors of the building. The apartments are arranged around an internal street that serves as the main axis of the entire structure and is repeated on alternate floors; the apartments themselves vary in size from one-bedroom units to apartments suitable for a family of ten. On the

seventh and eighth floors the street leads to stores and collective services. A system of loggias with *brise-soleil* opened on the main front filters light to the double-height interior spaces, offering each resident a "garden" from which to enjoy the surrounding grounds. Le Corbusier employed a new measurement of scale, called the Modulor, to harmonize the measurements with which he proportioned the living spaces and the essential data for

human bodies moving through them, a measurement he also used in establishing the dwelling unit that is the basis for the entire Unité d'Habitation.

Le Corbusier 1887–1965

Chapel of Notre-Dame-du-Haut, Ronchamp, France
1950–1954

"One begins with the acoustics of the landscape, taking as point of departure the four horizons. They are what dictate the orders . . . and to them the chapel turns"
(L.C.)

The great change that came over Le Corbusier, redirecting the language of the great master of the Modern movement from the purist and rationalist to an unexpectedly plastic and expressive treatment of architectural volumes, is usually dated to the building of this chapel at Ronchamp. In truth, however, what most distances this construction from the right-angled, blocky volumes of rationalist doctrine is neither the unusual treatment of the surfaces nor even the shell shape of the roof, which are really not that different from certain purist avant-garde experiments of the 1920s. What marks the change is the relationship with the features of the site. The detachment from nature, understood as the loss of the most typical values of a place and translated, by certain rationalist architecture, into a transposition of architectural forms and typologies, seen as being equally valid in every international field, is here replaced by Le Corbusier with an attentive listening to the "visual acoustics" of the site, with the result that the sinuous forms of the chapel are based on the undulating line of the surrounding landscape.

The chapel stands on the foundation of an earlier Gothic church. Its interior includes a central nave that leads to the main altar, facing east, and three small chapels, all of them so well separated that services can be held at all four simultaneously.

Three small towers facing in different directions "pick up" solar light and filter it onto the altars in the smaller chapels. The sanctity of the central nave, the floor of which, following the natural slope of the hill, is inclined towards the altar, is accentuated by a system of natural lighting, which enters in part through a gap between the curvilinear walls and the membrane of the shell-roof and in part through an apparently random arrangement of small holes in the thick wall facing south. The walls that form the curvilinear shape of the layout are dressed, inside and out-, with rough cement sprayed with a layer of fine cement, while the cement shell of the roof, composed of two membranes of reinforced concrete, separated by an inner cavity of 2.26 meters, is left untreated. To further emphasize the relationship between this sanctuary and the surrounding nature, there is a small outdoor altar located on the eastern side of the building, under the shelter of the overhang of the shell. This outdoor altar permits more than 10,000 pilgrims to attend services in the field around the chapel. The treatment of the walls, the use of natural light, and the unusual shape of the roof, similar to a nomad's tent, make the chapel reminiscent of various buildings of the Mediterranean culture and contribute to creating what Le Corbusier himself called "a vessel of intense concentration and meditation."

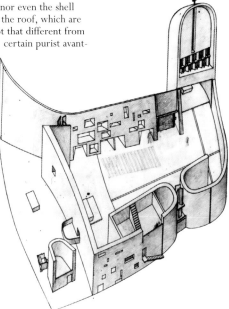

Waiting room and funeral chapel, cemetery east of Malmö, Sweden
1916–1974

"A primary and absolutely necessary condition is the utilization of the natural monument of the ridge, which must be used as the basis of the orientation of the project"
(Competition Jury)

The allusion to ancient Roman necropolises and to their layouts, marked by funeral buildings inspired by classical antiquity and the Mediterranean civilization, is a primary characteristic of the cemetery east of Malmö, a project whose various phases were destined to involve the professional career of the architect Sigurd Lewerentz until 1974. An unbreakable requirement of the 1916 competition for the project was the preservation of the Bronze Age burial mound dominating the grassy slope that was to be the site of the cemetery buildings, and this requirement gave Lewerentz the idea for an ideal fusion of architecture and landscape following the rhythms that regulate the various phases of the funeral rites involved in the practice of cremation. The elegant blend of Nordic landscape and Mediterranean architecture, which can be attributed to the long trip to Italy that the architect made in 1909, was soon put to good use in a great number of cemeteries in Sweden. In this cemetery east of Malmö it reaches such a high level of harmony that it implies a symbolic relationship between

nature and death. Cleverly entitled "Ridge," Lewerentz's design proposal, winner of the international competition in 1916, in its first version as much as in the final version of 1931–1936, provides for the orographic undulations of the site, with the proposed funeral and service buildings adapted to their shape. Lewerentz arranged these buildings along a route inserted in a "landscape that frees and lifts the spirit." The various buildings that mark the steps of the funeral ritual, and whose creation, protracted over time, represented the chronological phases that led to the final arrangement of the layout, are arranged along a main route that, sheltered by the slope of the ridge, divides

the cemetery complex in two parts.
From the main entrance the long route crosses the cemetery and leads to a circular plaza made for outdoor ceremonial services; it then leads to the main chapel (1920–1924) and at the far opposite end the crematorium (1923–1936), symbolic fulcrum of the entire complex.
The waiting pavilion (1922–1923) and the funeral chapel (1923–1926), located on an alternate route located downhill from the main route, are both partially inserted in the slope of the surrounding landscape and have colonnaded fronts. Composed as autonomous fragments of an ideal classical civilization, and

solidly adapted to the reality of the Nordic landscape, the two building nearly blend into the hill surrounding them and are perceptible only frontally and from close by.

The short distance that separates them, along with the different functions that the two small buildings were made to serve, throws into stark contrast the difference between the "city of the dead," and the places made for those who are still in life, where the humility of waiting is comforted by architecture inspired by the absolute values of a classicality outside time.

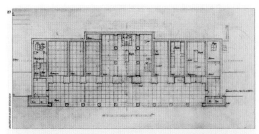

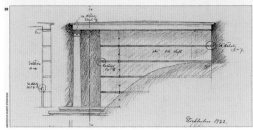

Casa Malaparte,
Capri, Italy
1938–1943

"Little by little, the house began to rise from the rock, wed to it, having taken its form, and it revealed itself as the most daring and intelligent and modern home on Capri"(Curzio Malaparte)

The attribution of Casa Malaparte is a complicated and as yet unresolved enigma. The only version of the project signed by the architect Adalberto Libera, and dated 1938, bears little correspondence to the shape of the final design. There is then the exuberant personality of the buyer, who may also have been the true designer of the house, the writer and Fascist intellectual Curzio Malaparte. These facts have kept the attribution in a continuous oscillation between a celebration of the house as the fruit of the rationalistic poetics of the architect or, in a different light, as an autobiographic expression of the buyer.

Setting aside the complex investigations that would be necessary to resolve the question of the building's attribution, there remains the question of why Malaparte, when looking around for an architect to build him a refuge on Capo Masullo on the island of Capri, should have chosen, at least for the first version of the design, the architect Libera.

In 1933 Malaparte had been accused by the Fascist regime of subversive activity. The cause was a series of satiric pamphlets he'd written, the title of one of which, *Une femme: Hitler*, should give a sense of their spirit. He had found himself condemned to five years of exile on the island of Lipari. Thanks to the favoritism he enjoyed among the followers of Il Duce, the period of confinement was drastically reduced, and when he was once again free, Malaparte bought Capo Masullo and decided to have Libera build him a house on its rocky coast that, rising from the reefs, would relieve the "melancholic nostalgia for space" that he had suffered during his years of forced exile.

While it is a modern house, at the same time it preserves the highest values of Mediterranean architecture; it is a sort of fortress-sanctuary located on the shore of the sea. It was this very theme, this clash between the apparently irreconcilable values of tradition and modernity, that was leading, during those very same years, to the major Italian contribution to rationalist architecture, a contribution that succeeded in reconciling the honesty and the functional values demanded by the new European architecture with the traditional values preserved in the minor, spontaneous architecture of the Mediterranean coasts. It was Gruppo 7, the association founded in Milan in 1926, which included in its ranks, among others, Libera and Giuseppe Terragni, that took the lead in the architectonic exploration of this no-man's-land suspended between tradition and modernity. The members of the group achieved a synthesis of the two values by evoking a New Archaic Epoch in which architecture would be reduced to a few fundamental types and to an extreme purity of form. Thanks to this formal reductionism, the Casa Malaparte, even in its first version, represented an archetype of the Mediterranean house, characterized by the typical terrace roof served by a spectacular external stairway that, like Holy Stairs, leads to a contemplation of the horizon of the sea.

Adapted to the physical shape of the hillside, the pure geometry of the building, with its narrow, elongated rectangular body (28.00 × 6.60 meters in the design by Libera), disguises the home's three floors. The lower floor is used as a storeroom and for services; the ground floor has the kitchen and guest rooms. The floor beneath the terrace is occupied by the large and unadorned living room, after which follow, as in a royal mansion, Malaparte's bedroom, that of his favorite female, and a room not unlike the private study of a Renaissance prince that looks out over the bright, ancient waters of the sea the Romans knew as Mare Nostrum.

Jewish Museum, Berlin, Germany
1989–1998

"The basic concept is very simple: erect a museum about an empty space that extends through the entire building and is physically sensed by visitors"(D.L.)

The center of the paradigm of the New Architecture seems to lie in the theoretical postulates and irregular folds of fractal geometry, according

diagram in which the urban layout, with its monumental projections and public spaces, can be reduced to vector signs and schematic lines of force. The rational approach to design, based on the classical tools of urbanistics, is therefore replaced by what in the realm of technology is called a fractal landform, the product of a generic convergence of physical and social forces.

The critical reconstruction of

to which the shape of the cosmos itself cannot be reduced to the primary forms of Euclidian geometry (cubes, cones, spheres) and leads instead to the complexity of the "nonlinear" dynamics generated by the encounter between the forces and resistances within the material of objects and the flow of climatic and ecological factors on their exterior. The city itself can be read as a vast dynamic field, an enormous

the city thus opens itself to new theories, freed of every relationship with the course of history but at the same time capable of bringing together in an architectural organism all the urbanistic matrices and deposits of a city's development. In this regard the words of Daniel Libeskind prove useful: "Most architects and urban planners have concentrated on the visible aspect of architecture, concerning themselves with

showing what was already evident . . . in doing so they have neglected the deeper understanding of architecture."

The new Jewish Museum in Berlin certainly aspires to a deeper dimension of architectural phenomena. With its tortuous sculptural shape that has all the intensity of a lightning bolt, it "bursts" in the heart of the baroque city not far from the Rondel, the famous intersection formed by Linderstrasse with Wilhelmstrasse and Friedrichstrasse. Entirely dressed in modular metal panels, the museum has no visible entrances or other means of communication with the exterior. There are only the irregular zigzag cuts in the zinc panels that set off an infinite series of fissures of continually different lengths. The entrance is below street level and leads to an underground tunnel that symbolically connects the Jewish Museum to the nearby Berlin Museum. The layout of the museum disguises a complex and ambitious system of symbolic references, first among them being those generated by distortions of the star of David, the hexagon of which is "deconstructed" in the irregular forms of broken, twisting lines. An empty and impassable open space runs along the building, crossing it for its entire height. Illuminated by natural light, this compact enclosure within tears in the reinforced concrete can be looked into but not entered or crossed, a dramatic symbol of the absence of a people and of that people's extermination.

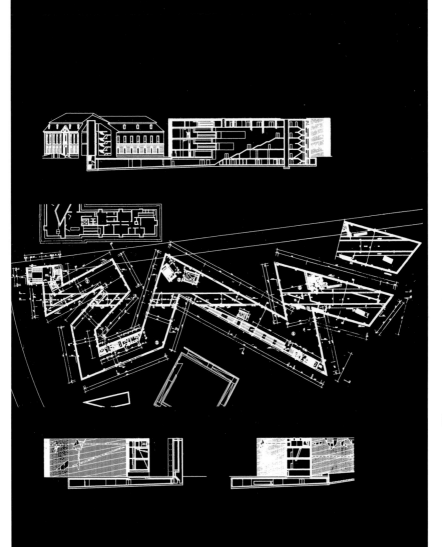

Daniel Libeskind 1946

Steiner House, Vienna, Austria
1910

"The house has to please everyone, contrary to the work of art, which does not. The work is a private matter for the artist. The house is not. The work of art is brought into the world without there being a need for it. The house satisfies a requirement" (A.L.)

The crusade that Adolf Loos carried on against the members of the Vienna Secession, and in general against any kind of artistic decoration applied to an object of daily use, took place against the background of turn-of-the-century Vienna. The crusade's main objective was the purification of architecture, meaning the removal of every trace of decoration, and, indeed, to Loos ornamentation was a kind of crime since its creation meant a waste of materials and human resources. For Loos, the incompatibility between "art" and functionality in the same object inevitably came to involve the discipline of architecture, which he claimed could not be reduced to any artistic principle, as is clear in his famous statement, "Only a very small part of architecture belongs to art: the tomb and the monument. Everything else that fulfills a function is to be excluded from the domain of art." Stripped bare of any

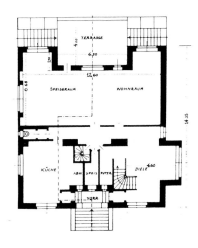

decoration and of any individualistic quirk, the Steiner House in Vienna testifies to Loos's important contribution to the birth of Modern architecture. Its creation was in part a response to local building codes, according to which the main façade of a house could have a maximum height of one floor. Exploiting a difference in height between the street side and the back garden, the Steiner House succeeds in rising to four floors on its back façade, which is connected to the single floor on the street side by way of a curved roof covered in copper. The austerity of the rear façade, with its two symmetrical projecting bodies that frame the central area, which is divided horizontally into two parts, differs from the side faces, on which an apparently casual arrangement of openings in reality follows the arrangement of the internal spaces. The interior rooms are laid out on the basis of a *Raumplan* according to which the height of a room is related to the amount of floor space it takes up, such that the final cross-section reveals a fitting together of volumes of varying height, all of them connected by a series of ramps.

Competition for the Chicago Tribune Tower, Chicago, USA
1922

"The large Greek Doric column must be built. If not in Chicago then in another city. If not for the Chicago Tribune *perhaps for someone else. If not by myself, then by another architect"* (A.L.)

When Adolf Loos, as his entry in the competition for the design of the new headquarters of the *Chicago Tribune*, presented a monumental parallelepiped serving as the base for an immense Doric column, its shaft rising twenty-one floors with offices for the most famous daily paper in the city, many thought the design had to be some kind of joke. Looked at more closely, however, Loos's 1922 proposal is an accurate response to the requirements of the competition, which, calling for the construction of "the most beautiful business building in the world," set off a lively public debate in which the eminently symbolic and communicative function required of the new architectonic object acted not only as a form of advertising for the great editorial corporation, but also, and most of all, bound the construction of the skyscraper with popular opinion, to the distracted judgment of the man in the street. The provocative enlargement to an urban scale of such a classical element from architecture, with its tripartite division of base, shaft, and capital dressed entirely in smooth black granite, did indeed evoke the

category of the classical. According to Loos, that sense of the classical, combined with the universality of its language, would restore to architecture its lost collective dimension and save it from the vagaries of taste and style. The technique of the leap in scale was not all new to the typology of the skyscraper, but the fact that it would have rendered the classical elements of the Doric column in a giant size led Loos to imbue the entire project with a fantastic dimension, although in doing so he did not create new forms of architecture but

rather reused the classical forms of the architect's daily work.

In this sense, despite the question of its buildability, Loos's design for the Chicago Tribune Tower seems related to his generally somewhat subversive attitude. He hoped to remove all artistic prerogatives from the discipline of architecture, which he wanted to see reorganized on the basis of sound practical and theoretical thinking, based in particular on the solid principles of economy, order, and "non-artistry."

While Loos's proposal for the new headquarters of the *Chicago Tribune* received no recognition, the winning design, by John Mead Howells and Raymond M. Hood, selected by the jury and by the readers of the paper from among the 263 designs submitted, led to the construction on North Michigan Avenue of a "comfortable" neo-Gothic tower: hence Loos's prophecy could be considered confirmed. Other architects, working for other companies all around the world, continue to repeat the forms of the immense column.

162

Adolf Loos 1870–1933

Glasgow School of Art, Glasgow, UK
1897–1909

"In an error, if it is honest, there is hope. But it is no longer there in the frigid perfection of style" (C.R.M.)

The many local variations of the international Art Nouveau movement, meaning the "new art," shared certain basic constants, first among these being the rejection of any imitation of stylistic elements from the past. Because of these shared constants, between 1890 and 1920, these new artistic movements in Europe began to take shape as an authentic new international style. Putting aside any formal distinctions, the German Jugendstil, the English Modern style, the Viennese Secessionstil, the French Art Nouveau, the Spanish Modernismo, and the Italian Liberty share the same ambitious goal of updating the applied arts and architecture to match them to the progress made in the sciences and arts, thereby creating a new style that, within the totality of its expression, would truly represent the new, modern society. New artistic methods, created by the abolition of the hierarchical distinctions between "major" and "minor" arts, joined to new technical abilities made possible by the advances made in engineering at the end of the nineteenth century, such as the use of shaped iron, converged to turn the organism of a building into a total work of art in which the design of the furnishings and the details blended with the design of the architectural shape of the structure to create a stylistic unity, one that is often compared to the kind of organic whole found in nature.

It was with the ornamental possibilities offered by the curving line based on such biological and vegetal forms as the vine tendril that the first manifestations of Art Nouveau expressed their radical rejection of the codes and stylistic elements of the past. A major contribution to the anything-but-linear route that leads from the earliest manifestations of Art Nouveau to the reality of Modern architecture was made by Charles Rennie Mackintosh and his geometric reductionism, thanks to which the floral decoration so typical of Art Nouveau was translated into abstract linear compositions and thus into the geometric and schematic fitting together of architectural planes and volumes. The Glasgow School of Art, made between 1897 and 1899 and then enlarged between 1907 and 1909, is one of the outstanding examples of an abstract-geometric variation of the Art Nouveau language in which it is possible to make out anticipations of many traits of the future modern architecture.

A very simple and linear floor plan distributes the classrooms on two floors above ground and on one basement level, each floor served by a long central hall. On the ground floor and first floor, the rooms are arranged asymmetrically with respect to the entryway. As a result of this the regular rhythm of the large windows of the classrooms is interrupted by the asymmetrical central body of the atrium.

The windows are made with iron frameworks, the rectangular frames of which can be partially opened. They are themselves framed by simple architraves set in the stone that dresses the walls. The central body is an autonomous entity, composed of the sculptured entryway connected to the street by a curving stairway and framed by traditional polygonal windows. At its summit, a tall prismatic shape, positioned on a terrace moved back from the level of the façade, evokes the image of a medieval tower.

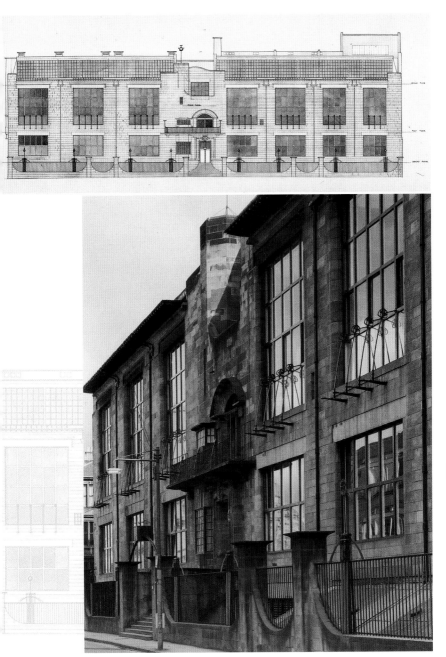

Charles Rennie Mackintosh 1868–1928

Bridge over the Val Tschiel, Switzerland
1925–1926

"The engineer was so used to using those same elementary materials, which provide support for only a single dimension, that they had become second nature to him and prevented him from exploiting other possibilities" (R.M.)

"Marco Polo describes a bridge, stone by stone. 'But which is the stone that supports the bridge?' Kublai Kan asks. 'The bridge is not supported by one stone or another,' Marco answers, 'but by the line of the arch that they form.'"
Thus does Italo Calvino, in his book *Invisible Cities*, reveal the building principle that governs the distribution of weights and thrusts in the construction of a bridge, describable as the line of the supporting arch along which the elements of the bridge are arranged. The same generative principle, although making use of different construction materials, is behind the bridges with which the Swiss engineer Robert Maillart managed to span the ravines of remote Alpine valleys, in so doing making invaluable contributions to developments in the use of reinforced concrete and to the progress of modern civil engineering. Following a basic theory that rejected the building principle that divides elements into those supporting and those supported, he arrived at a new building system in which all the elements were united.

The more than forty bridges that Robert Maillart made in his career resulted from a process of reduction with which he abolished everything that was not functional from the typology of the bridge. Broken down to those elements that could not be further reduced, the bridge thus became for Maillart the preferred field for experimentation with the rigid slab as a dynamic supporting element in the construction of the bridge. Based on the isostatic scheme of the open three-hinged arch, the bridge on the Val Tschiel is composed of a thin curving slab of reinforced concrete, joined to the horizontal slab of the bed by means of thin vertical stiffening walls that, connecting the two elements, contribute to the overall rigidity of the whole.
The 55-meter open space between the rock walls is spanned by a thin rigid arch that, reacting to the occasional overloads on the horizontal bed to which it is structurally connected, as well as to the permanent load, creates a new spatial configuration destined to celebrate the expressive potentials of reinforced concrete. The sense of artifice resulting from the gesture of spanning the natural gap in the rocks seems to be almost nullified by the system of thin concrete slabs, both flat and curved, that, sized not schematically but according to the forces transmitted by the load, join the two rocky walls following a natural balance that Maillart is said to have calculated in the space of a few hours.

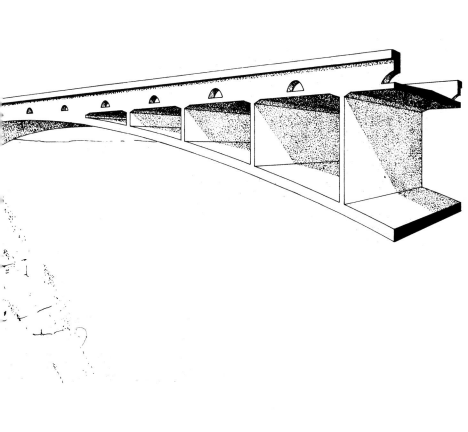

Robert Maillart 1872–1940

Fujisawa Municipal Gymnasium, Fujisawa, Japan
1980–1984

"In the case of Fujisawa, many say that it resembles a helmet, a frog, or a beetle, etc., but in planning it I gave no thought at all to a helmet or a frog or a beetle . . . some have called it a space ship, a frog, a fox, and I don't know what else. But I only wanted to make a very dynamic building"(F.M.)

Recent and very rapid modernization is the distinguishing feature of the urban landscape of much of Japan's cities, which—in the opinion of Fumihiko Maki— are composed essentially of industrial objects with inexpressive profiles, fragments scattered about without any sense of organization. In describing these contemporary cities Maki makes use of an apt simile, comparing them to a cloud in which the parts and the whole are in an unstable and precarious equilibrium. In the Fujisawa Sports Complex the expressive potential of stainless steel used in the audacious roof becomes the symbol of a remote or proximate industrial progress. Composed of two gymnasium buildings joined by a connecting body, the sports center is remarkable for the extreme asymmetrical tension that is created between the

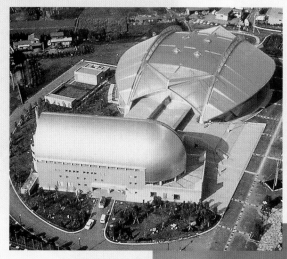

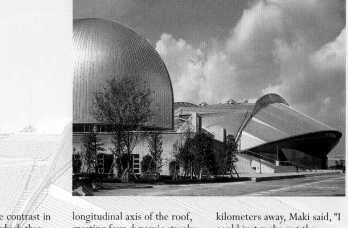

two bodies by the contrast in the elements of which they are composed and built. The roof of the larger gymnasium is supported by a network of steel girders on which the stainless-steel shell rests, while internally the space of the enormous hall has a strong sense of expansion because of the opposition of the vertical and longitudinal lines, the centers of which seem to hold up the perimeter walls. Four narrow skylights run along the longitudinal axis of the roof, creating four dynamic streaks of natural light inside the grand hall.

The second, smaller, gymnasium is striking for the sharp contrast between the surfaces made of different materials. The spherical vault of the metal roof rests directly on perimeter walls, with a longitudinal space running along the point of juncture. After observing his construction from a few kilometers away, Maki said, "I could just make out the profile of the sports complex, and it was exactly like a crescent moon at midday." By curving the roofs and extending the perimeter walls of the municipal center, Maki has achieved a billowing architectonic form that performs the symbolic role of an artificial sky or, even better, of a link between earth and sky.

Fiat-Lingotto Factory, Turin, Italy
1916–1925

"The importance of the building demanded a construction that was related to the use it was to serve … for many years to come"
(G.M.T.)

In 1925 Le Corbusier expressed his approval of the new Fiat factory: "Here is the solution of a well-put problem," he said, indicating that in the Lingotto factory the form of the building was perfectly matched to its function. Close examination reveals that the layout of the factory was unquestionably

based on the proper functioning of the whole and its parts. Inspired by the progress then taking place in American industry, the Lingotto factory outside Turin is one of the first examples of an architectural layout designed to serve the various stages of an industrial production cycle.

In designing the new factory, the industrial engineer Giacomo Mattè-Trucco and the top-level management drew their inspiration from the principles of assembly-line mass production, transforming the Fiat works from a garage into an authentic factory. The need immediately arose of giving the factory a modular, and thus repeatable, structure; Mattè-Trucco satisfied this need with a layout of twin halls and enclosed courtyards based on a bay type with a grid of 6 × 6 meters, each composed of a framework of beams and columns in reinforced cement.

The result was an extremely flexible system composed of long, well-ventilated work spaces in which the movement of materials from the outside in was entrusted to freight elevators easily accessible from the inner corridors. The flexibility of the system, repeated on all four factory floors, each with a capacity of 1,500 kilograms per square meter, proved functional until 1982, until that date meeting the requirements of a modern

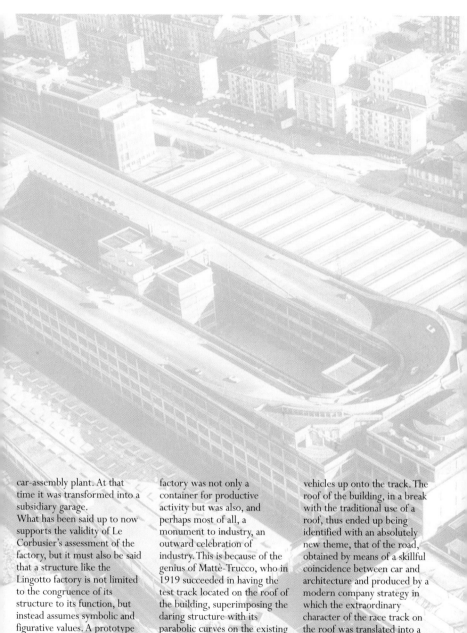

car-assembly plant. At that time it was transformed into a subsidiary garage.

What has been said up to now supports the validity of Le Corbusier's assessment of the factory, but it must also be said that a structure like the Lingotto factory is not limited to the congruence of its structure to its function, but instead assumes symbolic and figurative values. A prototype of modernity and a metaphor of progress, the Lingotto

factory was not only a container for productive activity but was also, and perhaps most of all, a monument to industry, an outward celebration of industry. This is because of the genius of Mattè-Trucco, who in 1919 succeeded in having the test track located on the roof of the building, superimposing the daring structure with its parabolic curves on the existing support structure and creating two steep ramps to lead the

vehicles up onto the track. The roof of the building, in a break with the traditional use of a roof, thus ended up being identified with an absolutely new theme, that of the road, obtained by means of a skillful coincidence between car and architecture and produced by a modern company strategy in which the extraordinary character of the race track on the roof was translated into a hymn to the world of the automobile.

Douglas House, Harbor Springs, Michigan, USA
1971–1973

"My main regulating principles have to do with that purity that is derived in part from the distinction between nature and artifice, a distinction the serves to bind them in a complementary relationship"(R.M.)

As was true of the other members of the New York Five (Peter Eisenman, Charles Gwathmey, Michael Graves, and John Hejduk), Richard Meier's first commissions as a professional architect were for the construction of single-family homes for well-to-do, sophisticated private clients. It was with this theme, more than any other, that Meier succeeded in revealing the guidelines of his coherent and personal expressive style which, parallel to the formulations of the other members of the New York Five, proposed a "pure" architecture, oriented towards classical modernism.
Having discarded every formal reference of Beaux-Arts derivation along with those drawn from the rest of the historical patrimony of the past, Meier turned to the legacy of Modernism, principally the architecture and styles of the great masters of the International style since, as Meier himself stated, "I see myself as a continuator of Modern architecture; there are still valid explorations to continue in its syntax."
While the reuse of this syntax explains the distinctive traits of his architecture—such as external volumes reduced to bare surfaces, planimetric

regularity as opposed to the concept of symmetry, perfection of detail opposed to the use of decorative apparatus, the use of white as a synonym for purity and brightness—the same linguistic principles create a certain atopic relationship with the environmental context, which, projecting Meier in the most classical tradition of architecture, leads his single-family homes to fill up with universal and abstract values, thanks to which the relationship with the site becomes subtle, or at the most allusive.

The Douglas House appears to be "beached" on the side of a steep slope covered by tall conifers overlooking Lake Michigan. The white walls and the artificial sense of its functional "mechanisms" are thus inserted in the middle of nature and can be distinguished from it by way of contrast, which at the same time makes possible the contemplation of their nature. Because of the hillside, access to the house is by means of a walkway that leads to its roof; from there, along with an interior stairway, a series of stairs, passages, and footbridges leads down to the level of the living room and then, continuing to descend, to the private beach along the lake. The permeability between building and nature is further enhanced by the use of large windows and skylights that, as from the deck of a ship, offer exceptional views of the lake.

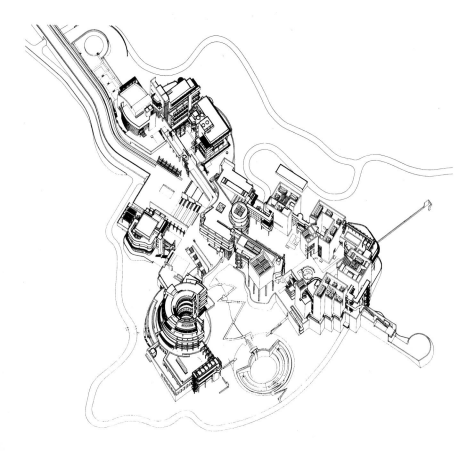

Getty Center, Los Angeles, California, USA
1985–1997

"I work with surfaces and volumes, with the manipulation of forms under light, with sudden changes in scale or point of view, with movement and with stasis"(R.M.)

The encounter between architecture and landscape, played out on the inevitable opposition between the natural and the artificial, reached new

heights in the design for the Getty Center museum installation, which involved the biggest numbers for any architectural project signed by a single architect in the history of the twentieth century: 88,200 square meters over a surface of 440,000 square meters with an overall cost of more than $(US)1 billion. Architect Richard Meier resolved the complicated relationships between the value of the surface area covered by

the Getty Center and the hilly, typically Californian, landscape by means of a system of landscaping that integrated the new cultural center in the physical geography of the site while repeating the landscape inside the center with a series of gardens and "spontaneous" pathways marked off by a series of fountains and water courses that flow into the natural watershed along which the city of art is arranged. Dressed, according to their

function or shape, in either Roman travertine or in metallic panels with an opaque finish, the various bodies that compose the Getty Center are very low in height in accordance with the restrictions of the local building code, according to which the complex was not to exceed the height of the highest nearby hill, which is 273 meters.

A cable car provides public access to the center, taking visitors from the parking lot up to the central square. A large stairway leads from there up to the museum itself. The route through the complex extends across several levels and moves among six buildings, on the upper floors of which are the galleries of the museum, illuminated by a system of skylights. In addition to the museum, the Getty Center is composed of several other buildings, including one with a cafeteria and restaurant, conveniently located on the central square; one with an auditorium with seating for 450; the building of the Art History Information Program; those for the Getty Center for Education and the Getty Grants Program; and finally the Center for the History of Art and the Humanities, the circular layout of which includes reading rooms, studies, offices, and a library containing one million volumes.

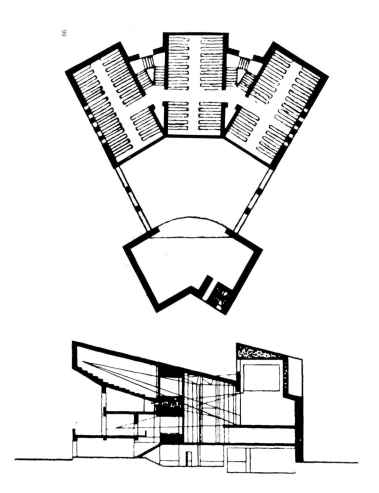

Rusakov Workers' Club, Moscow, Russia
1927–1929

"After centuries of imitation, architecture once again shows off its natural beauty, the powerful muscles of its force, the elastic leap into airy places, and it does so with the impetuous forms of the building of the Rusakov club" (K.S.M.)

The fervor of avant-garde Soviet Constructivism enjoyed sporadic but highly emblematic physical expressions in the five workers' clubs that the architect Konstantin Mel'nikov made in Moscow between 1927 and 1929. Characterized by a high level of technology, these clubs were somewhat like "social condensers" in which all the plans and the programs for the future communist society flowed together and were given shape in accordance with the various basic figurative rules proposed by Russian Constructivism. Constructivism, a Russian art movement that lasted from around 1917 to 1932, took its inspiration from the styles of various European avant-garde movements and promoted a new figurative language that, seeking a utopian combination of the forms of art and those of life, celebrated on a grand scale symbolic elements derived from the morphology of the machine and

mechanistic constructions, which were used as metaphors to transmit a dynamic tension to the architectonic organism. Without doubt, the best known of Mel'nikov's workers' clubs is that of the trolley employees. Its layout is based on the geometric figure of the triangle, and the blocks of three auditoriums that project from the body of the building give it a sense of the toothed gears of a mechanical engine. The ground floor of the building is taken up by the large main auditorium with its orchestra area, over which stand the three smaller auditoriums, each of which can be divided off from the larger hall beneath by a system of retractable wheeled partitions.

The street face, with the three projecting auditoriums, rests on a high base made accessible by two large stairways.

The overall volume of the building, aside from suggesting the dynamic image of a machine, has a sense of monumentality, a typical component of Soviet architecture destined to transform itself into authoritarian classicism with the advent of the Stalinist dictatorship.

Einstein Tower
Astrophysical
Observatory,
Potsdam, Germany
1919–1921

*"Einstein personally gave his
scientific judgment: 'Organic' . . . I
understand what he meant: that
you cannot change or remove any
piece of it without destroying all
of it" (E.M.)*

Einstein's statement, made
during the inauguration of the
Einsteinturm (Einstein Tower),

elements, based on plant
forms and in widespread use
at the beginning of the
twentieth century in the
stylistic elements of Art
Nouveau, continued their
formal evolution in the
reformist style of German
Expressionism, according to
which an original creation
inspired by the forms of
nature had nonetheless to
transform itself into a work of
global art.
Similar expressions of global
art, characterized by dynamic,

extreme rapidity of execution,
take the shapes of buildings
whose construction seems
improbable, with masses that
seem to contract under a
dynamic flow, as though
generated by a process of
osmosis originating in the
interior of the organism of the
building. These graphic
gestures by Mendelsohn are
the Expressionist avant-garde's
most concrete contribution to
the affirmation of a "dynamic
construction," in opposition to
the rationalist canons that
regulated and controlled the
"functional construction." Even
so, Mendelsohn was well
aware that in the construction
of an actual building, the
emotional aspects must be
made to accommodate the
purely functional
requirements.
Indeed, it must be kept in
mind that aside from being a
compendium of highly
expressive plastic forms, the
astrophysical institute in
Potsdam is a fully functioning
instrument for the study of the
deviations of cosmic rays at the
basis of Einstein's theory of
relativity. The energetically
molded body is designed to
serve a specific operational
purpose and houses a
telescope, a vertical shaft, a
horizontal spectroscope, and
an underground laboratory.
Although often compared to
the image of a flowing mass of
elastic cement, the
observatory tower is made
traditionally enough of bricks
covered with plaster, and only
the base with the doorway and
the dome at the top of the
tower, designed to catch solar
rays, are made of reinforced
concrete.

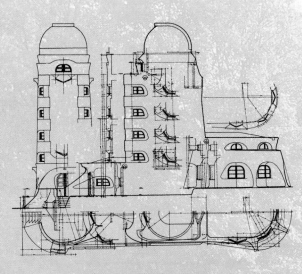

attributes a precise biological
and living characteristic to this
construction, which has been
unanimously defined as the
masterpiece of the German
Expressionist architect Erich
Mendelsohn. The attribute
"organic," fruit in part of the
wonder Einstein experienced
at seeing the dynamic profile
and plastic shape of the tower
that still bears his name,
demonstrates how certain
curvilinear and irregular

all-encompassing forms in
which the perception and the
construction of the work are
bound together, appear in the
series of imaginary drawings
and fantastic sketches
Mendelsohn made between
1914 and 1918 and of which
the Einsteinturm in Potsdam
seems to have been an
unplanned concretization. In
those works, lines in
continuous evolution, traced
with firmness but also with

**Church of San Giovanni
Battista, Autostrada
del Sole, Campi Bisenzio,
near Florence, Italy**
1960–1964

*"I have never thought of drawing
'inspiration' from a natural form,
much less imitating one ...To me
such thinking seems like an 'a
priori' negation of the
architectural fact"(G.M.)*

Giovanni Michelucci's career
extended across the entire

difficult span of the twentieth
century to arrive at the
achievement of a highly
personal language marked by
great expressive freedom and a
powerful sense of plasticity.
The Santa Maria Novella train
station in Florence, which he
built between 1933 and 1935
in collaboration with the
Gruppo Toscano ("Tuscan
Group"), testifies to
Michelucci's involvement in
the Italian rationalist
movement, but over time he

went through a slow and
radical process of revising his
thinking in regard to every
aspect of architecture, and that
process led him to an
independent, highly personal
style.
It would be limiting to
consider his masterpiece, the
Autostrada del Sole church,
only in terms of the expressive
codes of organic architecture,
for this architectonic organism
came into being from a far
broader and more far-reaching

ideological and religious
viewpoint. Built to
commemorate the workers
killed during construction of
the Autostrada del Sole, the
Church of San Giovanni
Battista gives architectonic
expression to a vast series of
evangelical and biblical images,
all fitted beneath the
primordial tent that the daring
shape of the copper-dressed
roof evokes. The rustic
support walls for this roof are
made of a layer of reinforced

concrete strong enough to
bear the forces of traction and
dressed in stones from San
Giuliano; the roof is made of a
thin membrane of reinforced
concrete, supported by a
system of branching pillars
connected to beams made of
reinforced concrete.
The story of the building of
the Church of San Giovanni
Battista was marked by the
difficulty of translating the
fantastic forms that Michelucci
had given his graphic image

into the solid forms of a real
building, making this work of
sacred architecture one of the
first Italian contributions to
"informal" architecture.

German pavilion
for the International
Exhibition of Barcelona,
Barcelona, Spain
1929

*"I believe that architecture
has little or nothing to do
with the invention of interesting
forms or with personal
inclinations.
True architecture is always
objective and is the expression
of the inner structure of our time,
from which it stems"(L.M.)*

Can modern architecture,
aspiring to represent the spirit
of its time and thus forever
breaking with tradition and
with the architecture of the
past, ever be classical? The
pavilion that Ludwig Mies van
der Rohe designed for the
International Exhibition in
Barcelona in 1929 delivers an
affirmative response to this
question.
Although designed by Mies van
der Rohe to last a long time,
the pavilion, like all the

ephemeral constructions set up
for the exhibition, was
dismantled at the conclusion of
the exhibition. In 1989 an
exact replica was built, so
today it "returns" to physically
document the compositional
and typological methods that
guided its construction.
The pavilion is easily
schematized, being made up of
a base of travertine marble,
part of which is taken up by
the structure set up for the
exhibition, itself composed of a

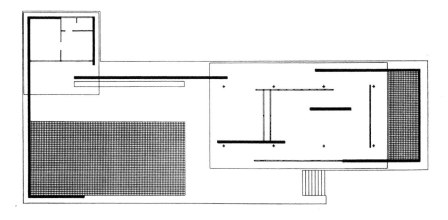

roof slab supported by eight cross-shaped steel columns, and the rest of which is taken up by two pools of water enclosed within wall slabs dressed in marble of different colors. Thus the pavilion lends itself to multiple readings and interpretations. Its presentation of a collection of slabs that only partially enclose the covered space involves a process of decomposition that is typically De Stijl, marked by the modern rejection of closed volumes in favor of permeability between interior and exterior spaces; at the same time, however, the distribution of the pavilion could be based on a typological rereading of the classical central-courtyard house, the formal configuration of which Mies van der Rohe would have partly contorted. The reading of the pavilion as a "house composed of a roof and an enclosure," attributable to the theories of Antonio Monestiroli and Carlos Martí Arís, reduces the construction to a series of enclosed areas open to the sky and distinguished by the theme of water and comparable to the courtyards of a closed-court typology. The purity that characterizes the style of Mies van der Rohe disassembles and remodels classical architecture, demonstrating the objectivity and the current applicability of the typological approach to the practice of architecture.

Seagram Building, New York, USA

1954–1958
(with Philip Johnson)

"My conception and approach to the Seagram Building were no different from those towards all the buildings I have made. My idea, or, better, the direction I go in, is towards a structure and a clear construction"(L.M.)

Compositional clarity and constructive synthesis, both leading back to the lucid slogan created by Ludwig Mies van der Rohe, according to which "less is more," which leads architecture to reduce itself to a few fundamental building types capable of responding to specific and essential functional roles, were the constant qualities in the production of Mies van der Rohe in America, where he emigrated in 1938, not long after Germany fell into the hands of the Nazi regime. Thanks to the universality of his building theories, Mies van der Rohe had no trouble integrating with the productive processes of the New World, and he soon took on the typology of the skyscraper, the preferred field for experiments with structural skeletons.

The construction of the Seagram Building can be seen as the completion of a theoretical and practical concept that Mies van der Rohe began forming in Germany around the 1920s and that concerned the building of offices. Even then (as in his competition design for a glass-and-steel tower for the Friedrichstrasse Station in Berlin), Mies van der Rohe saw the office building as "a house for work, for organization, for clarity, and for economy," whose supporting skeleton was covered by a not-bearing wall: in substance, "buildings of skin and bones."

It thus seems clear that for Mies van der Rohe the design of a skyscraper, based on functional adherence to purpose, had to be based on principles of anonymity and not artistry, indispensable components for every authentic manifestation of modernity.

Thirty-nine stories high and dressed in a curtain wall of bronze and colored glass, the Seagram Building stands back 27.5 meters from Park Avenue. The space between the building and the avenue serves as the pretext for the creation of a plaza paved in pink granite and furnished with plants and pools of water. From its base the parallelepiped of the skyscraper rises, its layout rectangular, with a ground floor lobby 7.30 meters high marked by the columns of the bearing structure and the elevator shafts.

The way the building is set back from the street, an unusual situation given the cost of Manhattan real estate, emphasizes the volume of the building, the classical geometry of which contrasts with the surrounding eclectic-style skyscrapers.

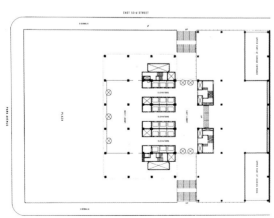

**New municipal building,
Murcia, Spain**
1991–1998

*"The initiation to architecture
should include today, in my
opinion, a strong familiarity with
history, a history that is no longer
merely a storehouse of forms or a
laboratory of styles but that
simply offers the material for
thinking of both the evolution of
architecture and the way in which
architects worked in the past"*
(J.R.M.)

There are certain
contemporary architects who
instead of unconditionally
drawing forms and figures
from the stylistic patrimony of
the architecture of the past
establish a different kind of
relationship with the past,
which they use as a stimulus
for the critical advancement
of the architectonic discipline,
using history as a true "raw
material" for further creations.
Standing out among these
architects is José Rafael

Moneo, whose theoretical and
practical contributions have
sought to free the destiny of
contemporary architecture
from the domination of the
fantasy and rampant creativity
of the generation of new
artist-architects and to return
the architectonic discipline to
the practice of the values of
wisely made constructions that
are capable of enduring over
time since, "an architectonic
work, if it is successful, can
erase its architect."

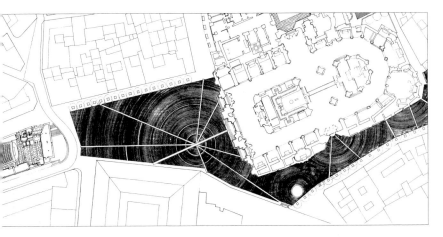

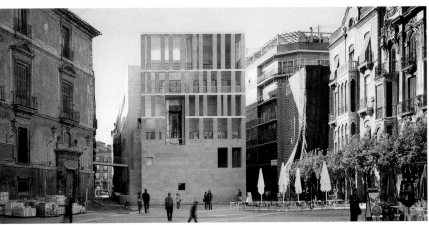

One work that has certainly been successful is the way Moneo, rebuilding the town hall of Murcia, has morphologically reworked the historical Belluga Plaza, dominated by the city's eighteenth-century cathedral and by the archbishop's palace. The guiding principle behind the creation of the city hall, which faces the baroque façade of the cathedral, was defined by Moneo himself: "We are convinced that the plaza should maintain its baroque celebratory spirit and therefore propose a building that will become one more spectator instead of being the protagonist of the plaza, a role reserved for the cathedral and the cardinal's palace." These are the premises behind the design of the new town hall. The façade's modern geometric arrangement, created as "a numerical musical score," was inspired by a monumental retable, or altarpiece. Its classical compartments are stylized in openings and divisions that, dematerializing, increase in number upwards, towards the top of the building. Thanks to its dressing in local sandstone, the building fits well with its surroundings, and perhaps to keep this new headquarters of civil power from imposing on the pre-existing religious buildings, its main entrance is not on plaza Belluga, but along the nearby calle Frenería.

Sea Ranch Condominium, Sonoma County, California, USA
1964–1968

"Californian architecture varies as much as its geography, and all the styles, from the vernacular to the colonial, from the neo-Gothic to the neoclassical to the neo-Victorian to the trends of the Bay region and the Modern, have left their mark on its cities and countryside" (C.W.M.)

This residential complex, located on a stretch of rugged, panoramic coastline three hours by car to the north of San Francisco, has ten living units arranged around a central courtyard. An expression of Charles W. Moore's constant efforts to make his works of architecture fit their settings, whether in cities or elsewhere, the Sea Ranch Condominium is so well integrated with its spectacular location that it has the sense of having always stood just that way along just that stretch of coast. Designed to reflect California's most traditional and vernacular styles of architecture, the condominium's ten living units form a single volumetric composition well harmonized with the vastness of the site. The living units are arranged around a central courtyard in part to protect it from the strong winds that constantly

blow in this coastal region. The strong winds also explain the absence of drainpipes and gutters on the buildings, since such attachments are easily subject to vibrations as a result of wind. Each unit is based on a 7 × 7 meter cube. The structure and external dressing are in roughly finished wood, while the kitchens and bathrooms, which in some cases extend to more than one floor, are made of perfectly finished wooden frameworks. By repeating the traditional building styles of popular American architecture, the Sea Ranch Condominium, aside from being perfectly integrated within its natural surroundings, succeeds in evoking an architectural image rooted in the collective memory of the people of California.

Charles W. Moore 1925–1993

Piazza d'Italia, New Orleans, USA
1975–1978

"The role of the architect consists, properly, in assembling a series of familiar settings that give those who live in them the chance to reconnect to everything around them by means of a series of surprises that make them more greatly aware of where they are"(C.W.M.)

Postmodern architecture overcame the basic principles of the Modern movement by way of an expressive liberty derived from the eclectic reuse of styles of the past, often applied with irony and an abundance of decoration. In the architectural creations of Charles W. Moore, Postmodernism runs into the kitschy aspects of the metropolitan landscape. In this way the reuse of the architectural values of history, rejected by certain Modernist architecture in favor of a language fully centered on technical and functional values, mixes with symbolic and figurative values that flow outwards into a multitude of allusions, not only perceptible but also psychological. Greeted by Paolo Portoghesi as "the end of prohibitionism," this renewal of the language of architecture takes on extracommunicative and extradisciplinary values in the famous Piazza d'Italia that Moore designed in New

Orleans as a simulacrum of the homeland of the city's large community of Italian immigrants. The most classical and monumental aspects of the Imperial Roman style, replicated and distorted in a variety of forms and materials in a series of fragments of exedrae and colonnades arranged around the circular space of the piazza, mix with expressions of populist and national identity, the whole culminating in the stepped fountain shaped like the Italian peninsula.

Here, as never before, architecture combines with a promotional message whose success is proportional to the legibility of the architectural contents, assimilating effective techniques of persuasion from the principles and culture of entertainment.

Underground Showroom for the Turin Automobile Exhibition Center, Turin, Italy
1958–1959

"The main purpose of my research has always been to achieve the best results in terms of style and from a technical point of view"(R.M.)

The statics of bridges and their many applications seem to have been a constant factor in the career of the Italian engineer Riccardo Morandi. Morandi worked out the statics needed to cover incredible open spans and did so in a different way each time, fitting his solution to the specific problems of the individual situation. There was the theme of the arched bridge, that of the girder bridge, the portal bridge, the balanced beam, and finally that of the cable-stayed bridge (as in, for example, the Polcevera Viaduct at Genoa). Morandi built magnificent bridges and viaducts in Italy and elsewhere, most of all between 1950 and 1970. What most of them have in common is the use of prestressed reinforced concrete, of which Morandi was the uncontested pioneer in Italy. A result of efforts to reduce the amount of iron necessary in cement frameworks, the experiments in prestressing were directed at giving cement the strength to resist tensile stress, that by nature, it does not have. The technique of the prestressing the steel framework, patented in 1949 by Morandi himself and widely used in the construction of bridges, allowed his structural research to "free itself from the concept of balance of gravitational masses," enriching it instead with thin, ropey images composed thin, light, bent elements.

Morandi applied the image of the bridge and its fundamental components to his works of civil engineering, thus establishing an almost programmatic relationship between bridges and industrial or civil buildings. It was with a civil-industrial building, an underground showroom in Turin, that Morandi succeeded in creating a space in which the rules of statics are translated in dynamic figures and architectonic elements that give the underground space a highly expressive quality far from the anonymous feeling that usually typifies such settings. Created for a large exhibition of industrial vehicles, the showroom occupies an area of 151 × 69 meters located 8 meters below the street level of Valentino Park. The park itself was not compromised by the construction beneath it since the zone over the roof of the pavilion was turned into a playground for children. A cross-section view of the pavilion reveals that it is, in fact, shaped very much like a bridge, constructed using the scheme of the balanced beam. Morandi met the demands for maximum free space on the ground and minimum thickness of the roof cover by setting thin pairs of support beams made of prestressed, reinforced concrete on pairs of intermediate struts inclined so as to defray the point of maximum stress. The tie beams of the struts are joined by small connecting rods to the side walls of the showroom, appropriately sized to counter the horizontal thrust of the surrounding earth. The pairs of ribs diverge and interweave, reducing in thickness towards the middle of the span, thus creating a lozenge-shaped mesh designed to react to transversal stress. In this three-dimensional space, the similarity to a bridge that the cross-section of the showroom unquestionably reveals undergoes a sort of vertiginous multiplication created by the serial repetition of the inclined connecting rods and the articulation of the ribs of the ceiling, which add up to give the space the surprising drama of an underground sepulcher.

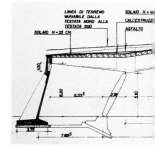

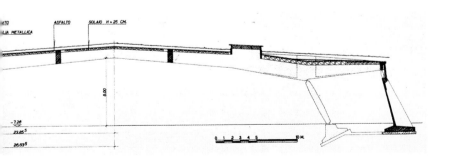

Riccardo Morandi 1902–1989

Power Station,
Trezzo D'Adda, Italy
1905–1906

"A completely virgin problem, free of all those connections . . . that usually impose themselves on an architect, paralyzing every spontaneous idea"(G.M.)

The use of iron as a building material led the discipline of architecture to concentrate on the essential constructive and structural elements of the

architectonic organism. A long time was required to create an esthetics of engineering in keeping with the spirit of the Modern era at the beginning of the century. The primary obstacle to its creation was the lingering prestige of academic architecture based on imitative styles applied as decoration to buildings. When, in 1905, the Lombard industrialist Benigno Crespi commissioned the architect Gaetano Moretti to

build a power station at Trezzo D'Adda, concerns about protecting the landscape along with the representative character of certain eclectic architecture led him to stipulate that the station should be made to "fit with the natural surroundings and not create any sense of discord with the Visconti castle that towers over the site."
The power station, which opened in April 1906, is today ranked as one of the most

important examples of Italian architecture between the nineteenth and twentieth centuries, for it is a synthesis of eclectic architecture and plant engineering. It was a revolutionary theme for the architecture of the period and was destined to become a recurrent typology in the culture of the modern. The "building" of the power station is composed of three integrated bodies. The four above-ground floors of the central and tallest body host the rooms with the control and distribution boards. To the side of this are two lower buildings, narrow and elongated. One contains the turbine hall with its ten groups of generators; the other has the large steam power station. These side bodies are joined to the central nucleus by way of two large specular stairways. The buildings are decorated with blocks of local rustic stone, and the way this decoration successfully blends with the site is a result of the rational composition procedure that Moretti applied to the entire design of the power station. Thus, different stylistic canons, with medieval, Syrian, Oriental, or Art Deco attributes, are applied to the loose articulation of the volumes, quite simply based on the functional and planimetric arrangement that was needed for the power station.

Simpson-Lee House, Mount Wilson, South New Wales, Australia
1989–1994

"People interest me as individuals, not as anonymous consumers of architecture" (G.M.)

In 1991 the Finnish architect Juhani Pallasmaa provided a definition of a new form of ecological architecture known as ecological functionalism: "Today I cannot imagine any other perspective than an ecological form of life in which architecture returns to the initial ideal of functionalism, based on biology, and would take root again in its cultural and regional substrate; one might call it ecologic functionalism . . . After the decades of wealth and of abundance, we

will probably return to an esthetics of need in which expression and installation blend; utility and beauty are again united."
Although in its specific quality as a rational product of industry, functionalism has very little to do with the best use of natural resources or with the use of ecological materials that characterizes a good deal of contemporary bioecological architecture, the term "ecological

functionalism," despite its apparent ambiguity, can be useful to understanding the special private homes designed by the Australian architect Glenn Murcutt, a highly-skilled builder of modern functional "refuges."
Far from any kind of ecological mimicry—in which the forms, volumes, and colors of architecture are selected to achieve harmony with the surrounding environment—Murcutt's compositional and constructive style can be considered ecological in the sense that he rejects all traces of individualistic expression and uses artisan skills to apply the best aspects of ecological technology to his constructions so as to obtain the optimal use of natural elements while fully exploiting atmospheric phenomena. Thus intersecting and natural ventilation systems, basins for the collection of rain water, and the use of natural light—physical qualities of the Australian landscape—have become integral parts of his architecture, which in most cases is made with an iron and steel framework that is then dressed in inexpensive or scrap materials like aluminum panels.
Located 150 kilometers northwest of Sidney, in the heart of the Blue Mountains (named for their bluish mists), the Simpson-Lee House stands on two panoramic lots of more than seven acres. The layout of the house folds in order to conform to the natural shape of the setting, which it fits closely without changing the natural, original lie of the land. The planimetric

arrangement of the construction follows a horizontal line suggested by the arrangement of the lots, which puts in communication the two separate pavilions of which the house is composed. As though a natural extension of the direction of the nearby road, the pathway first reaches the small structure used as a garage-studio and then, by way of a footbridge that crosses the basin used to collect rain water, the home itself. It finally loses itself in the surrounding woods. In order to best enjoy the view offered by the site, the façade of the house overlooking the valley has the areas of the living and dining rooms and is shaped like a large window, in part openable, and completely closable by means of six large aluminum panels. The bedrooms, each one with its own bath, are located on the side of the house facing the mountain, under the lowest part of the roof, giving each a sense of enclosed domesticity.

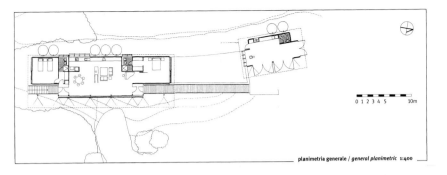

planimetria generale / *general planimetric* 1:400

Glenn Murcutt 1936

Hangar in reinforced concrete with a geodetic structure, Orbetello, Italy
1939–1942

"Building is an art even in its most technical aspects, those that involve structural stability"
(P.L.N.)

In his *Manifesto of Futurist Architecture* (1914), Antonio Sant'Elia wrote, "Calculation of the resistance of materials, the use of reinforced concrete and of iron preclude architecture in the classical and traditional sense. Modern construction materials and our scientific knowledge do not lend themselves at all to the discipline of historical styles." These lines make abundantly clear the sharp division that puts Art and Technology on opposing sides in a competition to be the dominant force in the creation of a building. One direct consequence of this way of thinking is the formation of two antithetical professional figures, the engineer and the architect.

While what Sant'Elia prophesized may well have come true, in the sense that the birth of Modern architecture resulted from the unquestionable supremacy of the mathematical-technical culture over the intuitive–artistic, it is also true that large works of architecture result from a necessary synthesis of the technical and artistic aspects. The works of the engineer Pier Luigi Nervi, which include architectural masterpieces along with beautiful lessons in the technique of construction, demonstrate how this synthesis can be traced to the coincidence between a sensitivity to statics and an elastic attitude that precedes the creation of every valuable piece of architecture. Highly dedicated to "integrity, truth, and correctness" in building, Nervi worked to improve the practical operations of the building profession; at each of his worksites he took on the roles of both designer and construction foreman, roles that he claimed were all too often artificially separated in the course of an architectural undertaking.

The true originality of the methods employed by Nervi as an engineer was the concept of an architectural intuition that would permit the solution of problems without recourse to calculations. Nervi believed that mathematical calculations could, at the most, provide a useful a posteriori check of an already assembled structural system; they could not themselves provide a solution. Very illuminating in this regard are the roofs Nervi made of prefabricated elements for the hangars of Orbetello, an experiment on the theme of the roof taken as an organic shell formed of the elastic weaving of the ribs. The geodetic structure (the line of minimum length that joins two points on a surface) covers an open surface of 100 × 40 meters and is composed of a lightened structure made of a latticework of prefabricated elements supported by six concrete buttresses anchored to the ground. The joints formed at the juncture of each four prefabricated elements of the latticework structure were made by welding the reinforcement bars and by casting prestressed concrete. Ascertaining the exact strength of such a complex structure—as Nervi himself claimed—would have been practically impossible. Thus the first rough calculations of a structural system undoubtedly inspired by the anatomic membranes of a skeleton were followed by experimental research into the effects of stress applied to a celluloid model. The laboratory tests proved accurate. In fact, after the retreating German army blew up the hangars, knocking down the six buttresses, Nervi found that the prefabricated joints, although no longer connected to anything, had remained intact.

Kaufmann House, Palm Springs, California, USA
1946–1947

"One thing is a living plant whose roots draw liquids and nutriments from the soil, one thing is a static structure that rests on an impermeable foundation of cement" (R.N.)

Unlike the great German masters of the Modern movement whom the Nazi regime forced into exile overseas, Richard Neutra emigrated to American quite voluntarily, in 1923. Born in Vienna and trained at that city's Technische Hochschule, after the years of his academic studies Neutra chose Adolf Loos as his master, working in that architect's studio for about two years, up to the outbreak of World War I. Apart from personal and financial reasons, Neutra's decision to move to America can without doubt be attributed to the influence of his great master, who had himself spent the years 1893 to 1896 in the United States and who spoke of that country as the ideal location for the development of a positive model of modernity. A second "American seduction" was the work of Frank Lloyd Wright, which, by 1910, was quite well known in Europe and so fascinated Neutra that before opening his own studio in Los Angeles in 1927 he spent three

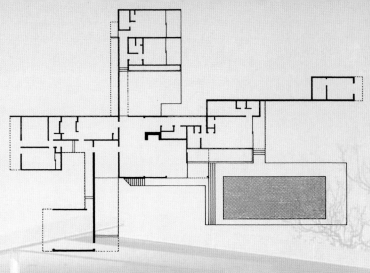

months in the refuge-school that Wright had founded near Taliesin, Wisconsin. Neutra's American work can be said to have resulted from the tumultuous and in part discordant background of his training, blending a technical education based on the triumph of the technological potential of the modern with a refined sense of the relationship between architecture and nature, although unlike the organicism of Wright, Neutra did not attempt to present his buildings as products of the earth but instead concentrated on the relationships between humans and nature, introducing through the needs of a new technique, improvements in the comfort and standards of living of his Californian clients.

The Kaufmann House in Palm Springs is a pavilion structure that rises from the surrounding rocks and plants as a series of horizontal planes marked off by transparent surfaces. Its rectangular layout has no sense of geometric schematics; spreading open in a series of rooms and halls offering spectacular views of the surrounding landscape, the arrangement not only inserts the house in the landscape but also dispels any sense of the rectangular shape.

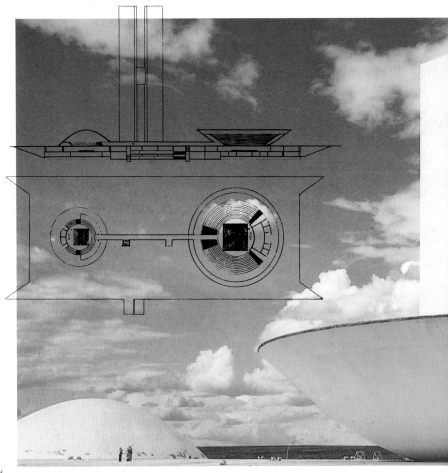

Plaza of the Three Powers, Brasilia, Brazil
1958–1960

*"My principal concern in the
Plaza of the Three Powers was
unity . . . making sure I gave the
whole that sense of conciseness of
the great plazas of Europe within
the scale and values set by the
splendid project by Lúcio Costa"*
(O.N.)

Modern architecture's version
of a great metropolitan utopia
has had but few opportunities
for physical expression, and
those in the vast open spaces
where economically backward
societies have embraced the
large-scale dreams of
modernity, importing the
modes of urban growth
worked out in Europe by the
masters of the Modern
movement.
In the hope of relocating the
economic center of Brazil
from the costal strip to its
interior, various attempts have
been made since the end of
the 1700s to set up a new
capital deep inside the
country. This effort met with
success only in 1957 with the
construction of Brasilia,
established by President
Kubitschek as symbol of the
rebirth and integration of the
entire national collectivity.
Product of the artistic
gestuality of the Brazilian
architect Lúcio Costa, the
pilot plan for the development
of the city assumed the shape

of a giant bird, which, generated by the juncture of two main guide routes, one of them, curving, measuring 12.5 kilometers, negated every sense of the right-angled grids of cities with colonial histories. Inspired by urban studies that Le Corbusier made in 1929 of several South American cities, the pilot plan foresaw the orderly arrangement of large-scale architectural installations along the two regulating lines.

The celebration of the new capital was to be entrusted to the monumentality of this architecture.
The architectural installations, designed by Oscar Niemeyer, culminate in the Plaza of the Three Powers, the fulcrum of the urbanistic layout, where the political institutions (government, parliament, and justice) are given suitable architectural settings. The immense horizontal area of the plaza is dominated by the

paired bodies of the administration building, at whose base stand the palace of the Senate, in the shape of a dome, and that of the Chamber of Deputies, in the shape of a saucer; there are then the palace of the parliament and the seat of the supreme court.

Institut du Monde Arabe, Paris, France
1981–1987

"A cultural position in architecture is a necessity. It involves the refusal to use key-in-hand solutions or easy alternatives, thus permitting an approach that is at the same time global in its conception and specific in relation to the site"(J.N.)

If it is true, as Jean Nouvel has stated, that "a building must communicate the anxieties of an epoch," we can interpret the headquarters of the Institut du Monde Arabe as a condensation of the dialectic energies resulting from the encounter between oriental culture and European culture and also, most of all, from the superimposition of two architectural elements usually considered difficult to reconcile: decoration and the typology of the glass prism. This modern building, made in conformity with the programmatic needs that the then minister of culture André Malraux prescribed for every *maison de culture* destined to stand on French territory, hosts spaces for shows, exhibitions, conferences, and debates. There are also a library, movie theater, and center of Arab studies. The institute occupies a triangular lot, with its northern face following the curve of the Seine River. On the windows

of the north-facing wall the outline of the surrounding city with its famous monuments has been reproduced in enamel, almost as through making a comment on the reproducibility of images of Western culture. On the south-facing side, the encounter between different cultures is reproduced by means of a functionally decorative apparatus. Defined by Modernist culture as a thing without purpose and thus rejected because of the lack of correspondence between its form and any given function, the decoration, in its variations of geometric arabesques, achieves an absolutely contemporary form of expression on the windows of this face. The grid between the glass panels repeats the arabesques of Islamic culture, and by means of photoelectric cells it directs the flow of daylight to illuminate the rooms of the institute.

Secession Building, Vienna, Austria
1897–1898

"Walls had to become: pale and splendid, sacred and chaste. Everything had to have the same stately dignity. A dignity without blemish: like what I felt approach me and look inside me when, at Segesta, I stood alone in front of the endless remains" (J.M.O.)

The Viennese contribution to Modern architecture may well be contained in the "stately dignity . . . without blemish" that permeates the volumes of the Vienna Secession Building. The artistic movement known as the Vienna Secession (Wiener Secession) was founded in Vienna in 1897 around the figures, among others, of Gustav Klimt, Otto Wagner, Josef Hoffmann, and Joseph Maria Olbrich, designer of the pavilion made to display the works of the members of the Secession. The story of the pavilion leads directly to the heart of the Vienna Secession, one aspect of which was great displeasure with academic art and all historicist decoration; for that reason, it can be associated with the larger Art Nouveau movement. On the other hand, however, it made recurrent references to classicism and the continuity of history. Within the context of a debate between abstract ornamentation and the permanence of floral

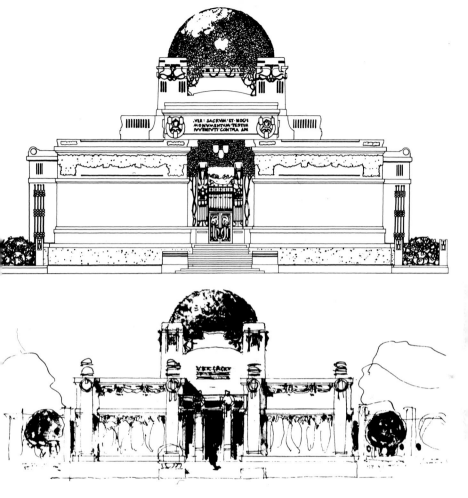

decoration, the Secession Building seems to point in the direction of an alternate route, to a form of architectural composition based on the values of "mass" or "proportion," of which the ornamentation, when added to the construction, could at the most reveal the guiding principles.

Attributable to the trip that Olbrich made to Italy and North Africa in 1893 after winning the Prix de Rome, the cubic forms of the pavilion allude to a Mediterranean purity that moves away from certain vegetal decorations or from the typically Art Nouveau exhibition of the metal structure. The building occupies a triangular lot with a Greek-cross layout, based on the joining of four rectangular bodies. The main façade, with vertical slits that mark the main entrance, is composed of the body that houses the rooms for the artists and the offices.

The other bodies are arranged around this central nucleus, with a system of flexible mobile walls so they can be divided to form exhibition spaces. They are illuminated by skylights in the roof. On the roof, directly above the atrium of the entryway, is a dome surrounded by four short stone pylons; at the top of the dome is a metal sphere that filters the light into the vestibule through a dense mesh of metal laurel leaves.

Town Hall of Stockholm, Sweden
1909–1923

"During the construction . . . both the personnel of the architect's studio and all the other people busy doing creative-type work had their workshops on the site"(R.O.)

The recent proliferation of adjectives applied by contemporary critics to architectural works includes the succinct and efficacious "edifice-city." The idea behind this architectural typology involves the complex relationship, both physical and symbolic, that a building

traditionally tied to the stylistic elements of folk and vernacular forms of architecture.

Without doubt, a certain romantic aura guided the arrangement and organization of the work on the building site, ideally inspired by that inimitable fusion of arts and crafts that was practiced by medieval guilds.

In 1918, with the construction of the town hall in full swing, the worksite resembled an immense laboratory, and, as Ragnar Östberg himself explained, the close cooperation of architects, sculptors, painters,

of the building, a clear result of its medieval inclinations, must be added a parallel contemporary reading, one that sees the town hall as a fragment of the city, sees it as, in the words of its designer, "a compendium of the city," in which nature and architecture blend in the unity of the constructed organism. Symbolically located on a flat stretch of land along Lake Mälar, the town hall is arranged in a compact layout around two courtyards. The first of these, open to the sky, is known as the Grand Court and can be crossed from several directions, thus assuming the role of city square. The Council Chamber and the Golden Chamber face the inner perimeter of the Grand Court, with access provided by a portico that connects the closed space of the court with the banks of the lake.

The second courtyard, called the Blue Hall, also functions as an urban space. Its interior location beneath the system of roofs is in a certain sense negated by the fact that the internal walls around it are illuminated by a horizontal strip of windows that evokes the exterior façades of which the town hall is composed. A ramp of marble stairs leads to the balustrade that connects the Blue Hall to the Golden Chamber, which is on the second floor. In a continuous play of historical references, the town hall, standing in the contemporary world, evokes the history of the city, and with its high tower becomes a symbolic element in the city of Stockholm.

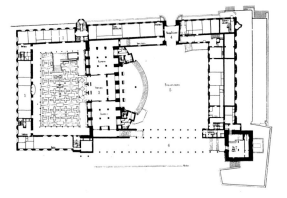

manages to establish or simulate with the image of the city in which it stands, to the point that the urban metaphor becomes the true expressive subject matter of the architecture. Among the many possible readings of the Stockholm Town Hall, the dominant one—as seems reasonable, since its creator was the leading exponent of Swedish National Romantic architecture—is the romantic, which sees the town hall as

ironworkers and copper workers, textile artisans, carpenters, and bricklayers "achieved the most felicitous results."

Every detail of the town hall reveals the patient work of craftspeople. The building is dressed with rough, dark red bricks made by hand and set in place using a technique similar to the one used in the construction of religious buildings during the Middle Ages. To the Romantic reading

Café de Unie, Rotterdam, Netherlands
1924–1925

"An architecture rationally based on the circumstances of life today would be in every sense opposed to the sort of architecture that has existed up till now" (J.J.P.O.)

The picturesque and local traditions that the Amsterdam school evoked using a few simple building materials applied to expressive, creative forms, were repudiated by the avant-garde movement that took the name of neoplasticism. The birth of the movement dates to 1917 and coincides with the foundation of the magazine *De Stijl* ("The

Style") by the painter and writer Theo van Doesburg. The Dutch artists who soon gravitated around the magazine included the architects J. J. P. Oud and Van t'Hoff, the painters Mondrian and Van der Leck, the poet Kok, and the Belgian sculptor Vantongerloo. Derived from Mondrian's pictorial experiments and based on the exclusive use of the right angle and the three primary colors, neoplasticism proposed the

achievement of a new form of plastic representation through the use of an abstract procedure that limited the expressive vocabulary to the geometric figures of the square and the rectangle and the volumes of the parallelepipeds and that shrunk the color palette to the fundamentals (yellow, blue, red).

Behind this drastic avant-garde reductionism was the ideal of achieving a new unity in the figurative arts, which, freed of all traces of individualism and sentimentality, would have enabled the plastic arts to better express the new universal values of life. This new form of esthetic expression, based on neoplastic painting, naturally evolved towards a new architectonic language, destined to influence a good deal of the nascent European rationalist movement in architecture.

Taken by the members of *De Stijl* as the main objective towards which all the figurative arts should be made to converge, architecture soon acquired a new experimental stance of Cubist derivation, translated in the decomposition of architectural volumes into colored planes; in the elimination of the window as a hole in a wall, its space now being generated by the sliding together or apart of planes; and in the elimination of the hierarchy applied to the façades of a building, replaced by an overall vision of the architectural organism without any favored angles.

Oud's brief membership among the ranks of *De Stijl* dates to between 1919 and

1921; however, the intersection of planes and their interpenetration, inspired by the Cubist formula, were to remain constants of his architectural style. As city architect for Rotterdam he was able to apply this style to the broad range of typologies used in public housing. In the same way, the Café de Unie can be taken as the manifesto of the *De Stijl* morphology, a genuine neoplastic canvas produced by that ambitious process of close identification between painting and architecture, joined side by side in the "universal creation of the beautiful."

Standing between two neoclassical buildings in the historic center of Rotterdam, the Café de Unie faces the Calandplein with an abstract façade, on the surface of which fields of red, blue, and yellow are presented, along with the black and white of the background, as organic parts of the architecture and from which project the trade signs of the café, done up with typically *De Stijl* graphics.

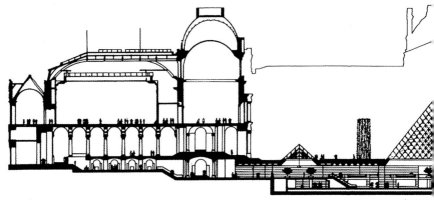

Grand Louvre,
Paris, France
1983–1993

"I believe that architecture is a pragmatic art. For it to become art it must be built on a foundation of necessity" (I.M.P.)

The "museum of museums," Le Grand Louvre, largest museum institution in the world, has been functionally adjusted and is now capable of supporting the astonishing number of visitors it receives thanks to the ingenious design of the American architect Ieoh Ming Pei. Originally built as a royal palace, the Louvre had long fallen short as a museum space, lacking spaces flexible and adequate enough to house the services and halls required of a modern, functioning museum. Promulgated in 1981 by the then president François Mitterand, the program of readjustment called for the modernization of the national monument and its integration within the city of Paris, without jeopardizing its historical and cultural integrity.

Pei's design satisfied these requirements with an undertaking that was to involve two phases of work. The first, begun in 1983, involved the creation of a new main entrance, beneath the vast surface of the central courtyard, the Cour Napoleon, which Pei created by way of an underground addition of

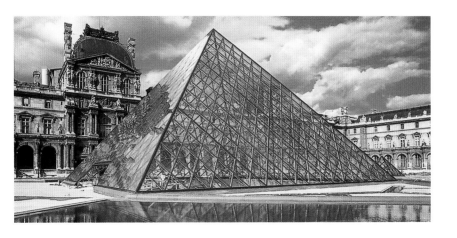

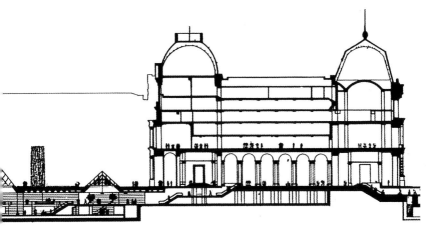

46,000 square meters that divides the throng of visitors into three routes that connect to the three wings of the museum. This is also the site of a series of necessary technical services: the entry and information services, a restaurant, an auditorium, and two galleries for temporary exhibitions. This first phase of construction also involved the simultaneous adjustment and reworking of the U-shaped building that surrounds the central courtyard. The second phase, which reached completion in 1993, involved converting the Richelieu Wing, until then occupied by the offices of the ministry of finance, into exhibition space. Doing so added 36,000 square meters to the Louvre's floorspace. The decision to feed natural light into the underground area of the main entrance by way of a glass pyramid 21 meters high that would stand in the center of the Cour Napoleon, accompanied by three smaller glass pyramids, made Pei's design one of the most controversial in Europe. The lightness of the metallic structure and the transparency of the surfaces of the volumes operate an effective process of dematerialization of the solidity of the archetypical pyramid, reworking the established image of that elementary geometric figure by way of the instruments of high-tech language.

Bibliothèque Nationale de France, Paris, France
1989–1997

"It is necessary to keep history in mind, but only as one more fact among others, and what is determinant in this history is that it produces a certain type of geography" (D.P.)

Several results of the recent minimalist trend in architecture are edifying

reference to established symbolic formalisms, much less to high-tech exhibitionism, it does not exclude recourse to certain archetypical and classical values of architecture, albeit reduced to minimal gestures purged of every explicit analogy to figurative models of the past.

So it is that France's new national library is a monument stripped bare of every historicist connotation that

middle area taken up by a luxurious plaza-garden; this is surrounded by four monumental L-shaped towers, one at each corner of the base. Among them, these towers have space for 400 kilometers of shelves, along with the administrative offices of the library.

The reading rooms and specialized libraries are arranged around the central garden and thus enjoy natural light as well as views of this fragment of nature transplanted to the center of an artificial organism. The stairs and necessary services for the library are located towards the outer perimeters of the buildings.

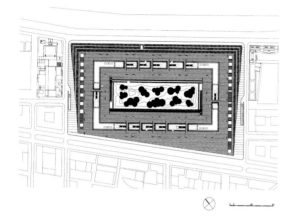

demonstrations of the truism that what is new in architecture is quite often difficult to separate from what is antique; and in the field of minimalist architecture Dominique Perrault ranks among the recognized leaders of the international field. Minimalism subjects the repertory of forms and figures of the architectural language to a process of formal and cultural reduction. While this means that it excludes any

stands, as its designer has declared, "in a site inscribed within the continuity of the series of large, open spaces connected to the Seine, such as the Place de la Concorde, the Champs de Mars, the Invalides."

The new installation, large enough to accommodate 4,000 readers and 20 million volumes, stands in an industrial area of the XIII *arrondissement*. At its center is a rectangular base, its open

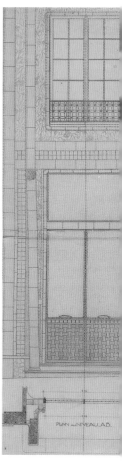

PLAN AU NIVEAU A.B.

House in Rue Franklin, Paris, France
1903–1904

"In the beginning architecture is only wooden framework. In order to overcome fire one builds in hard material. And the prestige of the wooden frame is such that one reproduces all the traits, including the heads of the nails"(A.P.)

The slow process, beginning at the end of the nineteenth century, by which the revolutionary building technique of reinforced concrete came to assume formal independence, originated in the rational building techniques developed by French culture. A result of the need to provide buildings with a combination of the resistance to compressive forces provided by ordinary cement and the resistance to tensile forces provided by a steel framework, the technique of reinforced cement was first applied in Europe in experiments conducted by François Hennebique and by Anatole de Baudot. Aside from its static advantages, the new building method also accelerated the installation of the load-bearing structure of a building, breaking it down into pillars, beams, and floors that were no longer necessarily related to the interior layout of the building. The new method also began to display its expressive values, applicable to

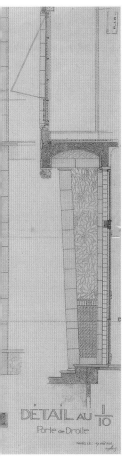

DÉTAIL AU $\frac{1}{10}$

Porte de Droite

PARIS LE 17 JANVIER 1903

all the categories of architectural language thanks in large part to the works of Auguste Perret.

Since it is made using wooden forms, reinforced concrete is comparable to certain wooden structures of antiquity, so the new building system became, for Perret, the pretext for giving constructions a compositional articulation based on the relationship between load-bearing and borne structures. The apartment building in rue Franklin is borne by a frame in reinforced concrete that, because it is visible on the façade, permits the resolution of certain esthetic and functional questions. The scarcity of natural light, limited by the front, is resolved by putting a U-shaped recess in the middle of the façade, thus making possible a double system of windows and balconies angled at 45 degrees. To the sides of the central body, a symmetrical system of bow-windows, overhanging the line of the façade, rises for six floors, up to the terraces of the last two floors, which are pulled inward. Although clad with ornamental, glazed-tile panels, the structural system is revealed with surprising clarity by stylistic alterations in the decorative order: smooth ceramic for the beams and pillars, recessed ceramic panels with floral motifs for the curtain walls.

Palazzo della Civiltà Italiana, Rome, Italy

(with Giovanni Guerrini, Bruno La Padula, Carlo Romano)
1936–1942

"If you want to be pedantic about it, we could say that all great Italian architecture has been only formal" (M.P.)

The decision made in 1935 to commemorate the twentieth anniversary of the Fascist era with a large universal exposition was a direct result of the strong-willed character of Benito Mussolini and his unwavering belief in the celebratory power of architecture. Meant to evoke the pomp of ancient imperial Rome, the exhibition was known as EUR (Esposizione Universale of Rome) or E 42, the latter because it was scheduled be held in Rome in 1942. Having named himself the great event's "spiritual father," Mussolini selected an immense area as the site of the exposition and its buildings (more than a thousand acres of countryside), making sure to locate the area between Rome and the sea so that it would require the draining of marshlands and would also restore to Rome its grandeur as capital of the waters of the Mediterranean. Located in the area of Rome called Tre Fontane, the exhibition's permanent buildings, after their use in the 1942 exposition, were meant serve as the beginnings of a new city quarter, which, located along an imperial road, would act as the strategic hinge in a monumental axis, joining, both physically and symbolically, the capital with the Tyrrhenian coast. The new street system was laid out in accordance with the Roman grid system of cardanus and decumanus, resulting in the creation of plazas and forums, with monumental buildings set down along the streets. The urbanistic plans and the many ideas that followed one another over time reached a kind of finalization in the plan laid out by Marcello Piacentini in 1937, but this soon led to a heated debate between the more reformist factions of rational Italian architecture and the more conservative classicism of Piacentini. In fact, the first urban plan for E 42, created in 1936 by Piacentini, Giuseppe Pagano, Luigi Piccinato, Luigi Vietti, and Ettore Rossi, had proposed a modern, functional city, not a replication of ancient Rome. That first plan called into being a grandiose, rationalist, and modernist settlement, inspired by the kind of technological triumphs that have marked every universal exposition. This first plan made use of Futuristic and quite improbable buildings made of crystal and steel facing limitless plazas and endless boulevards. Thus the rhetorical monumentalism of Piacentini, accused of imperialist leanings, was opposed by the rationalist modernism of Pagano. The palace of Italian civilization, however, seems inspired by a fully rhetorical language, in which the theme of the round arch is repeated so relentlessly that it dematerializes the subtle cage that encloses the reinforced-concrete framework of the building. Along with the elementary geometric forms of the cube and square, the design brushes aside every conceivable slavish citation of historical sources to move towards a "purity of abstract rhythm" that, applied to a work of art as an "anonymous work," opens the way to a renewed relationship between history, understood as the patrimony of the past, and modern culture in architecture.

Georges Pompidou Center, Paris, France

(with Richard Rogers, Ove Arup, and Partners)
1971–1977

"The building is a diagram. People read it in an instant; its insides are on the outsides, you can see them, you understand that people move in a certain way and the same goes for elevators, escalators"(R.P.)

According to the unwritten manual of traditional architecture, the physical plant of a building, with all its associated tubes and wires, should be hidden away behind the walls and floors. All of the network of tubes and wires that make up the "vital organs" necessary to the proper functioning of the building's "body" can therefore be seen and understood only by way of arcane and highly technical images or access points, through secret openings or sections that move farther and farther inward, right down to the bowels of the building. The Georges Pompidou Center, better known simply as Beaubourg, reverses this age-old building rule. By locating its support structure, technical plant, and elevator apparatus in full view outside the walls of the enormous (60 × 170 meters) building, it leaves its interior floors, each with 7,500 square meters of space, completely unobstructed and thus easily adaptable to every

type of exhibition or other museum activity. Endowed with this exceptional flexibility, a result of the thoroughly open floor plan, which is repeated on all six of the building's stories, the Georges Pompidou Center, going against every precept of the theory of "knitting up" the urban fabric, along with all concerns about matching a new building to pre-existing structures, exhibits its Neomodernist triumph in the historic center of Paris, applying a completely new architectural language to a container for mass-consumption cultural events. Although it is often associated with the high-tech trend that uses pieces of assembly-line mass production as elements in architectural structures, Beaubourg is really, as Renzo Piano has often explained, "a big, artisan-made product, a kind of big prototype made by hand piece by piece." The custom-built elements that compose the load-bearing structure in steel and cast iron, along with the technical equipment and the escalators, were made by hand individually, such that each one is different, a process that permitted, for example, making the Gerber girders that support the main structure in a single cast so that they are strong enough to span the distance of 50 meters without intermediate supports.

Jean Marie Tjibaou Cultural Center, Nouméa, New Caledonia
1991–1998

"The center for Kanak culture that we are building in New Caledonia is a project that I would call "frontier," composed of anthropology, geography, and local culture" (R.P.)

The Jean Marie Tjibaou Cultural Center stands on a curvilinear pathway that, following a ridge covered in palms and pines, separates a small lagoon from Magenta Bay, located to the east of Nouméa, the capital of New Caledonia. Rejecting any trace of "architectural colonialism" Renzo Piano created an evocative, multifunctional complex inspired by multicultural criteria that, paying heed to the deep roots of the local traditions, assumed the knowledge of the place and the surrounding plants as a necessary starting place for any design effort. Composed of an amphitheater, a library, a media center, and various teaching laboratories, the complex is divided in distinct nuclei, somewhat like "neoarchaic" huts, made in laminated wood and metal capable by means of a system of double screens and skylights of capturing the Pacific trade winds, transforming them into an efficient system of natural cross-ventilation.

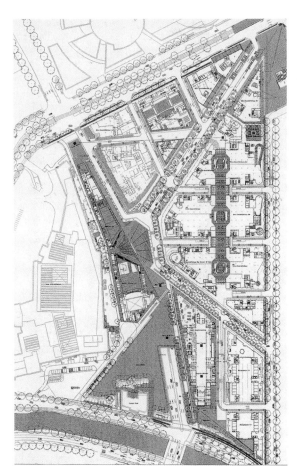

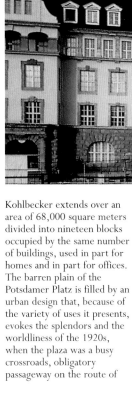

Reconstruction of a section of Potsdamer Platz, Berlin, Germany
1992–2000

"When I'm asked what the city of the future will be like, I answer: like that of the past, I hope. Our century has done terrible damage to that great human invention, the city. Its positive values—social life, the mix of functions, the quality of the buildings—are all leftovers from the past"(R.P.)

Symbol of the reunification of Berlin and its spiritual rebirth, the design for the reconstruction of Potsdamer Platz involved the Renzo Piano Building Workshop in an immense project of urban planning. Winner of the invitational competition published in 1992 by the Berlin Senate and the Daimler-Benz company, promoters of the undertaking, the volumetric plan presented by Piano with Christoph

Kohlbecker extends over an area of 68,000 square meters divided into nineteen blocks occupied by the same number of buildings, used in part for homes and in part for offices. The barren plain of the Potsdamer Platz is filled by an urban design that, because of the variety of uses it presents, evokes the splendors and the worldliness of the 1920s, when the plaza was a busy crossroads, obligatory passageway on the route of

anyone moving from the western quarters of Berlin towards the Mitte, the city center, site of a trolleyline terminus as well as a major train station. Effected by the necessary reworking of the connection between the Staatsbibliothek by Hans Scharoun, previously up against the Wall, and the monumental Mitte to the east, Piano's design used a new square as its hinge. Lined with new public buildings, this square forms an integrated and continuous whole with buildings of the Kulturforum complex. To the south of the square a new lake will be constructed using water from the Landwehrkanal, near which is the entrance to a street tunnel that crosses the area of the project. Many buildings will be constructed in the area, entrusted to various internationally famous architects. Standing out among these will be one designed by Piano himself, the Debis tower, the offices of the Daimler-Benz Interservice. Occupying the perimeter of a lot, the four buildings that make up the office center increase in height to end in the tower, which faces the Reichpietschufer. The structure evokes the lightness with which Mies van der Rohe dematerialized the surfaces of his skyscraper for the Friedrichstrasse Station competition in 1921.

Potamianos House, Filothei, Athens, Greece
1953–1955

"The work of the architect is not to invent ephemeral forms but to reveal the eternal shapes of tradition in the forms determined by the conditions of the present" (D.P.)

The history of the Modern movement is marked of by the punctual sequence of the CIAM (Congrès Internationaux d'Architecture Moderne) congresses. Founded in 1928 by some of the most famous and dedicated European architects, among them Le Corbusier, Walter Gropius, Ernest May, and Jacobus Oud, the congresses sought to give coherent theoretical expression to the various international

experiences of the architects of the Modern movement in the fields of town planning and architecture.
The first three congresses took place in cities—La Sarraz (Switzerland) for the first (1928), Frankfurt for the second (1929), and Brussels for the third (1930)—but the fourth CIAM congress, which took place in 1933, was held aboard a steamboat. On July 29, 1933, the *Patris II* weighed anchor in the port of

Marseilles and headed for Piraeus. This fourth CIAM, which took place in the water between the Mediterranean and the Aegean, was dominated by the charismatic figure of Le Corbusier. The central theme of the congress was the analysis of thirty-three cities, and in the course of heated debates the unusual passengers put forward their functionalist remedies for the future development of each of these cities. Le Corbusier later published this material anonymously under the name *Charter of Athens*. With its directives for the growth of the functional city, it later became famous.
The proposed remedies had in common the use of green belts to divide functional areas of cities and the regulation of the growth of residential building through the use of single typologies that would be repeated over and over, with high buildings located far from one another. Waiting for them in the port of Piraeus, among a crowd of Modernist architects, was a somewhat troubled Dimitris Pikionis. Attentive scholar of vernacular architecture and of the spirit of Greek tradition, Pikionis, sensing the wave of the rationalist renewal, immediately felt the need to distance himself from the esthetic conventions dictated by the Modern movement in an effort the achieve the difficult synthesis between tradition and modernity that he believed should accompany all good and efficient architecture.
Addressing the meeting of the 1933 CIAM, Pikionis warned the members of the congress

that if they were out hunting for Mediterranean images to apply to their functionalist lexicon, "This land is not like every other. Its spirituality is like a supreme principle that creates urgent demands to be satisfied . . . Naturally, I am not talking only about the natural landscape. I'm talking about the mental landscape." The Potamianos House, which stands on a panoramic hill in the Filothei quarter, not far from the city of Athens, can be taken as an expressive synthesis of Pikionis's analysis of the potential values of traditional Greek architecture and the new requirements of Modern architecture. In fact, it must have been the desire to fully exploit the panorama that led Pikionis to locate the bedrooms on the ground floor, giving enjoyment of the splendid view to the upper floor, used for receptions. Set on a solid base of local stone, the upper part of the house is lightened by large areas of plastered walls and by open loggias partly covered by roofs and by the projecting eaves. Extensive areas of glass contrast with the narrow openings on the ground floor and bring direct light into the rooms on the upper floor. The construction of the Potamianos House thus gives life to a structural organism in which the modern values of maximum comfort and rational use of space blend with the stones of tradition, Pikionis's favorite building material.

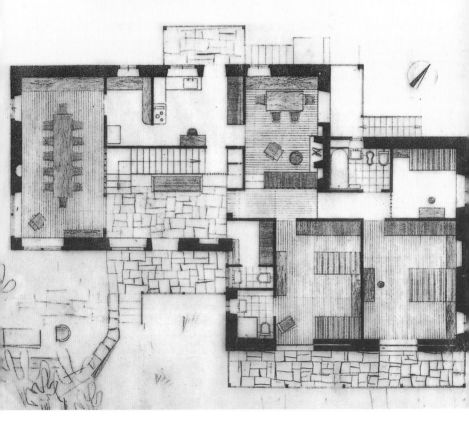

Dimitris Pikionis 1887–1968

Zale Funerary Complex, Ljubljana, Slovenia
1937–1940

"We Slavs have our own, singular power; even so, we still often find ourselves forced to go to Rome to find it" (J.P.)

In the history of Modern architecture the twin values of memory and invention have generated constructions that, although composed in accordance with the orders and conventions of classical architecture, appear up to date, very much in keeping with the spirit of their time. The most successful examples of this particular trend do not let their relationship with history exhaust itself in a simple return to the past, but instead manage to revitalize the symbols of the classical language (and more in general, of memory), inserting them in new, inventive compositions. Diametrically opposed to the radical innovations of the avant-garde, and yet modern in the sense of their invention, the works of Josef Plecnik were ignored by critics during his lifetime, and that critical isolation continued long after Plecnik's death.

Far from the experimentation that marked the beginning of the century, the avant-garde and Modern movement's furious drives to establish the "new as an absolute value," Plecnik's works always seem to follow an elegant integration between local artisan work and experimentation with forms. To the antihistorical motto "I do not want to know that there were other men before

me," adopted by Tristan Tzara to exalt Dadaist thinking (the most radical of all twentieth-century avant-gardes), Plecnik responds with his own guiding principle: "Like a spider, I want to attach my thread to tradition and then, beginning there, to weave my own web." The point of departure of this

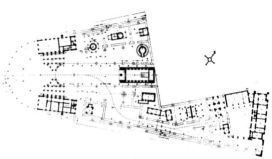

slow and tireless weaving is the artisan dimension, the essential aspect of his youthful training, to which Plecnik always gave a decisive role, even during the years of his collaboration with the great reformer Otto Wagner. It was the importance Plecnik attributed to the values of classicism, compared to which Modern architecture always seemed poorer to him, that distanced the Slovenian architect from the experimentalism of Wagner and the Vienna Secession. From 1921 on, Plecnik's works, divided among his birthplace of Ljubljana, Vienna, and Prague, acquired the traits of an autonomous and original force, a blend of the classical and archaic sources of the architectonic patrimony of the Mediterranean with the ideals of the rebirth of the new Slovenian nation, with

Ljubljana as its capital city. Made necessary by the strong demographic growth of Ljubljana, the Zale cemetery, composed of eleven chapels—one for each of the saints of the city's parishes, plus another reserved for non-believers—presents itself as a true city of the dead.

Distributed across a triangular lot, the chapels, together with various service buildings, present a kind of catalog of building types, small bits of architecture spread across the cemetery, all based on a classical and archaic architectural grammar. A collection of small projects, the Garden of All Saints, later called Zale, faces the city of Ljubljana through its monumental propylaeum, a metaphorical vestibule between the space of life and that of death. It is severe, classical architecture, but the double orders of columns and the grand central arch give it a sense of endless variations of rhythm and composition.

Grosses Schauspielhaus, Berlin, Germany
1918–1919

"In our poverty we must knowingly renounce wealth and try to make a harmonious blend of a few assonant forms"(H.P.)

The economic and social devastation suffered by Germany following its defeat in World War I make up the necessary background for the creations of the Expressionist avant-garde. The drive to present a program of rebirth and reform for a society finally freed led to an alliance between the artistic avant-gardes and the political left. Joining to form work councils (*Arbeitsrat für Kunst*), they chose Berlin as the new center from which to spread the word from the various avant-garde movements. The yearning for a social democratic utopia had at least one direct effect on the architectural postulates of avant-garde Expressionism: the sharp rejection of all symbolic references borrowed from the products of industry, including those mass produced or made in foreign countries. Favor was given instead to the idea of new "cathedrals of socialism," presented as dreamy crystal towers or improbable subterranean grottoes, locations set aside for the fulfillment of the great myth of the total work of art. The cave was an archetypical and mythological place,

capable of embodying the most remote identity of the German populations, and its myth went through a concrete transformation in the construction of the Grosses Schauspielhaus, a theater with 5,000 seats created through the reconstruction of the Karlstrasse circus in Berlin. Having miraculously survived the devastations of World War II, it was inexplicably demolished in the 1970s. The outer covering of the theater presented a system of hanging bows that, running the full

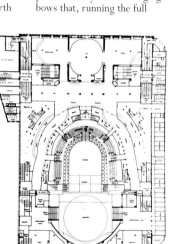

height of the building, soared upward to the top of the compact masonry mass of the building.

Inside, halls and foyers shaped like caves and caverns led into a "subterranean" world softly lit by a system of indirect lighting. The foreboding, ancestral atmosphere of these spaces was offset by the appearance of the central amphitheater, a vast concert hall crowned by a dome dripping with stalactites that,

arranged in diminishing order towards the height of the vault, optimized the distribution of sound waves among the spectators. The strong symbolic and expressive character of the vault was matched by the unusual semi-elliptical arrangement of the auditorium, which, breaking with the traditional type of the Italian theater, plunges the spectators into total participation in the theatrical performance.

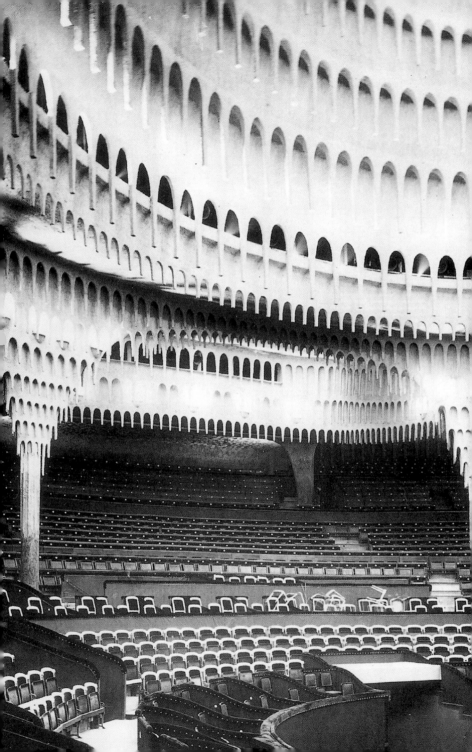

Mosque and Islamic Culture Center, Rome, Italy

(with Vittorio Gigliotti and Sami Mousawi)
1975–1993

"When I plan for a place I think of the place as a receiving station in which messages from a thousand other places near and far meet"
(P.P.)

The poetics of "architectonic listening," a constant in the

works of Paolo Portoghesi, promotes respect for the *genius loci* ("spirit of the place"). In opposition to the idea of a Modernist utopia created out of nothing, Portoghesi's architectonic listening makes use of the stratified values in the historical patrimony of every people's culture. The Mosque and Islamic Culture Center in Rome, fruit of the collaboration between Portoghesi, Vittorio Gigliotti, and Sami Mousawi, represents

the material expression of a dialogue between different cultures. Inspired by the union of two symbolic shapes, the square (metaphor for the earth) and the circle (metaphor for the sky and divine perfection), the great mosque, large enough for 2,000 people, has a square layout inscribed within a rectangle that is then broken down in turn into twenty-five smaller squares. A large dome rises over the nine central

squares, and sixteen smaller domes cover the sixteen smaller perimeter squares. The adjacent H-shaped building hosts the cultural center, composed of two unequal and slightly curved bodies, with a central courtyard formed where the two bodies cross. This is a square court, inspired by the traditional open space in front of an Arabian mosque (the *sahn*), where the faithful can gather for prayer in the open. The minaret, with four projecting bodies to hold up two circular rings, rises high above the center and is visible from the surrounding territory. The central body of the mosque is full of diffused light, filtered through the layers of domes, and as a result the area of the mosque has an abstract and transcendent atmosphere. The interwoven arches and the daring "biological" membranes of the columns are made of prefabricated cement mixed with crushed stone and marble sand from Carrara. The outer walls are dressed in straw-colored bricks with travertine and peperino inserts. Modeled on the archaic and classical typology of the Islamic *masjid* (place where the faithful prostrate themselves to their god), the large mosque of Rome is a physical space that is at the same time symbolic of a possible exchange between Islam and Christianity.

Climat de France Housing Complex,
Algiers, Algeria
1955–1957

"Perhaps for the first time in modern times we have sent men off to live in a monument. These men, who were the poorest in Algeria … understand this. They are the ones who baptized the square with the name 'the two hundred columns'" (F.P.)

Various movements within modern-day urbanistics suggest that the decay to which the outskirts of cities so often fall victim can be avoided by uniting those peripheral areas to the organism of the historical city by inserting within them new public spaces capable of evoking, by their form and content, the most immediately recognizable characteristics of the historic center. This union of the outskirts and the city center cannot be considered complete when it stops at the merely cosmetic (the outer areas of many cities are already loaded with decontextualized pediments and spires); to be complete it must have an effect on the fabric of the peripheral area that is the subject of the undertaking, giving that area a sense of collective values. Anticipating the core of this debate by about thirty years, Fernand Pouillon created a masterpiece in Algiers, a synthesis of urban qualities and constructive simplicity. "I organize my work spaces for the pedestrian, not for those who travel by airplane," Pouillon was fond of saying, thereby drawing a line between his works and the architecture of the 1950s that seemed designed to create urban spaces more pleasant to look at from the sky than from the ground. The Climat de France Housing Complex is located on a hill overlooking the sea, behind the Casbah of Algiers. It has a great courtyard with two hundred columns and a long pavilion that, curving in on itself, closes the complex off from the sea. The building with the great courtyard is 261 meters long and 66 meters wide. It is composed of residential units arranged along the two hundred columns of the portico, which wraps around the great space of the central courtyard. Set three meters away from the body of the building, the portico provides shelter for the shops located on the ground floor. Each of the two hundred columns is made of seven cubic blocks of limestone, joined by a long perimeter architrave one meter thick. Three floors of apartments take up the perimeter body of the building, which ends in a roof terrace with a slender loggia. The slope of the hillside on which the complex stands has been eliminated by the large open space of the courtyard, its perimeter marked off by a stately portico, while the outer structure towards the sea follows the slope of the hillside. Immense stairs and monumental ramps provide access for pedestrians and cars, giving the large open courtyard the role of a gathering place and also making it part of a route leading all the way down to the sea. Based on modular proportions—themselves based on the size of the columns—that are used to establish all the measurements of the construction, the building with the two hundred columns is the physical and symbolic center of a true historical citadel that has been relocated to an outer area of the city.

Dressed with square blocks of stone, this piece of popular building evokes the great columned spaces that enlivened the Roman forums of African cities, the courts of Arabian mosques and caravansaries, but, most of all, it seems located outside time, as though it had always existed. In fact, Pouillon succeeded in making a building that does not seem to draw its forms from an artistic and creative act and seems instead to be the result of an impersonal building system, an extension of the art of building cities. In so doing, Pouillon was following the teaching of the great master Auguste Perret, according to whom, "He who, without betraying the modern conditions of a program, or the use of modern materials, produces a work which seems to have always existed, which, in a word, is banal, can rest satisfied."

Fernand Pouillon 1912–1986

Casa del Farmacista, Gibellina Nuova, Sicily

(with Laura Thermes)
1980

"My Casa del Farmacista . . .
when it was no more than
a design it enjoyed great success
with critics. Once it was built,
a kind of generalized rejection
grew up around it that,
in my opinion, was caused
by the house getting off the piece
of paper" (F.P.)

With the construction of the Casa del Farmacista (Pharmacist's House) in Gibellina Nuova, Franco Purini and Laura Thermes knocked down the wall of the presumed incompatibility between architectural representation, the designs for buildings, and their physical realization. Although the two architects continue to affirm that an architectural design will always be "superior to the creation because of the quality

of the desire it expresses," the Casa del Farmacista, in the thickness of its walls, is a physical expression of Purini's long and diligent research into the theme of architectural representation and on the ties it can establish with built architecture, attempting to reveal the workings of the double code that the two disciplines have in common. Because of the problematic relationship between the practice of building and that of

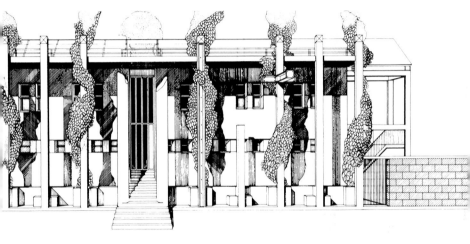

architectural representation, usually faced by architects who design and paint but do not become involved in actual building—which does not keep their figurative and pictorial creations from having an influence on the actual structure—Purini and Thermes open a building site only in those cases in which doing so is necessary to test the volumetrics that are the object of their research. "We are presumptuous enough to think of ourselves as architect-scientists who work in a 'construction laboratory,' where we mix ingredients, including dangerous ones, in the hope of finding new combinations." Located at the intersection of two streets in the center of the city, the Casa del Farmacista reacts with the chaos and the indefiniteness of the surrounding residential fabric by presenting itself as a "laboratory" of speaking forms. These forms are responsible not only for the representation of the pharmacist's house and the site of the town pharmacy, but also, and most of all, for the representation of fragments and simple architectural elements, made manifest by the double-height portico and by the archetype of the house with a sloping roof projecting from the line of the façade.

Lloyd's Building, London, UK
1978–1986

"We design every building such that it can be broken down into elements and subelements so as to result in an immediately legible order"(R.R.)

One of the constants of high-tech architecture is the authority and prestige it confers on individual building elements, in this sense agreeing with the spirit of much of nineteenth-century engineering along with the Modernist esthetic that takes the machine as model, with its pieces and elements transferred to the architectural discipline within the sphere of a sincere and widespread modernization of the processes that regulate the modernization and development of building. It thus follows that the preferred field of application of high-tech style is the industrial macrostructure or the advanced services sector. In these structures the steel supporting framework is visible, as are the physical plant and services. Also, such buildings generally display a marked extraneousness from their surrounding environment.

The construction of the new headquarters of Lloyd's presented Richard Rogers, the most celebrated protagonist of

the high-tech culture, with the problematic impact that the new construction would have, since it was going to stand in the historic heart of the City of London. The resulting building does indeed reveal its network of girders, its tubes, and its technical systems, but it nonetheless achieves a high level of suitability with the surrounding buildings, thanks to its clear and regular layout and its height, which varies,

according to its several façades, from a maximum of twelve stories to a minimum of six. Lloyd's requested flexible interior spaces, and Rogers provided them by placing every load-bearing element of the structure and all the tubes and ducts of its technical requirements on the façade, beyond the perimeter of the building, while the emergency stairs, elevators, and services are located in six external towers arranged

around the building. The mixed structure, composed of beams and columns in reinforced concrete and a structure in steel rings, forms a central opening, the heart of the building, known as the Room, where the trading takes place. This twelve-story-high volume is illuminated by natural light that pours down through a metallic barrel vault, homage to the structural engineering of the late nineteenth century.

Richard Rogers 1933

Theater of the World, Venice, Italy
1979–1980

"Architecture is theater, the architect is a director; there is then the event, the success, the hour that passes"(A.R.)

"A few profound things; the rest is vanity." Thus did Aldo Rossi direct his students towards a method of composition—based on the simplest, most elementary components of architecture—that was destined to take shape, between the 1960s and 1970s, as an authentic theory of architectural design. Pieces and parts, chosen from a simplified geometric selection, in a limited, restricted number, are brought together by Aldo Rossi to form new units by means of a combining technique that Ezio Bonfanti called his "additive procedure." The geometric archetypes of the sphere, the cube, and the cylinder add up to make the elements that are essential to construction, which Bonfanti listed as the "cylinder-column, pilaster, thin support wall, solid wall, limited openings, external stairs, triangular- and rectangular-sectioned bridge girders, and roofs that are flat or have a dome or cone." These are combined following a reductive process that proceeds by "succession" or by "superimposition."
An intimately autobiographical element, along with his rereading of the works of the history of architecture and the city—the essential background to each of Rossi's architectural scenarios—has kept his "additive procedure" from ever reducing itself to a mere

summation of geometric components; instead, it has engaged in unexpected relationships, filtered through the strength of analogy, with the typologies of traditional urban architecture, and, more in general, with the universal patrimony of the architecture of the past.
The Teatro del Mondo ("Theater of the World"), a floating structure, commissioned from Rossi by Paolo Portoghesi for the 1979 Venice Biennale "Teatro/Architettura," outlines, in the form of an ephemeral creation, the traits of Rossi's language that were destined to soon go around the world under the tutelary deity of a new classicism.
Drawn by a tugboat and challenging the norms that regulate all naval arts, the theater, more than 20 meters high, made its appearance off the tip of Venice's Dogana on November 11, 1979.
Built over a steel framework welded to a barge that gave it the unlikely ability to float, the theater was composed of a cubic body 11 meters high that ended in an octagonal roof 6 meters high covered in copper and crowned by a sphere and banner. The cubic body of the central structure, 9.50 meters on each side, was flanked on two sides by stairways that, arranged in three levels of internal galleries, led to a terrace located on the perimeter of the roof. At the bottom level, two tiers of seats faced each other from the longer sides of the central stage, used for small theatrical performances. Supported by the framework of metal tubes, the structure was covered by

wooden planks, and in fact the model for the theater was the wood-and-metal lighthouses that look out over the Atlantic coasts, a shape that frequently shows up in Rossi's projects and designs. The amazement of those who saw the floating theater was increased by the simple and familiar elements of which it was composed, almost as though it were a well-proportioned monument that, under its own power, had simply put out to sea.

Aldo Rossi 1931–1997

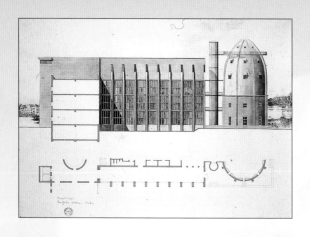

New building of the Bonnefanten Museum, Maastricht, Netherlands
1990–1994

"If we go through a museum several times, or have done so over the years, it seems to us like a city; perhaps our city or another place encountered because of distant events" (A.R.)

In an interview not so very long ago, the art historian Ernst H. Gombrich expressed his displeasure with the current trend, apparently on the rise, of museum architecture that "outweighs" the art on display. According to Gombrich, this is a kind of contemporary "sensationalism" that permits the museum building to "steal the show" from the individual art objects that should be the centers of attention. With this idea as background, we now describe a construction that by recovering the urban and municipal values traditionally associated with a city museum, succeeds in representing the figure of the museum as the authentic mirror of the city. The layout of the Bonnefanten Museum is quite simple, being composed of three longitudinal bodies joined at one end to a fourth, transverse body, at the center of which is the museum's main entrance. The open areas between the three longitudinal bodies have been turned into a series of

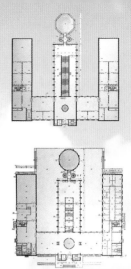

courtyards facing the Meuse River. The middle of the three longitudinal bodies houses the large stairway around which the entire layout is organized; this stairway ends on the side facing the river, site of a large dome dressed in metal, the materialization of a recurrent image in Rossi's sketches and designs. The use of iron and brick—simple, traditional building materials—gives the building a sense of a technological "deficit" that puts it in the same category as certain industrial and agricultural structures. This can be seen as further confirmation of Rossi's fondness for the simplicity of forms based on engineering and on respect for the laws of statics. Thus the most recurrent themes in Rossi's poetics concur to form a museum that is first of all an example of "civil architecture," a construction that, rising from the Dutch countryside, recalls the collective values of the city and the territory. A catalog of architectural forms, this museum is an "urban spot" par excellence, where the exhibition spaces and the internal collective spaces seem projected in continuity with the spaces of the city and where even the most distracted tourist will note signs of his or her own city or of those visited during the course of an exhausting tour and by now quite distant.

Residential building in Schützenstrasse, Berlin, Germany
1992–1998

"Roman monuments, the palaces of the Renaissance, castles, Gothic cathedrals constitute architecture; they are parts of its construction. As such, they are always returning, and not only as history and memory but as design elements" (A.R.)

Because of its setting and the methodology employed, this project by Aldo Rossi makes its own contribution to solving the complex problem of restoring buildings of the past and locating them near new

constructions.
In point of fact, the setting is near the former Checkpoint Charlie, around the westernmost end of the Mitte and at the end of the Tiergarten, where the Berlin Wall, projecting into the heart of the old city, already dealt a fatal blow by the ravages of the war, did even more damage to the city.
More precisely, the project concerned a lot between Zimmerstrasse and

Schützenstrasse and followed a program divided into distinct phases. In its first phase, the undertaking was restricted to just three lots on the Schützenstrasse, but in its later stages it came to involve the entire area of the block. From its earliest sketches, the project foresaw the restoration of two typical elements of the pre-war Mitte; the entire construction in Beaux-Arts style located along the Schützenstrasse and the base only of a nearby building, both of which had escaped the destruction of the war. The aim of the restoration, however, was not merely to give permanence to certain elements and fragments of the past but to return this section of the city's area to its nineteenth-century level of activity.
Within the compact, homogeneous grid at the center of Berlin, the building typology of the apartment house was constant.
Apartment buildings were constructed to exploit every free portion of the block on which they stood with the exception of the area used for the creation of the internal courtyard. The façades of these apartment houses rigorously followed the shape of the lot. Rossi's project evoked this close relationship between construction and lot and in fact used it as its logical framework. The internal courtyards belong to the buildings in the strict typological sense, since they create permeable spaces between the interior and exterior, served by entryways and pathways that make it possible to walk from one

block to another across the city.
The street façades, kept to a uniform eave height, create the sense of a composite architecture in which sections made of iron or glass stand beside restored portions. Outstanding among these are designs based on the Palazzo Farnese.
This is thus a true collection of building types, types that are in turn related to specific activities and functions. In fact, Rossi composed the façades of the block with a combinatory technique that makes the faces on the street present a selection of different building types in the logic of which the pre-existing fragments of the Schützenstrasse appear as indispensable signs of the growth and evolution of the city. Nor should the citation of Palazzo Farnese surprise anyone, for, within the narrative sequence of a collection of building types, it is an example of a typology, the synthesis of an original ideal model for European architecture: the sixteenth-century Italian palazzo.
In this way Rossi evokes fragments and models, physically or ideally pre-existing, with a technique that does not fall into the repetition of types but that reproduces the logic of certain building principles from the past.

Aldo Rossi 1931–1997

Ice Hockey Rink, Yale University, New Haven, USA
1956–1959

"Baroque architects took on the same problem of creating dynamic spaces. Within the limits imposed by the classical orders and by their technology they tried to see how far they could get towards an architecture beyond the static" (E.S.)

The architectonic restitution of a particular static condition, made possible by the proven technical abilities of reinforced concrete, led many works of Modern architecture made after the 1950s to elaborate structures and architectonic assemblies that, because of their plastic spatial configuration, are often compared to structures or forms based on the plant or animal worlds.

Such is the case with the hockey rink designed by Eero Saarinen for Yale University, which was baptized the "Yale Whale" almost the moment it was completed. As often happens in the creation of such complex structures, the "monumentality" implied by this nickname was the result of both the ingeniousness of the structure's engineer, the Norwegian Fred N. Severud, and the plastic and sculptural skills of its architect designer, Saarinen. The building's size is a response to a difficult and age-old dilemma—how to fit

the greatest possible number of people under a single covering, with the least possible number of intermediate supports for that covering. In this case, it was a matter of spectators seated around the oval shape of a hockey rink, leading to the idea of an oval sports arena with maximum dimensions of 101.5 × 56 meters, with a load-bearing structure in reinforced concrete that is surprisingly reduced to a parabolic arc, which is located along the longitudinal axis of the building, with low, undulating perimeter walls, 30 centimeters thick, leaning out 15 degrees towards the exterior of the building. The parabolic arch, which at its highest point stands 22.8 meters above the level of the sports arena, forms a continuous span, without intermediate supports, that projects fully 12 meters past the perimeter of the building, thereby creating a shelter for the main entrance to the sports complex. The wooden covering, composed of planks, is supported by a system of braces, composed of steel cables spaced center to center at a distance of 1.83 meters apart suspended between the parabolic arc and the ends of beams that project from the perimeter walls.

Helsinki Train Station, Helsinki, Finland
1904–1919

"Be honest in the form and the expressions, be honest in the material and the construction, and the future will admire your works" (E.S.)

The process of slow modernization with which, at the end of the nineteenth century, the countries of Northern Europe adapted to the progresses of industrialization and capitalism moved Finland towards a program of cultural rebirth that, as part of a growing movement for independence from Russian domination, led to an ambitious reawakening of the national identity.

As a result of this situation the experiments in Art Nouveau then being carried out in Europe made their way into Finland as part of the so-called National Romanticism Movement, which rejected academic and neoclassical stylistic elements in its drive to express the elements of popular tradition by means of a national, romantic language. In the first years of the twentieth century, the desire to create an architectural style capable of representing the identity of the Finnish nation was taken up by the architects Eliel Saarinen, Herman Gesellius, and Armas Lindgren, who, working as

associates, were later responsible for projecting Finnish architecture onto the contemporary scene of international architecture. The Helsinki Train Station is the fruit of this ambitious program. It was designed and built by Eliel Saarinen after he alone won first place in the competition published in 1903. A masterpiece of twentieth-century railroad architecture, destined to influence many later stations,

such as, for example, the central station of Stuttgart, designed by Paul Bonatz and Friedrich Eugen Scholer, the Helsinki station exhibits a classical and international language that, cleansed of every romantic superstructure, manifests its ties to the stylistic elements of the Jugendstil and the Wagnerschule. Dressed in granite and copper, the station has the monumental sense of an urban portal, emphasized

by the gigantic scale of the pairs of twin statues that flank the main entrance. This entrance leads to the central hall and to side halls covered by curving arches, while the high tower with its sense of a town hall stands on the right side of the building.

Power Station
1914, black pencil on paper
black, green, and red ink
31 × 20.5 cm
Paride Accetti Collection, Milan,
Italy
(formerly property of the
Sant'Elia family, Como, Italy)

"Calculation of the resistance of
materials, the use of reinforced
concrete and iron preclude
architecture in the classical and
traditional sense"(A.S.)

"Architecture breaks with tradition. It is necessary to begin again from the beginning." Antonio Sant'Elia expressed his Futurist passion in such declarations, and in his pamphlet *Manifesto of Futurist Architecture* (1914) he predicted the birth of a new architecture, one that would be based on the use of reinforced concrete and iron and that would lead to a new ideal of anticlassical, modern beauty.

Sant'Elia's pictorial studies for power stations, factories, hangars, lighthouses, bridges, and garages reflect this dedication to monumentality. It is a new monumentality, and he applied it to the new types of architectonic structures and infrastructures produced by progress made in the field of technology. These are new, isolated cathedrals of progress, the centers of a Futuristic revision of the urban world. With their powerful buttresses, oblique lines, and towering stacks—and unencumbered by any of the mechanical apparatuses that they would have required to actually function—electricity power stations, symbolic generators of the pulsating drive towards the rebirth of the city, rise to the level of new monumental symbols of the technological prophecy, replacing the traditional models evoked by the European avant-garde movements of the same period. The same monumental category would include the architectonic infrastructures, which are not isolated but are located by Sant'Elia in the metropolitan setting of the "New City," an immense worksite animated by advances in the field of engineering, such as elevators, pipelines, aerial and subterranean passageways, expressively exhibited as the stylistic elements of a new language foreshadowing functionalist architecture.

Antonio Sant'Elia 1888–1916

Brion Cemetery, San Vito di Altivole, Treviso, Italy
1969–1978

"The modern language should have its own words and its own grammar, exactly as happened in the case of classical forms. Modern forms and structures should be used following a classical order" (C.S.)

The strikingly individualistic character of Carlo Scarpa's work can be summarized as a general rejection of the homologizing attitude of utilitarian architecture carried out through the application of refined decoration with a close attention to architectonic detail. Scarpa's attention to detail is not expressed in an individualistic mannerism, however, and while it shows signs of the influence of Art Nouveau and the teaching of Frank Lloyd Wright, it takes the artisan tradition of making architecture and lifts it to the international reality of contemporary architecture. The high point of Scarpa's architectural career is the arrangement of the Brion Cemetery in San Vito di Altivole, a work that kept him busy during the last years of his life and that includes his own tomb within the area of the cemetery reserved for the members of the Brion family. The cemetery is a unitary and

organic arrangement composed of a series of architectural fragments and episodes that are grouped in smaller, independent arrangements complete in themselves. Arranged in a series within the boundary wall, along a path marked by water, are a cypress grove, a temple, a sacristy, crossed by the same footpath, a shrine, a propylaea, and an arcosolium. This last-named, inspired by a tomb in the catacombs, covers the sarcophagi of the Brions, husband and wife, with a pensile arch in reinforced concrete, associating a celebration of death with a eulogy to life.

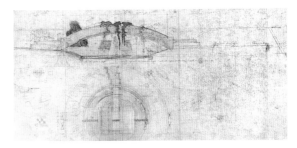

New Philharmonic, Berlin, Germany
1956–1963

"In the modern is also contained tradition, understood again as vitality. I speak in fact of those living traditions that are capable of conferring expression to architecture, because for me it must be, so to speak, stripped bare of every fixed exclusiveness" (H.S.)

The great "cathedral of socialism," the great collective building "of the people for the people," the structure that Bruno Taut and the members of the avant-garde Expressionist Novembergruppe and the Gläserne Kette began imagining in 1918, the building that was to be the headquarters of a future, authentically social-democratic society, finally took on a solid, physical shape many years after the avant-garde furors were spent, in the New Berlin Philharmonic that Hans Scharoun began working on in 1956 after winning the competition for its construction.

Scharoun was an active member of both of the artistic movements just named, but unlike many of his colleagues he did not abandon Germany during the years of Nazi power. Instead, working in complete isolation, between 1939 and 1945 he created an immense series of designs and watercolors in which a recurring theme was the enormous public building, a collective structure, with curvilinear and fragmented walls, enlivened by the enormous crowds gathered within them.

Among these pictorial sketches, the typology of the theater was very often presented under a new configuration, that of the "theater-form," which, inspired by the archetype of the cave, went against the classical, Italian theater model to wrap the spectators—or, more ideally, the entire German nation—in a single united organism in which spectators and orchestra alike, without distinctions of any kind, were projected in a mystical, cosmic abyss. Such were the theoretical and pictorial backgrounds of the New Philharmonic that Scharoun made between 1956 and 1963 close to the Berlin Wall, which at the time divided not only the city but also the entire German nation into a democratic part and a socialistic part. Scharoun's overturning of every classical type of theater also served the purpose of optimizing the acoustics; to this end he located the orchestra in the middle of the hall, with the platea and gallery arranged around it by means of a system of asymmetrical sloping platforms projecting over and converging onto the central space.

Nor is there anything conventional about the foyer, which is composed of a series of spaces and volumes connected by ramps and stairs that create a series of spaces arranged around the envelope of the concert hall, with passages and small walkways leading inwards.

Parish Church, St Fronleichnam, Aachen-Rothe Erde, Germany
1929–1930

"Clear and in the luminous purity of its austere youth is born a new order of the spaces and works, of the forms, and of the men on the ruins of aged memories, of pretexts made senseless, of misunderstood emblems" (R.S.)

So spoke the architect Rudolf Schwarz during the inaugural celebrations of the parish church of St Fronleichnam, the church of Corpus Domini in Aachen. The architect's speech celebrated the birth of a new architectonic order, which, given the boxlike elementary volumes of the church, could have been taken as a hymn to the Neues Bauen ("new building") preached by the doctrine of the Modern movement and institutionalized by Walter Gropius and by his teachings at the Bauhaus.

In reality, while Schwarz's church of Corpus Domini, with its bare white walls, presents traits of Modern architecture, freed from the traditionally symbolic eloquence of every other religious building, it is a programmatic building, created in response to the needs of worship dictated by the German liturgical movement, which wanted "the new order," of which Schwarz spoke, to mean the "rebirth of the architecture of poverty," diametrically opposed to every functionalist technicalism preached by the Neues Bauen. Planned as a single volume based on an elongated rectangular layout, the church of the Corpus Domini stands in a workers' suburb of Aachen. Its internal spaces are organized so as to give the faithful the closest possible participation in the celebration of the liturgy, with the space reserved for the faithful blending with that in which the priest stands to form one continuous, homogenous space. The church is composed of two elongated parallelepipeds. The larger of these is the main nave, 20 meters high, which is illuminated by a series of rectangular windows with an industrial appearance set along its longitudinal walls. The side nave, much lower than the main nave and attached to its side, serves as the confessional and includes the vestibule of the side entrance, since the main, central entrance is reserved for special ceremonies. The floor and altar are dressed in black marble that contrasts with the pallor of the walls and ceiling, the light from the few windows opened along the longitudinal walls of the main nave adding a spiritual sense. No structural element interferes with the bareness of the perimeter walls, which are reinforced internally by a support in reinforced concrete that serves every static function necessary to the building's stability. As the priest and theologian Romano Guardini noted, the configuration of the church does not evoke the esthetic category of an "emptiness," but rather of "silence," and "in silence is God."

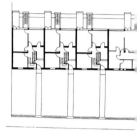

256

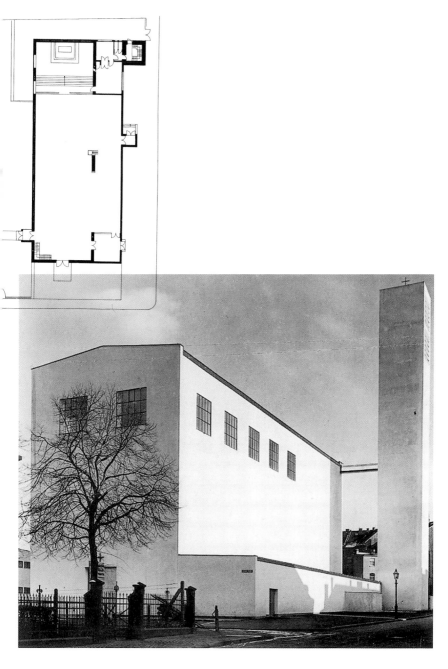

Rudolf Schwarz 1897–1961

Empire State Building, New York, USA
1931

"Building skyscrapers is the nearest peace-time equivalent of war"
(William A. Starrett, contractor)

It was the construction of the Empire State Building, long the tallest building in the world, thanks to its 380 meters of height, that brought about the internal metamorphosis of the compositional formulas of the

typology of the skyscraper in which the historical decorations applied to the surfaces, which followed an eclectic language drawn from a historical repertory ranging from ancient Egypt to the Mayan temples, moved towards rigid and elementary forms so that naturalistic and historicist ornamentation finally gave way to an authentically American "modernism."

The building, which can be seen as a celebration of the myths of verticality as well as the machine age, was made possible by advances in plant engineering and developments in elevators, the high speeds and safety of which were directly related to the birth and success of the skyscraper. The building's layout reflected the requirements of the city's zoning laws, which limited the portion of the building that could rise freely to one-quarter of the area of the site; the Empire State Building challenged the nearby Chrysler Building, completed in 1930, for the title of tallest building. It was built in accordance with a tough set of basic guidelines, which were described by the designer William F. Lamb: "A fixed budget, no space more than 28 feet [8.5 meters] from window to corridor, as many stories of such space as possible, an exterior of limestone, and completion of construction date of May 1, 1931, which meant a year and six months from the beginning of the sketches." Without detracting anything from the professional skills of the architects who made the Empire State Building the most eloquent symbol of Manhattan in the 1930s, a new figure emerges from these lines, that of the general contractor, audacious and authentic protagonist of that superhuman struggle against time that regulated the construction of the skyscraper. The notebook kept by Starrett Brothers & Eken records the history of the worksite and the ways in which the many problems were solved. The entire effort was designed to

meet the demands of speed and came to resemble a kind of assembly line, not unlike a system of direction based on Tayloristic principles. It was thus that 3,500 workmen created a total of 195,000 square meters of usable surface, served by 62 elevators, and did so in eleven months in accordance with a schedule that provided for the assembly of the more than 57,000 tons of steel that went to make the structural framework, all of it soldered and riveted according to a tight schedule that eliminated down time as far as possible, synchronizing the construction of the framework with the completion of the other elements of the building.

The rapid construction of the Empire State Building was thus a result of this highly centralized management, along with the specialized division of labor that was part of the growth of American industry. In fact, despite the loss of six workers, the building went up at the rate of one and a half floors per day during the periods of optimum worksite coordination.

Best Products supermarkets, Houston, Texas, and Sacramento, California, USA
1975 and 1977

*"Virtually all the work of SITE is built on the notion of opposites, on principles of the dialectic.
We strongly feel the relevance of this type of approach for a world without universal symbols"*
(James Wines)

With an approach that seems more in keeping with the provocations of a radical avant-garde than with an architectural discipline, SITE (Sculpture In The Environment), founded in 1969 by James Wines, Alison Sky, Michelle Stone, and Emilio Sousa, applied to the supermarkets of the Best Products chain a sort of esthetics of ruin, obtained by way of the paradox of the static collapse of various portions of the building, helped by the typically American predisposition for irony. Metaphors for the decline of consumer society and of the locales par excellence for the sale of its products, the Best Products supermarkets are—as James Wines announced—"De-architecture," a term he applied to his radical reworking of the "sociological and psychological elements of architecture."

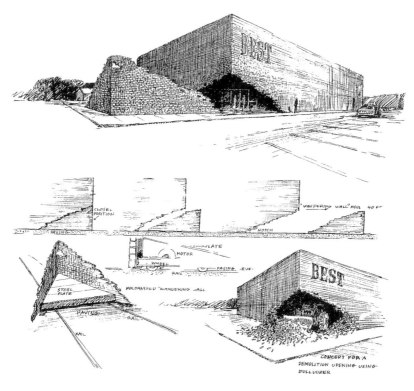

In the Houston store, the classical boxlike structure of a commercial space is surrounded by a broken wall that rises over the roof of the building but, at one strategic point, collapses, releasing an unlikely cascade of bricks over the doorway. In the Sacramento store, the idea of the ruin is given a theatrical twist, obtained by a mechanical contrivance that literally slides out a section of the corner of the building—with a weight of 45 tons—thereby creating a gaping hole in the structure that is the main entrance to the supermarket. The theme of the building in ruins is not new to the history of architecture, but what makes these structures memorably striking is the load of irony with which SITE destabilizes the myth of the consumer society and its place of worship, involving the patrons who drive by for a quart of milk in a sort of comedy.

**Bonjour Tristesse
residential complex,
Berlin, Germany**
1980–1984

*"In the life of today there
is a large dispersion tied
to the increase in information
and the augmentation of
exchanges . . . on the contrary
the architectonic project
and the construction must
overcome this situation and reach
a state of peaceful balance"*
(A.S.V.)

The IBA (Internationale
Bauausstellung; International
Building Exhibition) was
created in 1979 with the
expressed goal of refurbishing
two depressed areas of the city
of Berlin. Each of these efforts,
one in the area of Tegel, Prager
Platz, and Südliche
Friedrichstadt, and the other in
that of Kreuzberg, followed a
different theory of design,
although both had in common
the goal of creating new
buildings while also doing some

"cautious urban renewal." With
coordination from Josef Paul
Kleihues and Hardt-Waltherr
Hämer and financing from the
city of Berlin, the undertaking
was aimed at a "critical
reconstruction of the city,"
which was to be achieved by
reworking the city blocks of
Berlin as part of a vast repair
program of existing buildings,
all of it intended to restore
some of the city's urban
identity, which had been
obliterated by the devastations

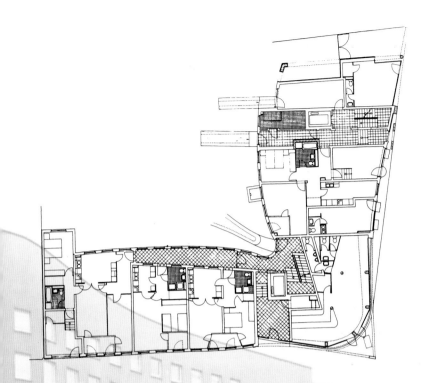

of the war.
Carried out by a group of internationally well known designers, the various undertakings began in 1987 and went ahead without interruption. Putting aside the unavoidable differences that reflect the differing personal languages of the various architects, the undertakings share the desire to achieve a dialogue between the traditional and the modern and thus can be included in that

stimulating critical category that Harold Rosemberg called "the tradition of the new." The Bonjour Tristesse residential complex—so-named following the words that some unknown person, but not without a certain poetic bent, painted on the top of the convex corner—stands at the intersection of Schlesischestrasse and Flackensteinstrasse, in the crowded heart of the Kreuzberg district. Seven

stories high, the building seems to melt into the complex urban and social fabric of the quarter in which it stands, balancing the Expressionistic note of its corner with the geometric rigor and with the right-sided rhythms of the openings that regularly mark off the façade, thus forming an urban organism inspired by the maxim of the Portuguese architect, according to whom "Architects do not invent anything; they transform reality."

Church of Santa Maria and Parish Center, Marco de Canavezes, Portugal
1990–1996

"I wanted to build a church that looked like a church, not a building with a cross inside it" (A.S.)

Álvaro Siza Vieira's contribution to developments in the recasting of the contemporary religious space has not been directed at the abolition of the building types and structural elements that, both traditionally and historically, have been associated with ecclesiastical buildings; rather, his activity has been designed to accord with a series of reflections on the reformation of the contemporary liturgical ritual. The officiating of the priest towards the faithful and the need for a communion space between the assembled faithful and the site of the liturgical celebration led Siza to lay out the Church of Santa Maria in Marco de Canavezes following a traditional single hall, 16 meters high and 30 meters wide, including, however, a convex apsidal wall that required the removal of the choir. The strictly symmetrical layout involves a pair of projecting bodies, 16.5 meters high, that serve as frames for the enormous area of the entryway (3 meters wide and 10 high). The mute walls of

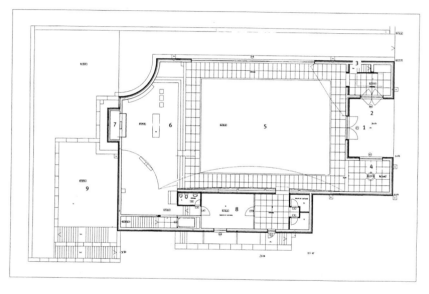

these bodies hide the bell tower and the baptismal font. The revolutionary convex shape of the wall behind the altar, externally expressed in the concave contractions at the corners of the building, is repeated in the convex shape of the northeast wall, which, bending in towards the central hall, offered Siza the opportunity to greatly increase the thickness of the wall in which to hide the openings that bring light into the central space. Along the opposite wall a long, narrow, continuous window, located at the right height, offers the faithful a view of the valley of Marco de Canavezes, renouncing the cesura, rooted in every religious typology, between the ascetic interior, site of the gathering, and surrounding nature. Two high, narrow openings in the wall behind the altar open onto a well of light that, in the form of a external courtyard, brings zenithal light into the mortuary chapel, on the underground level of which the entire structure rests. A base in gray granite welds the immaterial white walls of the church to the ground in this modest Lusitanian quarter. The building, along with the nearby auditorium and the Dominican school, give an urban identity to this fragment of Portuguese land where, as the nation's literary tradition states, "the earth ends and the sea begins."

House in Moledo, Portugal
1991–1998

"I thought that it would have been more natural, in Portugal, to design wooden shutters. For this reason, the roof had to be exposed, had to look like a new object, visible as though it had fallen from the sky" (E.S.)

Within the history of contemporary architecture, the idea of the Mediterranean is charged with values and references that go far beyond the geographical borders indicated by the term. By now many expressions can be considered synonymous with the term *Mediterranean* within the field of architecture. These many expressions include infancy of humanity, permanence of forms, wealth of tradition and memory, spirit of place, value of history, and crossroads of culture. Among these there are those adaptations of the environment that have resulted from the cultivation of land. The cultivation of land is an ancient gesture, deeply rooted in the Mediterranean culture, and it is commonly taken to include the construction of a shelter on an artificial terrace dug into the side of a hill to create an area for cultivation. Thus, the utilization of the natural conditions, made possible by difficult changes in topography, is perhaps the most ancient and fundamental act of

Eduardo Souto de Moura 1952

Mediterranean architecture. Portugal faces the Atlantic Ocean and not the Mediterranean Sea, but no geographer would disagree that the Moledo House by Eduardo Souto de Moura seems to derive its topographical collocation from this ancient and universal system. The unexpected impact on the environmental context, in which the house seems to almost naturally occupy a pre-existing slope of land, is in reality the result of a labor-intensive artifice. The exceptional element of the construction lies in the fact, as the architect explained, that "We had to rebuild the entire mountain, with new walls and platforms, which cost more than the house itself . . . The client, being an intelligent man, accepted this, and in the course of seven years the house began to be autonomous." At the specific request of the designer, the shutters facing the valley, facing onto the terraces, or protected by the space under the wall are made of cherry wood. To protect them, Souto de Moura made a projecting roof that became an autonomous element, separate from the organism of habitation, as though it had "fallen from the sky," the only constructed portion of a building that otherwise seems to have arisen from the soil around it by way of some age-old, natural process.

Goethenaum, Dornach, Switzerland
1913–1928

"The artistic, architectural, pictorial, and plastic styles that are used in the Goetheanum must differ from all the styles that until now have existed in the world" (R.S.)

Various extra-architectural components show up in many of the buildings attributed to the avant-garde "architectural Expressionism" movement, which came into being in Germany in the years leading up to the Great War. Because of the antirational architectonic qualities expressed in the various manifestations of its highly original and innovative message, the movement was destined to have important effects on the development of Modern architecture.
In fact, the main theories and background ideas of architectural Expressionism were derived from the literary and artistic avant-garde movements of the beginning of the century. These provided Expressionism's frame of reference, in particular its celebration of the emotional life and the spiritual dimension that put it in opposition to the widespread pragmatic and utilitarian values, which Expressionists blamed for the apparently unstoppable degradation of humanity.
The movement's more reformist and visionary wing embraced a view of the world based in part on the supremacy of artistic inspiration in the creation of a work of art, such that the work was thought to gush forth from the human spirit, more or less spontaneously, much like a plant from the soil. Another aspect was connected to the idealistic search for a grandiose architectonic model capable, again by way of an organic analogy, of connecting the material sphere and the human soul to the cosmos.

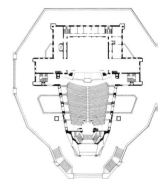

The designer and builder of the Goetheanum was not an architect, but rather a philosopher, the founder of the Free High School for Spiritual Science in Dornach, inspired by the principles of "anthroposophy," a mystical doctrine based on seven principles that accompany the human ego after a period of deep sleep and into a later incarnation, to the universal redemption of the pure spirit. As the headquarters of the confraternity the Goetheanum is a building that, basing itself on the "theory of metamorphosis" and on the related evolution of forms connected to their continuous evolution, is thought to establish a relationship with human thought and a spiritual image of the cosmos. To make it, Steiner applied to the construction the esthetic categories of the dynamic organic and of the living organic, obtained by way of an intricate continuity in the interrelationships that compose the building. Dedicated to Goethe and his thinking, the first Goetheanum (1913–1920) was constructed entirely in wood, drawn from seven different types of tree that, together with the seven capitals used atop each semicircle of which the outline of the building was composed, referred to the seven stages in evolution as outlined in the anthroposophical theorems elaborated by Steiner. Using a pentagonal layout, the curvilinear outline of the building was meant to reject any symmetry that might result from the use of a right angle, thus acquiring the semblance of a cave, covered by two large domes of painted wood. Completely destroyed by fire in 1922 the Goetheanum was rebuilt by Steiner between 1924 and 1928. Steiner entrusted the second version of the Goetheanum to the new technique of building with reinforced concrete, achieving fluidity in the walls and surfaces, inside which various "caves" host the rooms and spaces required by the esoteric ceremonies.

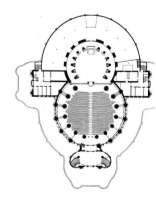

Rudolf Steiner 1861–1925

Lawson House, Quogue, Long Island, New York, USA
1979–1982

"In 1923 Le Corbusier proposed the challenge 'architecture or revolution.' For our times, I would like to propose a different challenge, in more conciliatory tones: tradition and modernity" (R.A.M.S.)

Postmodern architecture was born in America, and despite those who believe the United States possesses neither an authentic architectonic tradition nor a deeply rooted culture of living, it was America that advanced the first postulates against the Modernist doctrine. This was done through the revival, the shingle style. Widespread in the original American colonies between the seventeenth and eighteenth centuries, this type was based on the use of thin shingles with which those first colonists covered the roofs and walls of their homes along the Atlantic and the Pacific coasts. The style was the subject of a revival throughout the course of the nineteenth century—it was part of the Colonial revival associated with the popularity of Queen Anne domestic architecture—and for the generation of Postmodern architects, the shingle style came to represent the ideal raw material with which to re-establish the relationship between architecture and local traditions.

The points that follow, lucidly listed by Robert A. M. Stern, in the course of the 1970s, outline a new path for architecture that, in opposition to the rigors of functionalism, favors a "modern traditionalism": (1) applying decoration is not a crime; (2) buildings that draw inspiration from other buildings within the history of architecture are more meaningful than those that do not draw inspiration (this is called eclecticism); and (3) buildings that have relationships to those around them are more powerful than those that do not have such relationships (this could be called contextual integration). These points, together with

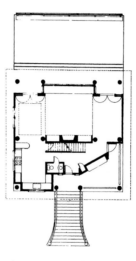

others, concur in the design of the Lawson House in Quogue, in which Stern, aside from making use of the most characteristic traits of the shingle style, draws inspiration from the classical beach cottages of the East Coast. The interior rooms follow a strictly symmetrical arrangement, while the top floor beneath the roof faces the Atlantic with a large dormer window, the sharply curving shape of which evokes certain classical forms.

Robert A.M. Stern 1939

History Faculty, Cambridge University, UK
1964–1968

"The specific way in which the symbolic-functional elements are put together can be the art of architecture"(J.S.)

Over the course of the 1950s, certain trends appeared within the world of Modern architecture that, following various linguistic variations based on the local or national traditions in which they took place, had in common a general rejection of the break with the past that was part of the doctrine of the Modern movement. These trends thus also rejected the consequent internationality of the Modern movement's linguistic code. The most obvious expressions of this discontent turned to Mediterranean architecture as a new source of inspiration— an outstanding example of this is the Ronchamp chapel by Le Corbusier—but thanks to the contribution of James Stirling, England began to draw on architectonic forms not only from its classical and neoclassical past but also from the patrimony of technical and engineering innovations that have long been rooted in the homeland of the Industrial Revolution. A new generation of English designers added to these elements the assimilation of ideas inherited from European Protorationalism and from Russian Constructivism, thanks to which modern English architecture has produced works with a new configuration, although it is one rooted in various national traditions.

Such is the case with the History Faculty of the University of Cambridge, in which the themes of the graduated greenhouse and the glass pavilion are joined in the creation of a highly modern library with space for 300 readers.

As stipulated by the competition, the design called for a large central space, that of the library, around which many smaller rooms were to be arranged, each grouping done in a different way. The result was a building with an inclined section where, in keeping with a constant aspect of Stirling's style, every part of the building is formally and autonomously defined according to its intended use. The rising line of the building's section follows the arrangement of the basement of the vast reading room, after which follow, tapering upward, the spaces for students, for seminarians, and for teachers, built in the L-shaped body that contains the distribution system for the building. This is composed of a series of halls that, arranged on various floors, run along the internal perimeter of the L-shaped body, looking through ribbon windows to both the outside of the building or the full-height open space of the reading room. The reading room is covered by a sort of graduated greenhouse that, supported at various heights by four metallic reticulate trusses, filters natural light into the center of the reading room.

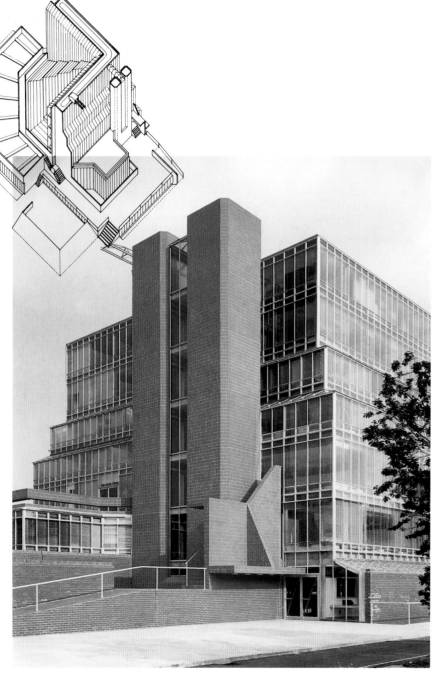

James Stirling 1926–1992

Neue Staatsgalerie and music school, Stuttgart, Germany
(with Michael Wilford & Associates)
1977–1996

"I believe that ninety-nine percent of modern architecture is boring, banal, and sterile, and in general disastrous and disharmonious if inserted in old cities" (J.S.)

Of all the various currents within contemporary

architecture, the Postmodern, because of its markedly historicist vocation, should be the one best suited for contending with the difficult dialogue between ancient and new that usually attends the insertion of a new building in a pre-existing urban fabric. The design by James Stirling and Michael Wilford & Associates for the Neue Staatsgalerie (New State Gallery) of Stuttgart, inaugurated in 1984, together with the design for

the music school, completed in 1996, forms a new cultural complex that, because of the heterogeneity of its architectural language, fits together well with the pre-existing Staatsgalerie of 1873 and with the overall complexity of the city of Stuttgart. Symbolic allusions to the history of the city—and more in general to the history of architecture—were applied to the architectural typologies used in the cultural complex,

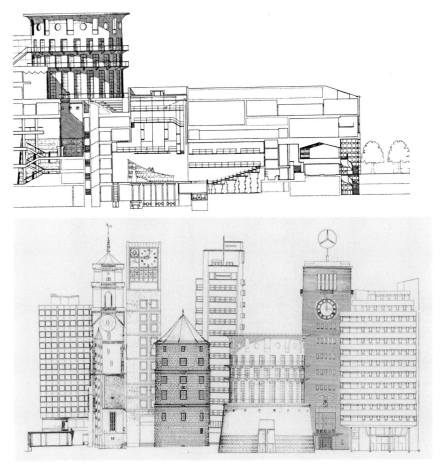

employing a technique that recalls that of collage. These allusions were skillfully fitted into a strategic urbanistic structure that used pedestrian paths as effective tools for integrating this new urban fragment within the city around it. The U-shaped layout and circular courtyard of the Neue Staatsgalerie recall the Altes Museum by Karl Friedrich Schinkel, while the shape of the tower of the music school, located at the center of a plaza, seems to be based on an entire catalog of tower shapes from all the towers spread throughout the city of Stuttgart, thus demonstrating the value of a design system based on the assembly of historical, time-tested forms put to good advantage within an impeccable urban structure that lets the new architectonic compositions blend with the stratifications of the pre-existing city.

Carson Pirie Scott & Co., Chicago, USA
1899–1904

"How to proclaim from the vertiginous heights of these strange, bizarre, modern roofs the peaceful gospel of feeling, of beauty, the cult of a more elevated life?" (L.H.S.)

The tall office building, archetype of the modern skyscraper, came into being in Chicago during the period between the last two decades of the nineteenth century and

the first decade of the twentieth. The city was then being almost entirely rebuilt following the devastating fire of 1871, and the Loop, its business center, was laid out following a regular grid of blocks, on the perimeter of which the enormous leap in real-estate prices, along with the adoption of new construction methods, led local businessmen to get the greatest number of offices in their buildings by increasing

the height, leading to a new building typology. Apparently the direct result of technical and engineering breakthroughs in the construction of elevators, which were first steam-powered, then hydraulic, and finally electric, and to parallel advances made in the iron and steel industry, including the creation of the double T beams used in the increasingly daring skeleton frameworks, the typology of the tall office building went through a period of elaborate

architectural experimentation. These many formal variations on the typology eventually led to the formation of an authentic school of architecture, the so-called Chicago School. The school carried out its research along the basis of two fundamental esthetic principles. The first, worked out by William Le Baron Jenney (whose Home Insurance Building some consider the first skyscraper), was based on an overtly

technical method that used the skeleton framework in metal to determine the formal appearance of the building; the second, a result of the works of Henry Hobson Richardson, employed that architect's eclectic version of the Romanesque in determining the stylistic definition of a building. A perfect synthesis of the new structural methods, genuinely modern and truly American, with enduring decorative and ornamental forms, the Carson Pirie Scott & Co. Store (originally built as the Schlesinger and Mayer Department Store) stands as the Chicago School's unquestioned masterpiece, as well as its most influential creation.

With its interior laid out according to the conventional typology of the large store, the building's façade reveals a framework that is rigidly structured in horizontal and vertical lines, an undisguised reflection of the metal skeleton behind it. The openings in the grid are filled with the large picture windows known as Chicago windows, their horizontal extension divided in a large fixed central sheet of glass between two narrower vertical windows with movable sashes for ventilation. The severe, modern rhythm of the geometric grid, dressed in white terracotta, contrasts with the ornamental strip of plant motifs on the first two floors, while the composite elements of the upper floors lead without variation to the special rounded corner of the building, designed in the image of a slender column.

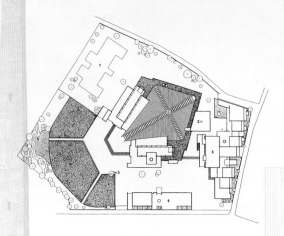

St Mary's Cathedral, Tokyo, Japan
1961–1964

"The strong symbolic impulse testifies to how architecture must have something that makes appeal to the human heart.
Even so, the basic forms, the spaces, the expression of the buildings must follow logic. A purely arbitrary architecture could not last long"
(K.T.)

During the 1950s, Kenzo Tange made a series of architectonic macrostructures using the most typical materials and products of Western technology and following a markedly structuralist style of Modernist derivation. He did pause occasionally for reflection in which the more experimental values of the Modern structural methods were combined with poetic gestures by which the architect imbued

his works with a strong symbolic force. St Mary's Cathedral, which Tange made in the Bunkyo-ku district of Tokyo to replace a Catholic cathedral destroyed during World War II, is the outstanding example of this symbolic aspect in his works. It celebrates the iconography of the Christian cross by directly evoking its shape.
The church, which is large enough to hold 1,500 people, stands on a cruciform base, the

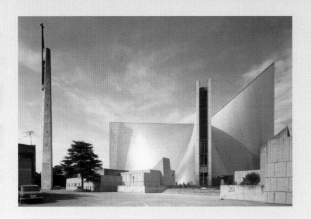

symbolic sense of which is
emphasized by the simple sail-
like structural elements that
rise over it to varying heights.
These elements, sheathed in
strips of corrugated aluminum,
are made with diagonal support
walls in reinforced concrete
that sweep upwards; where
they cross at their summit they
form a Latin cross, which,
together with vertical openings
in each arm of the cross, floods
the interior of the church with
natural light.

Newspaper and radio–television agency, Yamanashi, Kofu, Japan
1961–1966

"In an information society, technological considerations are of great importance to architecture and to the city. The development of so-called intelligent buildings is nothing other than a logical consequence, and contemporary society will want entire city quarters to be intelligent, in the same ways as individual buildings" (K.T.)

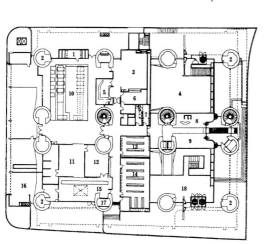

The introduction of modern architecture to Japan is usually attributed to the so-called first generation of modern Japanese architects, who, represented by the figures of Kenzo Tange, Kunio Mayekawa, and Junzo Sakakura, in the beginning of the 1950s, imported to Japan the mature style of the great masters of the Modern movement in Europe. The critical rereading of the architectonic works and urbanistic theories of Le Corbusier was of particular importance to this process, and when filtered through the practical and theoretical contributions of Tange, the manifestly plastic language of the French master blended into the spatial and symbolic influences inherent in the architectural tradition of Japan.

Over the course of the 1920s, Le Corbusier had proposed an urban utopia by way of universal urbanistic models that were meant to be indifferently applicable to every city on the planet. The feasibility of these plans would have been finally put to the test in 1960 with Tange's proposal for the expansion of the city of Tokyo. Directed at the specific problems created by that city's uncontrolled radial growth, Tange's plan proposed a model of limitless development achieved by way of a linear structure (called a "civic axis") that, leaping over Tokyo Bay, would have ended the traffic congestion by expanding the city beyond its center in a series of minor nuclei, organically unified to the city by means of infrastructures and megastructures. Although the plan remained on paper, it influenced Tange's later works. Always attentive to the relationship between architecture and urbanistics, Tange designed a series of megastructures in which the multiplication of functions and dimensions predisposes the building to limitless growth, in that way presenting the building as a fragment or portion of a virtual city.

The polyfunctional Yamanashhi center is headquarters to three integrated companies: a journalistic agency, a radio broadcast center, and a print agency. The building's structural system is designed to simplify future enlargements. The technical services and elevators are located inside the sixteen external towers, each five meters in diameter; thus, the size of the complex can be increased simply by multiplying the number of floors set up among the towers.

Glashaus, Deutscher Werkbund Exhibition, Cologne, Germany
1914

"A building is the direct carrier of spiritual values, shaper of the sensibilities of the general public, which slumbers today but will awaken tomorrow" (B.T.)

The recurring debate about which is superior, a pragmatic and modern industrial civilization or a life dedicated to the celebration of "contemplation," a debate with deep historical roots in German culture, was pushed to extremes in the political crisis in Germany just after World War I, with the rise of a mystical and visionary attitude that, rejecting the "mechanization of the world," looked forward to a social-democratic utopia founded on collective and democratic values. Founded by Bruno Taut in the immediate postwar period (1919), the Gläserne Kette ("glass chain"), together with the Expressionist avant-garde, chose as their symbols, and as the utopian headquarters for the social democratic rebirth, certain improbable "cathedrals of glass" and Alpine architecture in which the crystal and its transparency replaced architectonic ornament, creating infinite prospects and plays of light and color. Taut repudiated Western culture

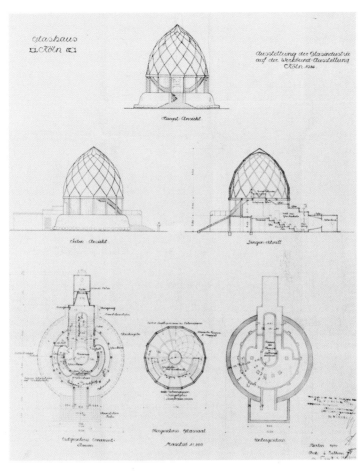

and its industrial progress in favor of Oriental traditions, hailed as bearers of a new light ("ex Oriente lux") capable of imbuing the arts and architecture with a new vital spirit. Otherwise confined to a pictorial and experimental dimension, the dreamy visions of the Gläserne Kette had already taken solid form in the Glass Pavilion that Taut had built before the war for the first exhibition of the Deutscher Werkbund in Cologne in 1914.

Raised on a circular cement base, its upper walls rounded off, the pavilion had a polygonal layout marked off by walls made of thick glass slabs, past which appeared an internal metallic stairway. The geometric structure of the dome with its exotic profile was composed of a lozenge-grid covered by panes of crystal that let natural light into the pavilion, inside which was a circular pool.

Casa del Fascio,
Como, Italy
1932–1936

"The concept that has kept me busy has been how to reconcile the two aspects of a new order: art and politics"(G. T.)

The difficult path taken by Italian rational architecture—a path that set it apart from similar national trends within the European Modern movement—resulted from the special relationship it established with tradition. The innovative abstract themes that were shared by the architects active in the new international rationalism can be said to lead back, in a general way, to the new symbolic values attributed to the use of glass and reinforced concrete. In Italy, however, these same themes became burdened with classical and archaic reminiscences that were extraneous to the international version of the functionalist avant-garde. The difficult political and cultural climate of the 1920s and 1930s, oscillating between evocations of Classicism and celebrations of Modernism, in particular the Modernism of industrial advances and new popular housing, provides the background to the construction of the Casa del Fascio by Giuseppe Terragni, a building that is an absolute masterpiece of Italian rational architecture.
Made to serve as the local headquarters of the Fascist party, the Casa del Fascio is the successful synthesis of two apparently irreconcilable architectonic matrices: the traditional urban typology of

the Renaissance palazzo and the construction method based on a supporting skeleton in reinforced concrete, in this case at least partially revealed. The prismatic volume of the building is dressed in white marble and bears no ornament. Each of its four façades is treated in a different manner, the various surfaces differing by the arrangement of the openings made in them; these differences disappear, however, in the areas where the pillar-pilaster structural scheme is plainly exhibited. The compact building, with its more or less square layout, is arranged around a double-height courtyard covered by a roof of concrete-framed glass blocks. By means of a system of galleries facing this central open space, the interior rooms of the building are made to revolve around this courtyard, which was meant to be the heart of the building and was the site of Fascist assemblies. The way the building is arranged around this hall, not exactly square and slightly off-axis with respect to the center of the building, has led some critics to say the compositional matrix of the building leads back to the typology of the Italian Renaissance palazzo. The idea that Terragni was reworking an historical typology in the design of the Casa del Fascio has led to a variety of readings. Among the many possible readings is that proposed by Diane Ghirardo, who sees the building as an audacious rereading of the typology of the late medieval communal palace. According to this reading, the monolithic wall at the corner turned towards the plaza is a stand-in

for the tower of a town hall, schematized and contracted, and the open spaces resulting from the indentation of the portico become the loggia of the medieval building. Concrete-framed glass blocks, marble, glass, and aluminum dress a modern building generated by the superimposition of an historically consolidated typology, the rereading of which Terragni purified so thoroughly that many critics, turning away in disdain, fail to recognize the original model.

Giuseppe Terragni 1904–1943

Jaques Dalcroze Institute for Rhythmic Gymnastics, Hellerau, Germany
1910–1913

"Good artisan work always fears originality, but not what is usual or what is only a repetition, which always brings with it its explanation" (H.T.)

The great building that rose at Hellerau, near Dresden, to host the Jaques Dalcroze Institute for Rhythmic Gymnastics occupies a highly delicate place in the history of the Modern movement. Although included within the current of Modern architecture known as protorationalism, this work by Heinrich Tessenow escapes every simple stylistic classification. The community building, made to "restore the spirit and art" while at the same time providing housing and a symbol for the new community, was designed by Tessenow to be not only the physical center of the new garden city of Hellerau, but also its symbol. The first solid creation on German soil of the utopian model of the English garden city, the design for Hellerau resulted from a synthesis of reformist and cooperative theories related to the generic Reform of Life movement that rose in Germany between 1900 and 1918. The birth of the first German garden city thus found a natural reference in the theory of disurbanization, supported by the building typology of the single-family home with small garden and associated with an aversion to large metropolitan areas

(*Großstadt*), which the movement saw as the cause of accelerated industrialization and as the "origin of all evils." The garden city proposed replacing the unhealthy and unhygienic situation of urban housing with life in the open air and in harmony with the laws of nature and even a return to the art of daily life. The building appears to be an arrangement of elementary geometric figures: square, rectangle, triangle, circle. The central body houses a large rectangular dance hall, made as a single parallelepiped and unencumbered by any fixed furnishings. On its exterior, this central body is topped by two steeply inclined pediments above a stately portico composed of large square pillars. The central body is flanked two lower structures that house the bathing halls and the two open courtyards (divided by sex) for outdoor gymnastic exercises. Tessenow's simple design, a response to the desire to "raise a celebrative building in the center of the garden city," uses essential and immediately recognizable forms to evoke the category of classicism. In fact, in its modern simplicity the Jaques Dalcroze Institute reveals the permanence of certain traditional and local building methods, such as long, narrow windows and pitched roofs—elements that were soon to be eliminated by the stylistic procedures imposed by the modern "international style." Tessenow took simple, traditional building elements and enlarged them, but did so in a way that enabled them to survive the leap in scale from their familiar, domestic size to

the giant, celebratory size required by the project for the dance institute. The use of various elements from the classical lexicon, such as tympanums, columns, and friezes—in some cases simply cited, in other cases more audaciously distorted—puts this work in a direct relation with the architectural patrimony of the past, demonstrating, in the end, how difficult it is to separate "the history of the new" from "the history of the past."

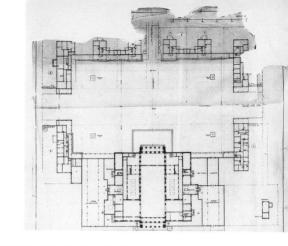

Heinrich Tessenow 1876–1950

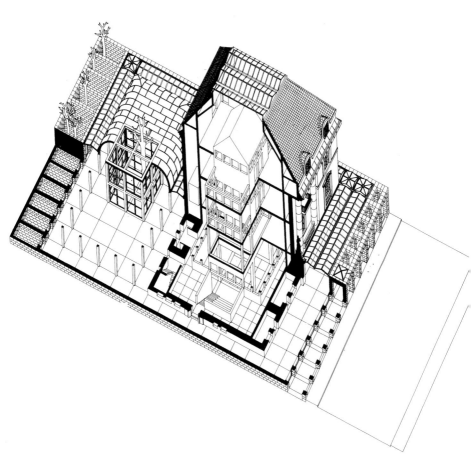

German Museum of Architecture, Frankfurt, Germany
1979–1984

*"Any building that does not have
itself as its principal theme is,
basically, a banality. Without
doubt it may serve purposes
and necessary needs and even
satisfy basic technical demands,
but if beyond mere functionality it
does not also create an idea, it
will remain a banal object"*
(O.M.U.)

Architecture was liberated
from the ingenuous rules of
functionalism by Oswald
Mathias Ungers, and he did so
by recourse to the rigorous
geometrics of the rationalist
language filtered by clear
references and allusions to the
history of architecture and its
past.
"The revival of the
architectonic archetypes" thus
came to be loaded with new
symbolic and semantic values
by being filtered through

metaphor and analogy, capable
of freeing the architectonic
phenomena from the primacy
of form over function. This is
what happened in the
construction of the German
Museum of Architecture in
Frankfurt, where a pre-
existing eighteenth-century
villa, integrated in the
construction of the museum,
was transformed into a
simulacrum in which certain
archetypical forms, repeated
and emptied of their original

function, set off a system of references that has for its principal theme the city and its architecture. Part of a large plan of urban renewal directed at valorizing the building fabric of an entire city district on the Main River, the project for the museum involved preserving the pre-existing eighteenth-century villa located at the intersection of the Schweizerstrasse and the Schaumainkai. The villa was surrounded by a wall into which niches, pillars, and trabeations were dug. Ungers demolished every bit of the interior of the eighteenth-century building, reducing it to a shell capable of hosting the necessary museum spaces. The large empty space thus created inside the pre-existing walls is occupied by a framework structure that, serving the various floors of the museum, evokes the structural and elementary archetype of the cabin, thus setting off a play of references that has for its object the representation and exhibition of architecture itself. The area outside the building that previously served as a courtyard has been integrated with the museum and is contained within its walls. In fact, much of this area is now part of the covered space of the museum since it has been roofed over by a system of skylights and by a vaulted roof.

Ungers House, Utscheid, Eifel, Germany
1986–1988

"Architecture is influenced by two fundamental references: the first is the reference to place—not only the actual place, but the cultural and historical—the second is the typological form that each building expresses"(O.M.U.)

This home was applied to the delicate slope of a valley deep in the southern hills of the Eifel region. The recourse to a classical form, the famous and stylized archetype of the building with a square layout (in this case 18.25 × 18.25 meters) and a sloping roof, loads this residential structure with an archaic value so that although it does not imitate the surrounding nature it absorbs its uncontaminated integrity. As its architect, Oswald Mathias Ungers, specified, it creates a relationship with nature of "dialectical opposition marked by reciprocal valorization." The site on which the house stands was previously occupied by the ruins of an eighteenth-century glassworks and its furnace, later converted into a farm; nearby is a stream fed by a natural spring. Along with the construction of the house Ungers undertook the rebuilding of a deconsecrated chapel and the creation of an atelier, crowded with relief models and feasibility studies

of his works. With its obsessive reduction of the composition to the theme of the square—a recurrent component in Ungers's rationalist language—the house evokes the category of geometric abstraction, but at the same time it entrusts the solidity and the gravity of its constructive system to the square blocks of white stone. With its window shutters hidden in the thickness of the walls and its eaves trimmed off to leave practically no projection, this modern building offers no perceptible indications of daily life. Far from every concept of style or fashion, the building seems to escape every temporal placement, since what counts for Ungers is "the continuity of ideas. Style means nothing. It is replaceable, tied to its time and thus ephemeral. The idea is everything."

Oswald Mathias Ungers 1926

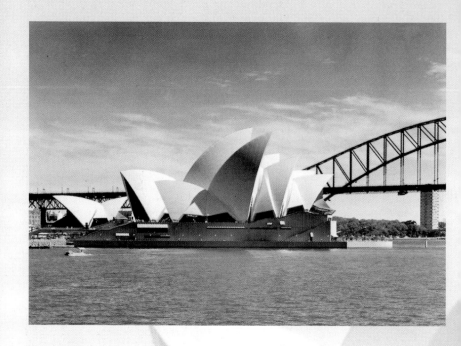

Opera House, Sydney, Australia
1957–1973

*"Sydney is a dark harbor ... There
is no white to take away the sun
and make it dazzle the eyes—not
like in the Mediterranean
countries or South America and
other sunlit countries. So I had
white in mind when I designed the
opera house" (J.U.)*

Only very rarely has the
identity of a city—and

perhaps even of an entire
continent—been so directly
related to a work of modern
architecture as has been the
case with Sydney, Australia,
and its Opera House. This
process of identification
should not be attributed to
only the spectacular shells of
its roofs, although they do
give the building an
unmistakable profile and are
readily compared to a bunch
of white sails opening across
the immense bay of Sydney.

But there is also the matter of
the ironclad will with which
Jørn Utzon succeeded in
adapting such a complex and
articulated structure in order
to make it transform the site
on which it was to stand,
integrating it, in a unitary
whole, with the metallic
structure of the nearby Sydney
Harbour Bridge. Unrelated to
every traditional theater
typology, the Opera House
can be divided into three
component parts that are

Jørn Utzon 1918

formally autonomous and complete: the base, the covering, and the auditorium. In a sense the Opera House is an audacious gesture of modern structuralism that gives concrete form to the visionary dreams and the impossible architectures elaborated during the opening years of the twentieth century by the organic and Expressionist avant-gardes. The complex undertaking of the creation of the roof shells,

in which the figure of Utzon was joined by the famous engineer Ove Arup and Peter Rice, did not meet with success until the architect succeeded in creating the curving surfaces of the various shells from a single geometric figure, a virtual sphere with a diameter of about 75 meters. Thus began a complicated test of the worksite, with the lack of financial returns finally forcing the Danish architect to abandon the site in 1966, but

not before having given life to the structures' ingenious form.

The shells are in fact quarters of a single sphere set on the curved ribs of a prefabricated framework, while the covering of the roofs was made by attaching more than 1 million white Höganäs tiles from Sweden to panels made of prefabricated vibrated concrete that were then secured to the superstructure of the roof shells.

Gymnasium, Losone, Ticino Canton, Switzerland
1991–1997

"I have often thought that there is only one model in architecture; it has remained the same for five thousand years and has always been reinterpreted. It is an 'international' model because it is about man, and not about place"
(L. V.)

The first scientific definition of an "architectonic type" dates to the *Dictionnaire Historique de l'Architecture* (1832) by Quatremère de Quincy: "A model, understood according to the practical execution of an art, is an object that must be repeated as it is; a type, by contrast, is an object that everyone can use to create works that may not resemble one another at all." This revolutionary definition of architectonic type can be taken as the starting point for the line of thought that has led through many and various reworkings to reach today as a school of thinking that sees the architectonic type as a work tool with which to achieve a refoundation of the discipline of architecture. Such a refoundation would give the architectonic type an unvarying formal character leading back to the elementary structure, repeated over time, of its form.

The repetition of certain eternal and elementary forms drawn from an architectonic typology and taken as reference thus lends itself to a process of critical re-evaluation in which the original configuration of the type, transgressed, is never cancelled and instead remains latent, almost like a sign of the paternity of the project.

This line of thinking goes against much of the artistic and creative approaches behind contemporary architecture in that it accepts the category of repetition as an indispensable element in the eventual success of an architectural project and rejects originality as an esthetic parameter and even less as a methodological parameter. The gymnasium that Livio Vacchini built in Losone is a temple, a *témenos*, or, as he himself said, a dolmen. It is the result of a process of reduction that began with an elementary constructive system based on a wall with regular open spaces that supports a flat slab as its roof. This building takes the archaic typology and turns it into an absolutely contemporary and functional building.

It can be said that the operation succeeded in creating a severe and monumental space without resorting to the theme of a formal analogy; instead limited itself to putting into practice an elementary building system through the use of the most advanced technology based on the techniques of reinforced and prestressed concrete.

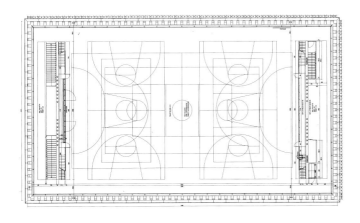

Livio Vacchini 1933

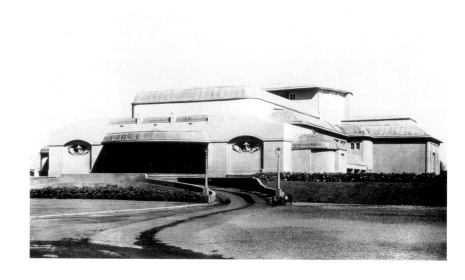

Deutscher Werkbund Theater, Cologne, Germany
1914

"The future of the 'new' is assured by the measure in which it draws on eternal methods from eternal sources. One creates, one finds the new only on the level of the eternal" (H.V.)

Henry Van de Velde's contribution to the development of Modern architecture begins with the heated debate within the stylistic current of Art Nouveau in which he opposed the ornamental use of naturalistic elements and applied instead abstract decoration involving clear, elastic lines. This leaning towards "moral" forms of ornament, capable at the same time of protecting the "creative freedom of the artist," would later be an aspect of Van de Velde's membership of the Deutscher Werkbund, the association of artists and industrialists founded in Munich in 1907. There was a conflict within the association between the ideals of permanence and the desire for change; the leading figure in the first camp was Van de Velde, that in the second was Hermann Muthesius.

The disagreement came to a head in July 1914 on the occasion of the first exhibition

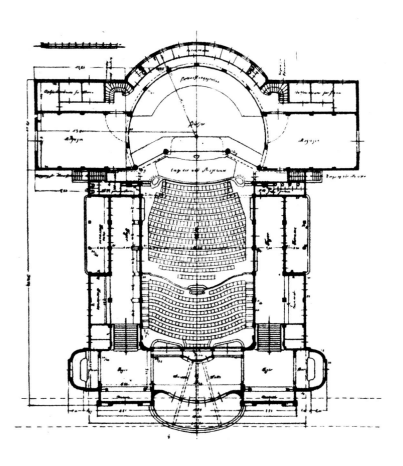

of the Werkbund, which was held in Cologne. Muthesius's proposal that the future products of the Werkbund be directed exclusively at industrial assembly-line production was contested by Henry Van de Velde, who spoke in the name of artistic freedom and rejected "every proposal for a canon or a typification." As seems clear, the premises of Modern architecture can be traced back to the heart of this debate, both in the rationalist variant of Modern architecture and in the protorationnalist version, in which the rejection of decoration and of the academic inheritance was often translated into a classical sense of forms with functional contents. This last current is related to the theater that Van de Velde designed for the first exhibition of the Werkbund, the volumes of which, although typically Art Nouveau in their sinuous curves, reproduce the classical symmetry of the internal spaces. Comparable to the outline of a church with a Latin-cross layout, the theater had an entryway that led by way of two symmetrical stairways to a pair of foyers located on opposite sides of the main central hall. The back of the semicircular stage was a wall in the shape of an apse, while the proscenium had a light tripartite screen.

Vanna Venturi House (Mother's House), Chestnut Hill, Pennsylvania, USA
1959–1964

"An architect's main job consists in organizing a single whole beginning with the conventional elements and judiciously adding new ones when the old ones seem improper" (R. V.)

Postmodern architecture's theoretical manifesto is Robert Venturi's *Complexity and Contradiction in Architecture* (1966). Greeted by the critic Vincent Scully as "the most important work on architecture since *Vers un Architecture* by Le Corbusier," the book expressed Venturi's assault on the orthodox language of Modernist architecture, carried out by way of a revival of the vernacular and traditional features rooted in the American landscape. For the first time, the rejection of the repertory of forms drawn from traditional, spontaneous architecture—a rejection openly espoused by functionalist doctrine—was officially cast aside in the name of a return to the ordinary and common architecture of the American landscape, the constructive and formal simplicity of which constituted, for Venturi, an invaluable repertory of images set in the collective memory on which to reflect and with which to work. Complexity and contradiction thus rise to become new paradigms within the discipline of architecture, and contrary to the dogmas of functional architecture they are capable of transmitting a plurality of symbolic and iconographic values from the patrimony of popular American architecture.

The vernacular architecture that Venturi revisited soon took on ambiguous features that subjected traditional typologies and elements to a process of formal distortion and reworking that was most often directed at the elaboration of architectural configurations more in keeping with contemporary reality. What Venturi theorized in his famous text he physically reproduced in his first series of single-family houses, the best known of which was the house he built for his mother in Chestnut Hill, Pennsylvania. The house is both simple and complex at the same time. It presents several of the features standard in an ordinary single-family home, such as the pitched roof and the fireplace rising from the center of the roofline, but at the same time it presents complex spatial and figurative correlations. The interruption in the peak of the roof and the fact that the windows are all of different sizes and shapes are a prelude to the complex arrangement of the internal spaces. Even the central position of the fireplace is contested by the staircase, which wraps around it while at the same time safeguarding the intimacy and traditional coziness of a domestic American setting.

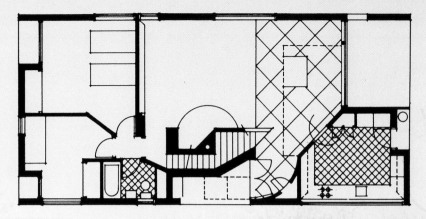

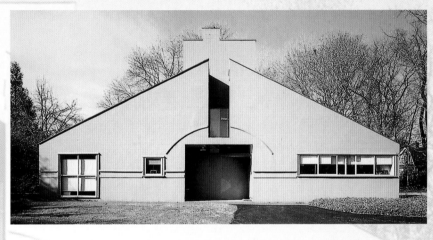

RCID Emergency Services, Disney World, Orlando, Florida, USA
(with Denise Scott-Brown & Associates)
1993

"In Las Vegas . . . we learned that mass culture and its symbols are essential components of architecture and that the commercial vernacular can be a source of inspiration just as rich as the industrial vernacular of the early Modernism"(R.V.)

With *Complexity and Contradiction in Architecture* (1966), Robert Venturi called for a revival of the vernacular and traditional features of the domestic American landscape. In *Learning from Las Vegas* (1972), he celebrated the popular and commercial architecture of the North American cities as a new source of inspiration for contemporary design.
The city of self-referencing signs, the product par excellence of the consumer society, is discovered to possess an infinity of stimuli and symbols capable of directing the architectonic practice towards a communicative process that has as its primary result the achievement of a popular dimension. What had been prophesized in the famous text was destined to inaugurate the Postmodern season, the architectonic manifestations of

which owed their popularity and symbolic impact to the revival of simple elements from the architecture of the past. With a difference circumscribable to variations in timetable, mechanisms of virtual animation similar to those that suddenly populate the Main Street of Las Vegas regulate every day the flow of thousands of Americans to Disney World, the city of movie fiction that is capable of making up for the lack of public spaces that typifies so many American cities. Thus, the architectonic stage-sets of the amusement-park city replicate the actual settings of a real place of meeting, and the vast phenomenon of popular culture is supported by efficient and also quite necessary support infrastructures. Among these is the office of the RCID emergency services, designed by Venturi, Scott-Brown & Associates for Disney World of Orlando to house the headquarters of the fire-prevention services. Behind what would seem to be a stage setting dressed in panels of glazed enamel and red bricks, the building hides a real fire station, although the appearance of its trucks in the streets of the amusement park would be unexpected and would have unforeseeable results.

Post Office Savings Bank, Vienna, Austria
1903–1912

"The bases themselves of the architectonic conceptions that are dominant today must be rearranged, in the sense that the only foundation of artistic creation must be modern life" (O.W.)

Fin-de-siècle Vienna was the setting for encounters among a wide variety of often contradictory early expressions of Modern architecture. The result of this foment was an artistic movement of unusual creativity known as the Vienna Secession. At the outset, its daring experimental reforms were directed at every level of Viennese society, but the movement was destined to expend its energies meeting the requests of a well-to-do cultural elite. Before joining the artistic movement, in 1899, Otto Wagner dominated the Viennese building scene, proposing new style ideas, in particular Nutzstil ("utilitarian style"). Taking its theories from the pages of *Moderne Architektur*, first published in Vienna in 1895, Wagner's Nutzstil replaced the canon proposed by Vitruvius of the triad—*firmitas, utilitas*, and *venustas*—with the revolutionary principles of style, composition, and construction by means of which the new modern style was to be liberated from academic stylistic elements and from the stereotypes of romanticism.

A perfect synthesis of art and technique, the Post Office Savings Bank stands in the southern strip of the historic center of Vienna, at the intersection of diagonal street axes. It occupies a large trapezoidal lot. Its layout, following the shape of the lot, grows from the inside out, exhibiting a close relationship between the layout and the façade.

The layout achieves maximum functionality by being based on an integration of distinct, readily recognizable parts: the large square of the banking hall, center of gravity of the entire structure, covered and illuminated by a light arched roof; the two wings for the offices, separated from the central hall by large courtyards; and the rear portion, added in 1912 to make room for new offices. Wagner's technical experimentation extended to the façade of the building, which is covered by a system of "prefabricated" plates attached to the perimeter wall by means of decorative rivets left visible. This innovative style of the dressing of the façade contrasted with the cornice of the building, composed of a decorative apparatus of two figures of angels, reminiscent of certain Art Nouveau decorations.

Robie House, Chicago, Illinois, USA
1908–1910

"More than any other country, America offers a new architectonic idea. Its ideal is democracy and its institutions are clearly conceived in the democratic spirit"(F.L.W.)

The drive for freedom from classical codes and from the lexical elements of Beaux-Arts eclecticism was carried forward by Frank Lloyd Wright during the initial phase of his astonishing creative revolution. He was destined to create the most successful masterpieces of organic architecture of the twentieth century, and he did so by way of the categorical rejection of the false ideals advocated by the culture of the Renaissance. These were guilty of drawing from the sources of history following the hasty method of pure imitation; Wright contrasted them with the value of the "Gothic spirit," source of the genuine correspondence between the means and the ends that would lead organic architecture to openly display the conditions of the social life that produced it in its forms.

An anticlassicist attitude thus came into being that sought to free America and its people from the domination of the styles of the past, which had been freely transported to the boundless American territory. These were to be replaced by way of the restoration of an architectonic style tied to an old local tradition, that of the prairie, in which the myth of the primitive origins of the entire nation could be identified. From these

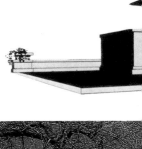

presuppositions flowed the series of "Prairie" houses that Wright designed for the flat landscape of the West and Midwest and of which the Robie House, despite its location in a Chicago suburb, can be considered the culminating triumph. In fact, although this single-family house is an elongated rectangle that follows the line of a large city street, it preserves the fundamental characteristics and the naturalistic references that characterize this typology. Its outline, in fact, arranged on three levels, presents an architectural space that begins at the central nucleus of the fireplace and expands outward in a series of rooms that, freed of the spatial configuration of the parallelepiped in box form, gives a new dynamic to the architectonic organism. The roofs display a marked horizontality on their different heights, with abrupt lateral projections that extend beyond the outer walls of the house, in this way verifying Wright's theory according to which "the horizontal line is the line of our house," referring here to the house of the American.

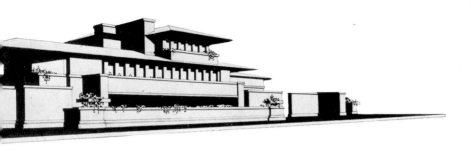

Frank Lloyd Wright 1867–1959

**Fallingwater,
Bear Run,
Pennsylvania, USA**
1934–1937

*"There was a big, tall rock
standing beside a waterfall, and it
seemed only natural to suspend the
house from that rock above the
falls."(F.L.W.)*

Frank Lloyd Wright's
contribution to the
development of organic
architecture, which in the most

generic explanation of its
doctrine calls for a building to
be in symbiosis with its
surrounding environment, can
be seen in all the writings and
the buildings that mark his
enormous artistic and poetic
production, where the very
concept of organic architecture
often ends up being identified
with that of Modern
architecture. In his search for
an architecture built at the
measure of man, in harmony
with the particularities of

place, and deeply rooted in the
collective values of the
American identity, Wright did
not look askance on the
advances made in technology
and modern industry. Rather,
he took them as expressions of
collective labor and as such
capable of assuring the
American population the
"dominion over a virgin land,
meaning comfort and
availability of means."
Fallingwater is the masterpiece
of organic architecture in the

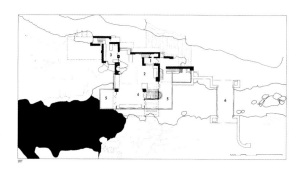

measure in which it projects the members of the Kaufmann family into the middle of the surrounding nature while at the same time holding them comfortably within its walls and the surfaces of its terraces. Following a dynamic process that moves, in keeping with Wright's habit, from the inside towards the outside, the layout of the building is broken down in a series of rooms that intersect around the central nucleus of the living-room

fireplace and that follow their ideal "embrace" of the surrounding nature by means of a system of projecting terraces, the horizontal outlines of which float in space, creating configurations that are different each time on each of the three floors of the house.

It was reinforced concrete that made it possible to "suspend the house from that rock above the falls." An iron armature was entrusted with

the overhanging terraces, extending in some cases to the problematic distance of 5.40 meters. It seems quite clear that this house over a waterfall is thus a highly successful synthesis of technique and nature, such that the outlines of the reinforced-concrete structure, thrillingly projecting away from the central body dressed in local stone, create an original and unequalled sense of artificial terraces suspended in the air.

Solomon R. Guggenheim Museum, New York, USA
1943–1959

"I did not come up with this design in order to subject the paintings to the building; on the contrary, it was to turn the building and the paintings into a marvelous uninterrupted symphony, such as has never before been created in world of art"(F.L.W.)

An artistic gesture destined to make the figure of Frank Lloyd Wright famous throughout the world, the Guggenheim Museum in New York stands as a compendium of the great master's organic poetics, opening new roads to developments in Modern and contemporary architecture. Inaugurated in October 1959, six months after Wright's death, the Guggenheim Museum stands on Fifth Avenue in Manhattan, where it openly displays its revolutionary, radical innovations. First of all, it breaks with the rigid grid of the city blocks; the unusual circular front of the museum, generated by the helicoidal ramp of its central hall, makes this immediately clear. This ramp itself is an innovation; the Guggenheim breaks with the long established typology of the museum by rethinking the most basic and classical of its compositional elements, the corridor, the true heart of every museum organism, the

form entrusted with creating the most direct relationship between the visitor and the exhibited objects. Once again the rejection of a historically determined model—in this case the gallery layout of the museum, typically composed of a discontinuous series of halls and exhibition spaces—is carried out by reworking the esthetic categories of the organic language, joined in the case of the Guggenheim, to concepts of plasticity and integral ornament. Wright himself threw light on these two esthetic categories, which apparently gave origin to the museum's novel shape: "This important word *plastic* means that the quality and the nature of the materials seem to 'flow' or 'spring' into shape, instead of forming a whole made of pieces cut and joined together." Thus was born the spiraling ramp that traces the new museum shape and lets it derive its forms from a process of organic growth in continuous becoming. Supported by eleven radial support walls in reinforced concrete, the ramp, which projects into the central space of the museum, takes the visitor along an exhibition route in which the illumination of the works is entrusted to the large central skylight and to those located along the outer shell of the building, integrated with incandescent sources of light.

Thermal baths at Vals, Grigioni, Switzerland
1991–1996

"An architecture of places without knowledge of the world is insignificant, as is an architecture of the world with no knowledge of places"(P.Z.)

In 1913 the Viennese architect Adolf Loos, in a short essay entitled "Rules for Him Who Builds in the Mountains," set down a series of principles to follow when building structures in high places. Among these is the following: "Be not afraid of being called unfashionable. Changes in the traditional way of building are only permitted if they are an improvement. Otherwise stay with what is traditional, for truth, even if it be hundreds of years old, has a stronger inner bond with us than the lie that walks by our side." This is preceded by a bit of advice that in its simplicity seems almost obvious: "A building on the plain requires a vertical articulation, the mountains demand a horizontal one." The thermal baths building at Vals, designed by the Swiss architect Peter Zumthor, stands at the foot of a pre-existing hotel complex to which it is connected by an underground passage. The shape of the construction, following a rigorously horizontal layout, is entrusted to a parallelepiped dressed with a "centuries old" local stone, green gneiss, extracted a little upstream from the thermal complex. The building is so thoroughly covered in this material, with thin strips and larger panels of the local stone applied to the surfaces of the façades and the internal walls, that the stone loses the sense of being a decorative material and seems instead to be the element from which the body of the complex was created, making it thus comparable to a large stratified monolith on the slope of the valley. At its interior, the archaic sense of the construction material is joined by the custom of the rite of the thermal bath, performed in the central basin inside the building and in the panoramic exterior pool. Halls and corridors lead past a series of technical spaces, services, showers, and dressing rooms, twisting and turning along the building to converge with sudden scenographic impact on the central pool, which one enters by way of four ramps set in four impressive parallelepipeds, inside which are further services necessary to the practice of thermal bathing.

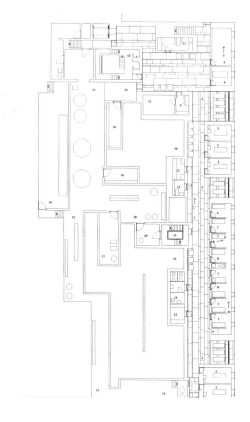

66

Following page:
Dominique Perrault
Bibliothèque Nationale
de France, Paris, 1988–1997

The architects

Alvar Aalto

(Kuortane, Finland, 1898–Helsinki, 1976)
Aalto earned his diploma in architecture from the Helsinki Polytechnic following studies from 1916 to 1921. After travels in Scandinavia, central Europe, and Italy, he made his professional debut in 1922 and opened his first studio, in Jyväskylä, one year later; in 1927 he moved to Turku. He gradually abandoned the neoclassicism of his first works to move closer to European functionalism, arriving at the formulation of a highly personal style that combined abstraction and naturalism. In 1935 he

established the ARTEK furniture design company. He held the position of Professor of Architecture at MIT in the late 1940s. On his return to Finland he set up office in Helsinki, and the postwar period proved to be the most original and expressive of his career. At the same time he also worked on many interesting urban projects outside his homeland.

Franco Albini

(Robbiate, Como, Italy, 1905–Milan 1977)
Albini graduated from the Milan Polytechnic in 1929 and opened his first studio in 1930 in Milan. Franca Helg joined

the firm in 1952, and their collaboration led to many interesting creations, including the La Rinascente Department Store in Rome. Antonio Piva joined the firm in 1962, and Albini's son Marco in 1965. Between 1963 and 1977 Albini taught at the Milan Polytechnic. From his earliest projects, Albini revealed a highly personal language, and although influenced by international rationalism, he applied this personal style to his entire artistic production over a period of more than forty years. His formal and geometric rigor, technical perfection, and attention to detail were visible in the fields of industrial design, restoration, interior design, and urbanistics, as well as in architecture.

Tadao Ando

(Osaka, Japan, 1941)
Before opening his first studio, in 1969, Ando made many trips to Europe, America, and Africa, and the impressions collected during these travels helped feed the ongoing synthesis of Orient and Occident that distinguishes his architectural production. From the introspective minimalism and geometric simplicity that were the outstanding traits of his earliest creations Ando passed to

increasingly more complex and articulated organisms, although fundamental aspects of his work remain his elegant and abstract use of simple materials and his desire to integrate and complete his architectonic forms with natural elements, such as water, light, and wind, as evidenced by the Japanese

pavilion for the World Exposition in Seville (1990–1992), with which Ando acquired international fame.

Erik Gunnar Asplund

(Stockholm, Sweden, 1885–1940)
After studies (1905–1909) at the Royal Institute of Technology in Stockholm, Asplund was among the group of young architects who founded (1910–1911) an independent school of architecture in opposition to the conservative teaching at the Academy of Arts. In private practice from 1911 until his death, he was also a professor at

the Royal Institute between 1931 and 1940, along with activities as a theorist and writer. His initial neoclassical period was followed, beginning in 1930, by adhesion to the Modern movement as filtered through the spiritualistic-romantic mood of the Scandinavian tradition. Asplund contrasted the usual heaviness of the Modernist language with light building elements, and in his last works, those made at the end of the 1930s, he achieved effects of grace and transparency that had an important influence on the international debate in architecture.

Carlo Aymonino

(Rome, Italy, 1926) Aymonino earned his degree from the University of Rome in 1950 and displayed close adhesion to neorealism during the first years of his career. From 1959 to 1964 he was a member of the editorial board of *Casabella-continuità*. The

works of that period reveal the influence of European Expressionism. In 1968 he became a professor at the Istituto Universitario di Architettura in Venice. His works and designs of the 1970s, often made in collaboration with other architects, show a

new language generated by a strictly limited variety of formal, typological, and chromatic elements. He was city-planning advisor for the historic center of Rome between 1980 and 1985. This experience marked the beginning of a stimulating and productive phase in which concern for the urban dimension of architecture, already an important aspect of his work, found realization in the practical field as well as in the theoretical.

Luis Barragán

(Guadalajara, Mexico, 1902–Mexico City, 1988) Barragán earned a degree in engineering in 1923 and began a career as a self-taught architect. The formulation of his personal style was deeply influenced by two trips to Europe, in 1924 and 1931; of the first remained the strong impressions made by the Arabian architecture and Mediterranean gardens of Spain and the ideas of the landscape architect Ferdinand Bac, whom he met in France. The second trip was important for the encounter with Le Corbusier and contacts made with new European movements. Several private homes he made after his return to Guadalajara in 1926

already revealed the highly original and sensitive blend of these European experiences with the forms and materials of Mexican architecture, a blend that would come to distinguish his style. His language gained increased precision through the combined use of plant and water forms along with simple volumes, a style that characterized the works he began making in Mexico City in 1936.

BBPR

(Gian Luigi Banfi, Milan, Italy, 1910–Mauthausen, 1945; Lodovico Barbiano di Belgioioso, Milan, Italy, 1909; Enrico Peressutti, Pinzano di

Tagliamento, Italy, 1908–Milan, Italy, 1976; Ernesto Nathan Rogers, Trieste, Italy, 1909–Gardone, Italy, 1969) In 1932, having just earned their degrees from the Milan Polytechnic, the four architects set up a studio in Milan. The studio was soon part of the lively debate of Modern architecture, as revealed by its architectural creations, its participation in the 1935 CIAM (Congrés Internationaux d'Architecture Moderne), and the theoretical activity of some of its members. Its stance attracted many international contacts, and its activity was varied, ranging from architecture to urbanistics to industrial design. The studio's postwar creations showed a progressive movement away from the rationalistic towards expressive values more attentive to environmental problems and traditional values, as well as concern for the insertion of architecture within a pre-existing historical context. The Torre Velasca in Milan, a typical example of this period, is considered by many to be the studio's outstanding creation. The works of the 1960s displayed less weight and formal effort.

Peter Behrens

(Hamburg, Germany, 1868–Berlin, 1940)
An outstanding personality among the pioneers of Modern architecture, Behrens' vast production, over a career of nearly forty years, reflected the many cultural and political changes of that period. He began his career as a painter and was a cofounder in 1893 of the Munich Secession. In 1898 he turned to industrial design and architecture. A fundamental period of his career covered the years 1907 to 1914, when he was design consultant for AEG of Berlin. Aware of the social impact of industry and its influence on all aspects of daily

life, Behrens made graphic studies, industrial objects, and large architectural projects for the company. After 1918 he abandoned the classical language on which his ideas of industrial culture had been based and moved towards Expressionism. His last works showed the definitive movement to rationalism.

Hendrik Petrus Berlage

(Amsterdam, Netherlands, 1856–The Hague, 1934)
After earning his degree at the Zurich Polytechnic, he traveled to Italy, Austria, and Germany. Returning to Amsterdam in 1881 he began work under the engineer Theodorus Sanders. His professional activity along with his theoretical works earned him a place among the founders of modern Dutch architecture. His activity can be divided into three periods. From 1881 to 1902 he made a series of buildings, including the Amsterdam Exchange, in which he demonstrated the

desire to return to authentic forms in opposition to the reigning eclecticism. In the following years he worked in urbanistics, presenting a series of plans marked by forceful unitary designs in opposition to the tendency towards decentralization; the creation of

these projects led to the formation of the Amsterdam School. In the last period of his activity he gave form to several works in a language similar to that of Frank Lloyd Wright, whom he had met during a trip to the United States in 1911; these works contributed to the spread of Wright's language and style in Europe.

Ricardo Bofill

(Barcelona, Spain, 1939)
After studies at the Escuela Técnica Superior de Arquitectura in Barcelona and at the University of Geneva, in 1960 he founded the interdisciplinary group Taller de Arquitectura, composed of

artists, economists, and architects. The team's many works revealed an initial adhesion to neorealist and neo-Brutalist language. Since the middle of the 1970s Bofill has worked primarily in France, opting for a decisive return to the classical language within the sphere of Postmodernism. The numerous works he made during the 1980s were highly regarded, most of all for their sense of monumental architecture that was strongly technological while at the same time respectful of local traditions. During recent years his works have revealed a certain distancing from purely historicist references and have assumed an increasingly international dimension, with works in America, China, and Japan.

Paul Bonatz
(Solgne, Metz, Germany, 1877–Stuttgart, 1956)
After studies at the University of Munich, he was a student and assistant to Theodor Fischer between 1902 and 1906, becoming professor at the Technische Hochschule of Stuttgart in 1908. In 1909 he opened a studio together with Friedrich Eugen Scholer. He moved from the reductionist historicism that characterized his first works to develop in later years a simplified architectural language oriented towards the Neue Sachlichkeit. From 1935 to 1941, during the period of the Nazi regime, he held the position of Reich consultant and returned to a monumental Expressionism, legible in his designs for the Autobahn and various large buildings in Berlin and Munich. Between 1943 and 1953 he lived in Turkey, acting as architecture consultant to the cultural minister of Ankara and working as a professor in Istanbul. In 1954 he returned to private practice in Stuttgart.

Mario Botta
(Mendrisio, Switzerland, 1943)
After several years of apprenticeship to a technical draftsman, Botta studied at the Istituto Universitario di Architettura in Venice between 1964 and 1969, graduating with Carlo Scarpa. During those same years he worked as an assistant to Le Corbusier and Louis I. Kahn. In 1969 he moved to Lugano and opened his own studio. The guidelines of his language have been recognizable from his very first creations: respect for the external landscape, orderly geometric shapes, and abundant recourse to craftwork. Various combinations of these elements

are clearly visible in the single-family dwellings he made during the 1970s and 1980s, and they are still part of his work, along with an increasing decomposition of the building into its component parts, as evidenced by the large-scale international commissions of the last years. Such formal experimentation is also characteristic of his activity as a designer. Since 1996 he has taught at the Academy of

Architecture in Mendrisio, which he founded.

Daniel Hudson Burnham
(Henderson, New York, USA, 1846–Heidelberg, Germany, 1912)
Burnham received his training in the discipline from the Chicago engineer William Le Baron Jenney and because of his contacts and talents was soon receiving important commissions.
In 1873 he went into partnership with John W. Root. Being a practical and excellent administrator, Burnham made the perfect partner to the versatile and imaginative Root. Both men performed important roles in the evolution of the Chicago School of Architecture, making several important works that were daring experiments in the use of new building technologies.
Worthy of note was the Flatiron Building in New York of 1901–1903, for a time the tallest skyscraper in the world. After Root's death, in 1891, Burnham dedicated himself to urban planning, adhering to the neoclassical style of the European Ecole des Beaux-Arts and becoming one of the leading exponents of the City Beautiful Movement with his 1907 plan for Chicago.

Santiago Calatrava

(Benimamet, Valencia, Spain, 1951)

Calatrava studied at the art school of Valencia from 1968 to 1969 and at the Escuela Técnica Superior de Arquitectura from 1969 to 1973. In 1981 he earned a degree in engineering from the Federal Institute of

Technology in Zurich. That same year he opened a studio in Zurich. This heterogeneous training, along with the strong influence exercised on him by the forms of nature, is clearly visible in the original oversized organic forms of his works in cement and steel, which blend art, architecture, and engineering. In recent years he has worked in Europe and America, constructing large-scale works, including airports and train stations, among them the station for the World Exhibition in Lisbon in 1998.

Arduino Cantafora

(Milan, Italy, 1945)

In 1971, Cantafora graduated from the Milan Polytechnic, where he was a student of Aldo Rossi's; between 1973 and 1976 he collaborated with Rossi on the preparation of competition projects. Over time he developed a firm interest in architectural representation,

destined to become the preferred field for his theoretical and pictorial method. In his paintings—exhibited at the Milan Triennale, the Venice Biennale, and in many personal and group shows—and in his writings he lucidly confronts the essential questions inherent in the poetic nature of living, the forms of which are portrayed in the disheartening unchangeableness of domestic interiors as well as in the rarefied monumentality of urban and collective settings. Cantafora has taught at Venice, Yale, and Lausanne, where he still introduces young architects to the techniques and the discipline of painting.

Eladio Dieste

(Artigas, Uruguay, 1917)

In 1943, Dieste graduated from the University of Montevideo with a degree in engineering and taught in the same university until 1973. After initial experience with the Ministry of Public Works, he opened his own studio in 1955. His work, for the most part carried out in close collaboration with other architects, engineers, and artisans, helped re-establish the idea that construction is an ideal field for blending architecture and engineering. In 1948 Dieste made his first works in reinforced ceramic, which together with brick became the primary material in his constructions. Combining ingenious structural and technological inventions with highly specialized manual labor,

Dieste created expressive works using limited materials and financial means. He has applied these highly evocative forms to industrial, religious, and commercial structures throughout South America.

Karl Ehn

(Vienna, Austria, 1884–1957)

Ehn attended the Akademie der Bildenen Künste in Vienna as a student of Otto Wagner. He worked for the city administration between 1908 and 1950, becoming one of the directors of the city residential sector. Ehn's stylistic evolution can be traced by way of the various building complexes he made during the 1920s and 1930s, inspired by English or Dutch models. From an initial language influenced by the Biedermeier style, as in the Hermeswiese installation of 1923, he moved to the

monumental expressionism of the Karl Marx-Hof of 1927 and then to the adoption of the strongly geometric formal elements of the Adelheid Popp-Hof of 1932. The end of the social democratic administration in 1934 marked the end of Ehn's professional career; after that date his production was limited to a few small-size homes.

Peter Eisenman
(Newark, New Jersey, USA, 1932)
Eisenman has studied and taught at several universities, including Cambridge, Princeton, and Cooper Union in New York, always accompanying his professional career with theoretical activity. During the 1960s he collaborated with Michael Graves on various homes and urban projects. During the 1970s Eisenman and Graves joined John Hejduk, Charles Gwathmey, and Richard Meier to form the New York Five. In 1966 Eisenman began

working on a series of single-family homes in which he drew inspiration from the rationalism of Giuseppe Terragni to apply a language that was completely unrelated to any contextual or functional reference. His design for Cannaregio, near Venice, in 1978, marked the turn towards the deconstructionism that characterized his increasingly articulate creations of the 1980s. The irregular, plastically deformed volumes of the architectonic and urbanistic projects of his most recent period indicate that his powerful visionary talent has not weakened.

Hassan Fathy
(Alexandria, Egypt, 1900–Cairo, 1989)
After completing his studies at

the Technical University of Cairo, Fathy began his professional career in that city in 1930. On the basis of his study of and respect for the monuments of ancient Egyptian civilization and vernacular Egyptian architecture, he sought to recuperate the building techniques and typological solutions of the Arabian architectural tradition. This effort led him to make,

between 1948 and 1953, his most famous work, the village of New Gourna at Luxor, the first of a series of installations made for rural populations that were recognized at the international level, more than the local, as models of an architecture capable of meeting the functional and financial requirements of such housing while also maintaining the formal and cultural appearance of the contexts in which they were located. Fathy spent the last period of his professional career designing villas and palaces for rich private patrons.

Sverre Fehn
(Kongsberg, Norway, 1924)
Fehn graduated from the Oslo School of Architecture in 1948 and set up his studio in that city; he taught at the Oslo School from 1971 to 1995. His first creations were distinguished by the constant effort to achieve a synthesis between a formal Modern language and local tradition. Fehn has always sought to establish intimate relationships between the nature of the site and his architecture, which is known for its smooth forms and refined details. With the Hedmark Museum in Hamar, during the 1970s, Fehn had to build alongside pre-existing architecture. He resolved the

problematic relationship between the old Bishop's Palace and the new cement-and-wood structure by making the points of contact between the two highly visible. An effort towards greater formal autonomy and the further articulation of details has been evident in the works of recent years.

Figini–Pollini

(Luigi Figini, Milan, Italy, 1903–1984; Gino Pollini, Rovereto, Italy, 1903–Milan, 1991)

The two architects, both students at the Milan Polytechnic and members of Gruppo 7, founded in 1926, began a collaboration in 1929 that was destined to last their entire lifetimes. Their first works, markedly rationalist, placed them among the more mature exponents of the Lombard School. From 1934 to 1957 they were involved in a profitable relationship with Adriano Olivetti. Apart from the factory at Ivrea, which stands as an unequaled model of

a modern industrial building, the works they built for Olivetti include designs for offices and homes. Their later works show a progressive movement from the purist forms of Italian Razionalismo to a greater expressiveness, accentuated by the structural solutions

adopted, the extrinsic quality of the materials used, and an increasingly refined balance between architecture and landscape.

Theodor Fischer

(Schweinfurt, Germany, 1862–Munich, 1938)

Fischer was involved in intense teaching and professional activity at Stuttgart and Munich, opening his studio in the latter city. In 1907, he became the first president of the Deutscher Werkbund. His work, characterized by the simplification of the eclectic language through the use of rigorous constructive solutions and the synthesis of elements of classicism and regionalism, was

fundamental to the passage from historicist tradition to the new rationalist esthetic in Germany. One of the first *Siedlungen* (large-scale, low-cost housing complexes) made with rationalist buildings was his Alte Heide complex in Munich, built after World War I. Fischer's vast production included many specialized buildings, such as offices, schools, and museums, along with urban plans that reveal his adhesion to the picturesque ideas of Camillo Sitte, but reworked to be more attentive to practical and functional considerations.

Norman Foster

(Manchester, UK, 1935)

After studies at the University of Manchester (1956–1961), he obtained his master's degree at Yale University in the United States (1961–1962). Together with Richard and Su Rogers and his future wife, Wendy Ann Cheesman, Foster founded Team 4 Architects in London in

1963. Several residential projects date to this period of his career. In 1967 he and Wendy Foster founded Foster Associates, beginning the most profitable and challenging phase of Foster's career. From the beginning his architecture has been neoproductivist in style. Over the years, his increasingly daring experiments in engineering have made him one of the leading exponents of high-tech architecture. Apart from the spectacular constructions that he has built throughout the world, Foster has made designs for smaller buildings of extraordinary elegance and refinement, such as the Sakler Gallery in London.

Massimiliano Fuksas

(Rome, Italy, 1944)

Fuksas got his degree in architecture in 1969 from the University of Rome and carried

out his professional activity in that city until the end of the 1980s. This Roman period of his career was marked by intense production of architecture based on a highly original reading of the Postmodern. He achieved international fame with the designs he made in France during the 1990s. Worthy of note among the many buildings he made there, all of them marked by strong formal characterization, is the Academy of Fine Arts in Bordeaux, made in 1995. His international fame was increased in 1998 when he was nominated to the post of Architecture Director for the Biennale of Venice.

Gabetti–Isola
(Roberto Gabetti, Turin, Italy, 1925–2000; Aimaro Oreglia d'Isola, Turin, Italy, 1928)
After completing their studies at the Turin Polytechnic, the two architects opened their studio in that city in 1950. The Bottega d'Erasmo of 1953, with which they began their professional activity, placed them among the promoters of neo-Liberty, which in Italy in the 1950s represented the opposition to the late

expressions of the Modern movement. Even the first works they made reveal the particular set of design characteristics that led them to achieve a quiet language known for compact, extended volumetrics. These characteristics include the close reading of the urban context, extensive knowledge of the history of architecture, and a

select reuse of the techniques and materials of the past in order to evoke traditional images. The works of their last years show traces of the composite methodologies that belong to the Postmodern.

Ignazio Gardella
(Milan, Italy, 1905–1999)
Gardella got a degree in civil engineering from the Milan Polytechnic in 1931 and opened his studio in Milan the next year. His career involved him in design projects for buildings of many different sizes, and his style reveals that his architectonic language was in constant evolution. The works of his first phase were markedly rationalist; the outstanding creation of his period is the tuberculosis clinic in Alessandria from 1936 to 1938. After World War II he gradually moved towards an increasingly personal and expressive language, the matrix of which was Milanese neoclassicism. As

different as they were, these phases of his career share a common aspect, which is the great sensitivity with which he always worked and which enabled him to insert a modern building in an old and highly typical urban context with great felicity.

Antoni Gaudí y Cornet
(Reus, Spain, 1852–Barcelona, 1926)
Gaudí completed his studies at the Escuela Provincial de Arquitectura in Barcelona, the city destined to be the principal theater of his professional activity. He initially followed the return to medieval forms proposed by the Catalan movement as the most genuine expression of vernacular Spanish tradition. Early on he met the wealthy industrialist Güell, destined to be his most important patron, for whom he made the first works

characterized by a daring combination of Gothic and Moresque elements. Such experimentation later led him to achieve a highly personal language freed from every reference to the past and full of formal, structural, and decorative inventions that surpassed every traditional compositional scheme. Busy until the last days of his life with the creation of the Sagrada Familia, he was long undervalued by official critics, and only recently have the greatness and the prophetic qualities of this isolated genius of architectonic creativity been recognized.

Frank O. Gehry

(Toronto, Canada, 1929)
Gehry studied at the University of Southern California and at Harvard and in 1954 began working for several architects. He opened his first studio, in California, in 1962, and his first works were influenced by the vernacular architecture of California and the work of Neutra and Wright. A series of residential buildings that he made during the 1970s, including his own home in Santa Monica, built between 1977 and 1979, revealed his growing tendency to dissolve the conventional compositional

and structural elements of architecture, leading to a sort of architecture of programmatic deconstructivism. His creations became increasingly sculptural during the 1980s and brought him worldwide fame. Created with the help of computers, his works of the 1990s took on even more irrational and plastic forms to the point of rejecting traditional perspective and perceptive values. In 1990 he received the Pritzker Architecture Prize.

Giorgio Grassi

(Milan, Italy, 1935)
After studying at the Milan Polytechnic Grassi began teaching there in 1965. From 1961 to 1964 he contributed to the magazine *Casabella-continuità*, together with Vittorio Gregotti, Guido Canella, and Aldo Rossi. From the beginning of his professional and teaching career he aligned

himself against experimentalism in architectonic styles, turning instead to the patrimony of history for appropriate models to meet design demands. His first works, inspired by Tessenow and Loos, revealed the tendency towards reduction and neutral monumentality that he was also to apply in the field

of restoration. It was in the reconstruction of the Roman theater of Sagunto, near Valencia, between 1985 and 1993, that his great talent for interpreting the original layout and volumes of the ancient monument and integrating them with a modern form gave life to a true masterpiece of contemporary architecture.

Michael Graves

(Indianapolis, USA, 1934)
Graves studied at the Universities of Cincinnati and Harvard, won the Prix de Rome in 1964, and opened a studio in Princeton, New Jersey, in 1964. In 1969 his work was presented at MoMA in New York by Kenneth Frampton, who included him in the New York Five. Graves's professional activity has gone through two distinct periods. The first was a purist phase in which he created a series of homes in "neo-Le Corbusier" style; the second has been a classicist phase, in which the many large-scale projects have assumed theatrical features with increasing references to the works Ledoux and Boullée. From an initial process of decomposition of the bodies of buildings, Graves has moved to questioning the regulating function of the layout,

ultimately resolving the discrepancy between layout and elevation by a historicist revival that permits him to freely combine columns, pilasters, and other elements from the past.

Vittorio Gregotti
(Novara, Italy, 1927)
Gregotti earned his degree from the Milan Polytechnic in 1952 and taught there from 1964 to 1978, moving in the latter year to the University of Venice. He combined his teaching activity with editorial

work for the magazines *Edilizia Moderna, Rassegna,* and *Casabella*. In his career as an architect he was originally one of the apologists of neo-Liberty; he progressively developed on interest in the concept of the megastructure. His interest in the large scale of landscapes found expression on the theoretical and practical levels in numerous projects and creations in the 1970s, and in 1974 he formed Gregotti and Associates. The designs he made during the 1980s revealed his increasing interest in an urban landscape based on large-scale architectonic infrastructures, as was also the case in his recent projects to transform the Bicocca industrial area of Milan.

Walter Gropius
(Berlin, Germany, 1883–Boston, USA, 1969)
After studies in Munich and Berlin, Gropius joined the office of Peter Behrens, from whom he learned the celebration of industrial development as a manifestation of a new culture. From 1910 to 1925 he worked with Adolf Meyer. The outstanding work of these years was the Fagus Works, a milestone in the Modern movement. In 1919 he founded the Bauhaus in Weimar, the crowning achievement of his teaching efforts to blend artistic creativity with the needs of industrial production. The school's relocation to Dessau, in 1925, began the technological era of Modern architecture, influenced by contemporary Dutch architects and leading to a series of works of international importance. Gropius left the Bauhaus in 1928 and began a period of experimentation in urbanistics and the typology of the home. With the advent of Nazism he moved to England and then, in 1937, to Boston, where the taught at Harvard and continued his professional activity, first alongside Marcel Breuer and then with the TAC group.

Zaha M. Hadid
(Baghdad, Iraq, 1950)
Having completed her studies in mathematics at the American University in Beirut, Hadid moved to the Architectural Association of London in 1972, where she was deeply influenced by the teachers Rem Koolhaas and Elia Zenghelis. In 1977 she joined with them to become a member of the Neosuprematist group OMA (Office for Metropolitan Architecture). In 1979 she began work on her own, taking

part in numerous competitions and winning world fame for her design of The Peak Club in Hong Kong, in 1983. In 1989 she was commissioned to build the fire station in Weil am Rhein, Germany. In 1999 she was commissioned to design the Museum of Contemporary Art in Rome. Since her debut, her architectonic language has been strongly expressive, dynamic, and chromatic and has stayed near the linguistic codes of deconstructionism.

Hugo Häring
(Biberach, Germany, 1882–Göppingen, Germany, 1958)
Häring studied at the Technische Hochschule in Stuttgart and Dresden before beginning his professional career in Berlin in 1921. He became a member of

several groups, including the Zehner Ring (Der Ring), disbanded by Hitler in 1933. Even so, Häring stayed in Germany during the years of Nazi rule, teaching in a private art school in Berlin. In 1943 he returned to Biberach to work. Although he made several notable buildings, such as the Gut Garkau farm complex in Lübeck, he is primarily known for his theoretical works, based on the spread of the organic language, which later influenced such very different architects as Aalto, Kahn, and Scharoun.

Zvi Hecker

(Kraków, Poland, 1931)
Hecker emigrated to Israel in 1950, where he studied architecture, engineering, and painting. Since 1959 he has had a private practice in Tel-Aviv, and in 1991 he opened a second studio in Berlin, dividing most of his time between those two cities. He teaches in the architecture faculties of numerous European, American, and Canadian universities. The theme of deconstruction, with its implicit revision of the spatial language of architecture and its postulates, is recurrent in his work, which is characterized by a poetics made of strong articulation of volumes, integration between internal and external spaces,

openness and attention to the natural setting, and a multidimensional figurative style. His more recent designs include the Spiral Apartment House in Ramat Gan, Israel, for which he won the Rechter Prize in 1998. His works have been exhibited in various cities

and in the Biennale of Venice in 1991 and 1996. He has won numerous architecture competitions and in 1966 won the German Critic Prize.

Herzog–de Meuron

(Jacques Herzog, Basel, Switzerland, 1950; Pierre de Meuron, Basel, Switzerland, 1950)
After studying with Aldo Rossi at the Technische Hochschule in Zurich, Herzog and De Meuron opened a studio in Basel in 1978. Their works immediately attracted great interest, leading to many large-scale international commissions. Among the most recent of these was the transformation of a power station on the banks of the River Thames into

exhibition space for London's Tate Gallery. Their extremely varied projects make clear an ongoing process of experimentation with new materials and new building systems, including the progressive detachment of the external envelope from the internal spaces. A singular aspect of their style is the use of traditional building materials and methods; these are entrusted with the expressive result of each project, with structures in reinforced concrete that give order to buildings while at the same time making them abstract.

Josef Hoffmann

(Pirnitz, today Brtnicze, Moravia, 1870–Vienna, Austria, 1956)
Hoffmann studied in Brno and then at the Academy of Fine

Arts in Vienna, where he was a student of Otto Wagner. In 1895 he won the Prix de Rome and went to Italy to study ancient monuments. Although strongly influenced by Wagner's teachings and by contact with Art Nouveau, he did not remain indifferent to the Mediterranean tradition and the products of England's Arts and

Crafts movement, aspects of which can be recognized in his first commission, a series of villas in Vienna. In 1903 he helped found the Wiener Werkstätte, an association of artisans that was active until 1932 and that created the furnishings for a series of highly elegant works characterized by the simplification of the formal elements and the refinement of the decorative and chromatic details. Hoffmann's production after 1905 saw the blending of different linguistic styles, running from classicism to Expressionism. During the last period of his career he was busy in a creative competition with the Modern movement and most of all with the work of the young Le Corbusier, who was active in his workshop for a certain period.

Hans Hollein

(Vienna, Austria, 1934)
After studies in Vienna and the United States Hollein set up a studio in Vienna in 1964. During the 1960s he matured his concept of architecture as a point of confluence of various creative activities, eventually coming to define architecture as any type of artificial control applied to the environment. In keeping with these principles, his first works—such as the Retti Candle Shop in the Kohlmarkt of Vienna, from 1964, which earned him international fame—are small-size spaces distinguished by attention to detail, the use of precious materials, and the design of the furnishings. These works, which placed him among the earliest critics of functionalism, anticipated the

theories of such groups as Archizoom, Superstudio, and OMA. His later projects, which have been larger in size and which accentuate the extravagant aspect of the use of citations and colors, made him one of the precursors of Postmodernism in Europe.

Victor Horta

(Ghent, Belgium, 1862–Brussels, Belgium, 1947)
After his studies and a period of apprenticeship in the studio of Alphonse Balat, Horta debuted in 1885 with a series of small works that immediately displayed his talent. The Hotel Tassel (Tassel House) in Brussels, from 1893, was a manifesto of Art Nouveau thanks to the introduction of revolutionary artistic, technological, and compositional elements. The use of iron as a material for

both construction and decoration as part of an architectonic program based on the open plan and the three-dimensional articulation of space—elements that also show up in his later works—represent Horta's original contribution to the development of the Modern movement in architecture. After a stay in the United States between 1916 and 1919, he fell back on a more traditional and severe style based on the classical.

Arata Isozaki

(Oita, Kyushu, Japan, 1931)
Isozaki studied at the University of Tokyo as student of Kenzo Tange and then worked with Tange until 1963. During the 1960s Isozaki's work went through a mannerist period, displaying a strong orientation to abstract forms composed of cubic and semicylindrical

elements in a clear break with the rationalist principles of Modern architecture. In the 1970s his works showed an increasing move towards historicism, with fragments drawn from Occidental architecture of the past inserted in a contemporary language. This trend towards eclecticism increased in the 1980s. His alternation of a high-tech language with a severely classical style made it difficult to identify a coherent line of development. Isozaki's works from the 1990s achieved a balanced synthesis of the earlier stylistic tendencies with a return to elementary geometric shapes, as for example in the Museum of Contemporary Art in Nagi.

Philip Johnson
(Cleveland, Ohio, USA, 1906)
As director of the Department of Architecture of the Museum of Modern Art in New York (1930–1936), Johnson became interested in European avant-garde architecture, promoting the first trips to the United States of Mies van der Rohe and Le Corbusier and publishing, together with Hitchcock, *The International Style: Architecture since 1922* (1932) in conjunction with an exhibit of Modern architecture held at the museum. Johnson's activity as an architect began in the 1940s with a series of works clearly influenced by rationalism. His language grew in complexity, involving the refined and unprejudiced use of classical elements inserted in up-to-date

technological solutions, making him a precursor of Postmodernism. He reached the height of his career in the 1980s with the AT&T Building in New York. The arrival of deconstructionism in the 1990s marked the conclusion of the architectonic experiments of his long professional career.

Louis I. Kahn
(Island of Oesel, today Saaremaa, Estonia, 1901–New York, USA, 1974)
Kahn emigrated to the United States in 1905 and graduated from the University of Pennsylvania in 1924. During the 1930s his interest in the living conditions in Pennsylvania led him to make numerous housing projects. His works from the 1940s make reference to the stylistic modules of the Modern movement, but in the next

decade he arrived at an original Brutalism, the outstanding example of which is the enlargement of the Yale Art Gallery in New Haven. This and his later works display all the characteristic motifs of his architectonic language: a preference for elementary geometric forms and compositions, the hierarchical separation of spaces, the

emphasis given secondary elements, and citations from the past. After the end of the 1960s he was able to apply his urbanistic and architectonic ideas fully with creations in India and Nepal.

Michel de Klerk
(Amsterdam, Netherlands, 1884–1923)
In 1898 De Klerk left his studies unfinished to work in the studio of Eduard Cuypers, staying there until 1910. During this period he took evening courses at the technical school and made a short but very important trip to London in 1906, where he encountered the early Arts and Crafts movement and the architecture of M. H. Baillie Scott, which greatly impressed him. These elements, together with his studies of Danish and Swedish rural architecture, were determinant in his formation and in the development of his personal style, thanks to which he was immediately accepted by the Amsterdam School. His first creation, made in collaboration with that group of young architects, was the Scheepvaarthuis Shipping Office in Amsterdam, of 1912, with its reinforced-concrete skeleton

hidden under dense artisan decoration. This style, which was the characteristic trait of his many residential buildings, came to be known as Dutch "brick Expressionism."

Rem Koolhaas
(Rotterdam, Netherlands, 1944)
After his debut as journalist and screenwriter, he studied architecture at the Architectural Association of London between 1968 and 1972. In 1975, together with Madelon

Vriesendorp and Elia and Zoe Zenghelis, he founded OMA (Office for Metropolitan Architecture), with offices in New York and London where, in open polemic with the functionalist city, he worked out a series of projects inspired by the experiences of the avant-garde Constructivists and Neosuprematists. In 1978 he published a series of utopian designs and suggestions, in which he expressed his theory of the "culture of congestion," which was destined to become the building concept of his work and which would find application in a series of urban designs for Paris, Amsterdam, and Lille, as well as great buildings, highly articulated and isolated from urban contexts, made between the 1980s and the 1990s.

Léon Krier
(Luxembourg, 1946)
After a period of apprenticeship at various professional studios, he began his activity as a self-taught architect in 1974. Together with Maurice Culot he began a theoretical reflection in favor of the city built to the measure of humans as opposed to the modern city dominated by commercial architecture that was destroying the historical centers of European cities; he then designed a series of urban plans in which a soberly classicalist style was joined to Postmodern citations. From the middle of the 1980s, his ideas had a preferred interlocutor in the Prince of Wales, for whom Krier became advisor and under whose patronage he designed some small

picturesque centers in Poundbury near Dorchester, UK. His first built structure was a tower villa in the classical language made in 1987 as his vacation home in Seaside, Florida.
He collaborated on various projects in the 1990s, including the competition for the Berlin Reichstag with his brother Robert.

Béla Lajta
(Pest, Hungary, 1873– Vienna, Austria, 1920)
Jewish by birth, Lajta changed his last name from Leitersdorfer. After earning his degree from the Budapest Polytechnic in 1895, he spent several years traveling throughout Europe, coming in contact with important architects, among them Josef Hoffmann and Adolf Loos. Upon his return to Hungary he began a close collaboration with Odön Lechner, founder of the

Hungarian Secession, the teachings of whom are apparent in his first creations. With the Budapest Institute for the Blind, a work of 1905–1908, he began to work out his autonomous language, influenced by Scandinavian and English Romanticism. The works of the following years, almost all commissioned by the Jewish community of the capital, display the definite passage to the poetics of rationalism. The outbreak of World War I ended his career, which had traced the route of the development of modern Hungarian architecture.

Le Corbusier (Charles-Edouard Jeanneret)
(La Chaux-de-Fonds, Switzerland,

In 1908 he graduated from the Göteborg Polytechnic. After a period of apprenticeship in the studios of Theodor Fischer and Richard Riemeschmid, he went into private practice in 1911. Over the following years he made various houses whose simple style makes evident the influence of the language of

1887–Roquebrune-Cap-Martin, France, 1965)
After studying engraving at the school of applied arts in his native city, between 1906 and 1914 he traveled in Europe and the Middle East, studying on his own the architectural culture of Europe and coming in contact with the most important architects of the epoch. In 1907 he met Hoffmann in Vienna, in 1908 he worked in Paris for the Perret brothers, in 1910 he was in Berlin in the office of Behrens. In 1917 he moved to Paris, where he opened a studio with his cousin Pierre Jeanneret. The following years were full of urbanistic projects, architectonic creations, and theoretical writings. The use of reinforced concrete and primary materials like iron and glass, industrialization of the worksite, the codification of certain technical prefabricated elements, and the use of pure colors are the distinctive traits of his new technical, typological, and formal language, represented in an emblematic way by the Villa Savoye of 1928–1931, which had a profound influence on entire generations of architects.

Sigurd Lewerentz
(Bjartra, Sweden, 1885–Lund, Sweden, 1975)

Tessenow. His works from the 1920s show a tendency towards an elegant revival of the classical along with the national vernacular tradition. His participation in the 1928 Stockholm exhibition marked his turn towards functionalism, enriched by attention to detail. This taste for details, joined to a refined use of traditional materials and formal complexity, led him to abandon functionalism in the postwar years in favor of a more poetic and individualistic language capable of creating architecture of greater intensity and evocation.

Adalberto Libera
(Villa Lagarina, Trent, Italy, 1903–Rome, Italy, 1963)
While still studying architecture at the University of Rome he was an active participant in the creation of a manifesto of Italian rationalism, which found its

expression between 1926 and 1927 in the magazine *Rassegna Italiana*. In 1927 Libera became a member of Gruppo 7; in 1928 and 1931 he organized the first and second exhibitions of rational architecture in Rome. In 1930 he promoted the formation of MIAR (Movimento Italiano per l'Architettura Razionale), of which he became secretary. During the following years he put his ideas into practice in numerous projects and creations in very different fields. In 1938 he won the competition for the palace of the congresses at the EUR with a classically designed structure that was fated to undergo great alterations during the construction phase. Dating to the same years is the Casa Malaparte on Capri, one of the most successful works of Italian rationalism. In the 1950s he was able to make use of the work on residential themes that he had started before the war.

Daniel Libeskind
(Lodz, Poland, 1946)
After studying music in Israel, in 1960 he moved to the United States. He obtained citizenship in 1965 and began studying architecture at the Cooper Union School in New York, later specializing at the University of

Essex in England. He made a name for himself in 1990 at the International Garden Exhibition in Osaka, when he and various other young architects were invited by Isozaki to design a pavilion. He later became known on the international scene, participating in numerous competitions and making

exhibitions and installations. His works, which fully reflect the theories elaborated and expressed within the sphere of his teaching activity, can be traced to the contemporary architectonic theories of deconstructionism. One of Libeskind's most important projects so far was the enlargement of the Berlin Museum between 1989 and 1998.

Adolf Loos
(Brno, Moravia, 1870–Vienna, Austria, 1933)
After courses at the Dresden Polytechnic, in 1893 Loos took a long trip to the United States, where he saw works by the Chicago school as well as expressions of the Arts and Crafts movement. Back in Europe, he began his professional activity in Vienna, creating works that were direct physical expressions of the

theories presented in his writings. In open opposition to the Jugendstil, the homes he built in the first two decades of the twentieth century were concrete manifestations of his theoretical vision as expressed in the essay "Architektur" (1910). Refined interiors of wood and marble contrasted with cubic exteriors with plastered surfaces left free of any ornamentation. In the 1920s he was made chief architect for the city, a position that permitted him to become involved in the area of public housing. Isolated from the architectonic culture of his time, he was closer to the protagonists of the European avant-garde. The revolutionary Tristan Tzara House, which he made in Paris is 1926, shows the influence of the Dadaists.

Charles Rennie Mackintosh
(Glasgow, UK, 1868–London, UK, 1928)
Mackintosh began his career working in the studio of John Hutchinson and taking evening courses at the Glasgow School of Applied Arts. In 1889 he was taken on as designer by the Honeyman & Keppie construction company, staying

there until 1913. There he met Herbert McNair and the two McDonald sisters, with whom he formed The Four, a group of artists active in the fields of graphics and engraving. Thanks to the elegance and originality of their designs, the works of what would become the Glasgow School became well

known at the international level. Meanwhile, since 1897, Mackintosh had been busy as an architect on his major commission, the Glasgow School of Art, where the geometric abstraction of the forms, united to the elegant combination of Gothic, Celtic, and Japanese decorative motifs presented an excellent synthesis of the elements of his artistic language. His fame is also tied to many designs for furniture exhibited in 1900 at the Vienna Secession. Problems with alcoholism forced him to move first to Suffolk and then to London and finally to France, where he dedicated himself to painting.

Robert Maillart
(Berne, Switzerland, 1872–Geneva, Switzerland, 1940)
After graduating with a degree in engineering from the Zurich

Polytechnic, Maillart worked for various studios before founding in 1902 Maillart & Cie, both an engineering studio and a construction company. In 1912 he left Switzerland and moved to Russia, where he worked until the October Revolution. He returned to Switzerland and opened studios in Geneva, Berne, and Zurich. His research into the use of reinforced concrete and in the ways of integrating the load-bearing and non-load-bearing elements in a single structure found its most successful and spectacular application in the forty bridges that he made between 1901 and 1940. His most important invention, which dates to 1908, was the mushroom slab, in which the supporting pylon flares as it rises to form a horizontal supporting ring, thus saving materials while also offering great flexibility of application along with light weight and an elegant exterior. This building system was applied in the warehouses of the Zurich Warehouse Association, making an important contribution to the building technology of the twentieth century.

Fumihiko Maki
(Tokyo, Japan, 1928)
Around the middle of the 1960s, after studies at the University of Tokyo and a stay in the United States, Maki returned to Japan, where he participated in the formation of the Metabolism Group and opened his own design studio. Without ever letting himself be drawn in by the utopian speculations of the other young members of the Metabolism

Group, he became one of the architects most sensitive to the rapid sociocultural changes then taking place in Japan and created an architectural style that was of great formal and functional interest. Although he prefers the use of high-tech, prefabricated, modular elements, all of his works display a clear tendency towards the continuity and coexistence of tradition and progress. His many creations in the 1980s and 1990s primarily involved school buildings and those made for public institutions, housing complexes, museums, and university settings, such as the Mita campus in Tokyo and the Shonan campus in Fujisawa in 1992.

Giacomo Mattè-Trucco
(Turin, Italy, 1869–1934)
Mattè-Trucco's interest in structural theories was clear as early as his studies at the Royal School in Turin; this interest soon led to experiments in the expressive possibilities of reinforced concrete used as a framework, and he made a precursor of the use of this material. His major contribution to industrial architecture was the idea of making the body of a building by assembling modular elements made of reinforced concrete. Use of this design method, which in theory would permit a building to grow infinitely, was given practical application in Mattè-Trucco's most important design, presented at the first "Architettura Razionale" exhibition in Rome in 1928, the Fiat-Lingotto factory in Turin, with its daring structure, most of all the ramps leading to the test track located on the roof of the building. This building proved to be an important Italian contribution to Modern architecture.

Richard Meier
(Newark, New Jersey, USA, 1934)
After studies at Cornell University in Ithaca, New York, he trained in the New York office of Skidmore, Owings and Merrill and with Marcel Breuer. In 1963 he opened his own studio in New York. His

first works were single-family homes and residential buildings that clearly showed the influence of Breuer along with an interest in Le Corbusier purism. Meier achieved fame with the 1969 exhibition of the New York Five, of which he was a member; in fact, the group was also known as the White architects because of his preference for that color. He was soon working on a series of important international commissions. In these buildings he freely combined his repertoire of geometric forms, within which he articulated complex spaces influenced by the compositions of the avant-gardes of the 1920s. Having become one of the most

sought-after architects in the world, he reached the apex of his career in the creation of the buildings for the Getty Center in Los Angeles, made between 1985 and 1997.

Konstantin Stepanovic Mel'nikov

(Moscow, Russia, 1890–1974) After earning his degree from the Moscow Academy in 1917, Mel'nikov was drawn to Constructivism, becoming a key figure within that movement and participating in the foundation of ASNOVA

(Association of New Architects). From his first works, including his home in Moscow, one of the most singular buildings of the 1920s in Russia, he displayed the movement's expressive flair, captured in a dynamic form. He acquired international fame with his pavilion for the exhibition of Constructivist objects with which he won the Grand Prix at the Exposition of Decorative Arts in Paris in 1925. He then worked on a series of projects emblematic of his original version of the Constructivist language, including the five workers' clubs he made in Moscow between 1927 and 1929, which were characterized by the interpenetration of articulated volumes mixed with symbolic and fantasy elements. He later became the target of Stalinist critics and ended his career on the outer margins of public architecture.

Erich Mendelsohn

(Allenstein, now Olsztyn, Poland, 1887–San Francisco, USA, 1953) Born in Poland, Mendelsohn studied architecture in Berlin and Munich. The drawings he made between 1914 and 1918, which show how profoundly

influenced he was by Expressionism, earned him European fame at the show held in Berlin in 1919. The highly symbolic force of these drawings appears in the architect's Expressionist masterpiece, the astrophysical observatory of Potsdam, built between 1919 and 1921. He then began a period of great

professional success during which he developed a personal style, characterized by forceful plasticity in the composition of volumes, supported by his extensive knowledge of the technical aspects of construction. A Jew, he left Germany in 1933, moving to England and from there to Palestine. In 1941 he emigrated to the United States, where he dedicated his last years to working on the creation of Jewish community centers.

Giovanni Michelucci

(Pistoia, Italy, 1891–Fiesole, Florence, Italy, 1990) Michelucci received his degree in 1911 from the architecture college of Florence and in the period between the world wars was an active participant in the Modern movement in Italy. In 1931 he made the Valiani House in Rome, considered by some

to be the first rationalist house in Italy. In 1933, together with the Gruppo Toscano (Tuscan Group), he won the competition for the Santa Maria Novella train station in Florence, one of the most important works of rationalism for its synthesis of the formal avant-garde language with the use of materials from the local tradition. His works from the postwar period reveal progressively greater attention to the problems involved in inserting new works in the pre-existing fabric, first directed at the renewal of the ancient city and later at the creation of a model for the formation of the new city. Finally, with the churches he made in the 1960s, he achieved the complete overcoming of the distinction between the architectonic structure and the urban space within which it is totally absorbed.

Ludwig Mies van der Rohe

(Aachen, Germany, 1886–Chicago, USA, 1969)
Mies van der Rohe did not study architecture but trained in the offices of Bruno Paul and Peter Behrens. From the latter he drew the classical severity of means, the purity of forms, the elegance of proportions, the taste for detail that, combined

with the use of modern industrial materials, characterized all his later work. He went out on his own in 1912, opening an office in Berlin. Effected by the sense of renewal following the end of World War I, he designed a series of revolutionary buildings that constitute a decisive

contribution to twentieth-century architecture in which he delineated the tendency to reduce the structure to a technical essential that could be freely organized within the architectonic space. His undisputed masterpiece is the German pavilion for the 1929 International Exposition in Barcelona, in which he achieved a spatial continuum coordinating internal and external space. After directing the Bauhaus from 1930 to 1933, he moved to the United States in 1938, where he applied his principle of "Less is more" to a few fundamental types, well suited to serve different functions.

José Rafael Moneo

(Tuleda, Spain, 1937)
After studies at the Escuela de Arquitectura of Madrid and a stay in Denmark at the studio of Jørn Utzon, Moneo returned to

Madrid in 1965 and began his professional career, designing while also teaching and carrying on intense work as an essayist and critic. The characteristic elements of his style were clear from his very first works: severity of language, classical forms, particular care for building materials, most of all brick, and rejection of the typological element as the point of departure in a design project. With the Bankinter (bank office building) in Madrid of 1973 to 1976, with which he gained great international recognition, he introduced the tendency to closely value the urban context while elaborating the enclosure elements, thus giving architects the new task of building for the

city by abandoning the notion of the building as container. Results of this were the design projects for the museums of modern art and architecture in Stockholm of 1997.

Charles W. Moore

(Benton Harbor, Michigan, USA, 1925–Los Angeles, USA, 1993)
Having completed his studies at the universities of Ann Arbor and Princeton, Moore began his professional career in 1962, in the early years working together with various associates. Beginning with the

idea that a contingent event is at the base of any design idea, his work has always resulted from a particular suggestion and thus cannot be defined in terms of any particular architectonic style. The single-family homes that he made in the 1960s, based on a rereading of domestic American architecture by way of the theme of the "house in the house," are complex solutions characterized by leaps in scale and spatial hierarchies. The decomposition of the building becomes more marked when the size and functional complexity increase, as, for example, his designs for residential and public buildings. A mannerist and folkloric lexicon is at the base of some of his works, such as the Piazza d'Italia in New Orleans of 1971 to 1978, which put him among the leading exponents of Postmodern architecture.

Riccardo Morandi

(Rome, Italy, 1902–1989)
After earning his diploma in 1927 from the school of applied engineering in Rome, Morandi dedicated himself to building earthquake-resistant structures in reinforced concrete in Calabria. In 1931 he opened an office in Rome. He made a name for himself for the

construction of innovative bridges, such as that on Lake Maracaibo in Venezuela, of 1957–1962. While all the major structuralists of the period following World War II tended towards a late rationalist purism, from the very beginning Morandi employed a personal revival of the Expressionistic

thematic. In certain bridges, in which he made use of tie beams covered in cement or of isostatic frameworks in plastic forms, he expressed an esthetic near Brutalism. One of his most notable works is the underground showroom for the automobile exhibition at Valentino Park in Turin, of 1958–1959, with its powerful and restless language based on the use of oblique supports that give the structure an almost dynamic movement.

Gaetano Moretti

(Milan, Italy, 1860–1938)
A student of Camillo Boito at the Brera Academy, where he

returned later to teach, Moretti trained by way of a rigorous philological study of the styles of the past, which made him without doubt one of the best and most learned representatives of eclecticism in Italy. First as collaborator and then as successor to Luca Beltrami, he carried on an intense activity as conservationist of monuments from 1891 to 1901. Details in his architectonic creations can be seen as anticipating the floral style; his most convincing work is the neo-Romanesque power station at Trezzo D'Adda of 1905–1906. The house in Milan at 15 viale Majno, of 1911–1913, reveals instead a prudent adhesion to Modernism.

Glenn Murcutt

(London, UK, 1936)
After studies at the University of New South Wales in Sydney he opened his own studio in that city in 1969. With the design for the Marie Short House in Kempsey, of 1974–1975, he abandoned the Modernism of his early works to develop a personal architectonic language directed at making each building harmonize with the environmental and cultural aspects of the site on which it would stand. The distinctive traits of his works include the use of simple materials that suggest lightness and permeability with the surroundings; the skillful union of planimetric simplicity with complex sections, including the use of mechanisms designed to control environmental conditions; and a constant

awareness of Aboriginal culture. In this way he has achieved an original interpretation of the legacy of the Modern movement and the traditions of colonial architecture in Australia.

Pier Luigi Nervi

(Sondrio, Italy, 1891–Rome, Italy, 1979)
In 1913 Nervi graduated in civil engineering from the University of Bologna; he then worked for the Società per Costruzione Cimentizia until 1923, when he opened his own studio in Rome. His constructions, considered ideal models by the section of rationalism interested in a direct relationship between form, function, and construction, were the fruit of a long and highly thought-out program to achieve balance between construction quality, expression, and the esthetics of

his preferred construction material, reinforced concrete. After a few initial works that immediately attracted attention, he dedicated himself to the creation of large-size roofs, beginning with those with a single span for the hangars of the Italian air force made between 1935 and 1943, for which he sometimes used a covering made of diagonal cement beams and sometimes a skeleton of prefabricated cement, finally arriving at the giant mushroom structure he used for the Palazzo del Lavoro at the "Italia `61" exhibition in Turin in 1961.

Richard Neutra

(Vienna, Austria, 1892–Wuppertal, Germany, 1970)
Having got his diploma in Vienna, Neutra immediately felt the fascination of American architecture, to which he was introduced in 1910 by Adolf Loos and then by the works of Frank Lloyd Wright, published in Europe in 1911. After his

first experience of work in Switzerland with the landscape architect Gustav Amman and in Berlin with Erich Mendelsohn, he emigrated to the United States in 1923 and two years later was in Wright's studio in Taliesin, Wisconsin. In 1926 he

moved to Los Angeles, where he collaborated with Rudolf Michael Schindler, before opening his own studio in Silver Lake. The series of private homes he made during the next years in California mark the passage from a synthesis of the building principles of the International Style with the Wrightian sensitivity to the environmental insertion to the development of his own expressive means, distinguished by simple, elegant forms and by the use of unusual materials. His participation in the CIAM conferences, his publications, his urbanistic designs, and those for buildings destined for collective services demonstrate the social concerns that have always been an aspect of Neutra's professional activity.

Oscar Niemeyer

(Rio de Janeiro, Brazil, 1907)
After studies at the School of Belles Arts in Rio de Janeiro, he worked in the studio of Lúcio Costa in 1935 and for Le Corbusier in Paris in 1936, the influence of whom is clearly visible in his first works. He went on to develop a personal style in which his original plastic organization of volumes and the introduction of curved lines alongside a rational grid, derived from Spanish baroque forms and from the natural landscape of Brazil, permitted him to overcome the teaching of Le Corbusier and to make buildings of great effect. His extremely expressive and antirational language earned him the position of chief government architect during construction of the country's new capital. Between 1956 and

1961 he designed all the most important buildings, the figurative elements of which, made enormous to fit the giant urban space, give the entire structure an unreal appearance. During the military regime, between 1964 and 1985, he emigrated to Paris, where he worked on many international projects. His last works indicated that his formal repertory was not yet exhausted.

Jean Nouvel

(Fumel, France, 1945)
In 1971 he graduated from the École Nationale Supérieure des Beaux-Arts of Paris, after having already worked for the architect Claude Parent and having opened his first studio in 1970. In 1976 he was co-founder of the MARS group, and in 1980 he planned and directed the biennale of architecture in Paris. In 1988 he opened Jean Nouvel,

Emmanuel Cattani et Associés, quickly reaching international fame thanks to an architectonic approach critical of traditional models and solutions and instead rich with metaphors and surprising, provocative images, made using light materials with colors taken from the daily life of the city and the periphery. The construction of the Institute du Monde Arabe in 1981–1987, a successful combination of the potentials offered by advanced technology and the possibilities of bioecological architecture, marked a fundamental point in his career and earned him many important commissions, making him one of the best known French architects in the world.

Joseph Maria Olbrich

(Troppau, Silesia, 1867–Düsseldorf, Germany,1908)
After studies at the Vienna Academy, in 1893 he won the Prix de Rome, which also led to his being taken into the studio of Otto Wagner, where worked for five years. In 1897 he was among the young avant-garde Austrian artists to found the Vienna Secession, for which he designed the Secession Building, between 1897 and 1898, which earned him immediate notoriety and numerous commissions between 1898 and 1900. He was soon recognized as the most gifted and inventive of the Secession architects. In 1899 he went to Darmstadt to help create the Mathildenhöhe artist colony, of which he assumed the direction and for which he

designed the buildings and the exhibition pavilion with its famous panoramic tower. His work placed him within the climate of figurative renewal promoted by Art Nouveau, but he succeeded in overcoming the limitations and weaknesses of that style by combining its fantasy appearance with spatial and distributive concreteness, thus anticipating the later formulations of the Modern movement.

Ragnar Östberg

(Oscar Fredriksborg, Stockholm, Sweden, 1866–Stockholm, Sweden, 1945)
Following studies in Stockholm Östberg spent quite a long time traveling in both Europe and America before beginning intense professional, cultural, and academic activity. His international fame was based most of all on his construction of the Stockholm Town Hall, a

building in a transitional style between eclecticism and the Modern movement, which he made between 1909 and 1923. In it heterogeneous ideas and citations, some based on the Doges' Palace in Venice and some drawn from the Swedish Romantic and Renaissance tradition, are combined in a personal style with which he hoped to achieve both a nationalistic expression and a meaningful relationship with the urban setting. This language, freely inspired by a variety of historical suggestions, transfigured and combined in an original way, informed Östberg's creations during the first two decades of the century; in the projects of his maturity that language gave way to an austere, monumental classicism distinguished by sharp geometric compositions and the extreme simplification of decoration.

Jacobus Johannes Pieter Oud

(Purmerend, Netherlands, 1890–Wassenaar, Netherlands, 1963)
After studies in Amsterdam and later at Delft, Oud worked for Petrus Josephus Hubertus Cuypers, the first Dutch "rationalist," and then worked for Theodor Fischer in Munich.

His 1915 meeting with the painter Theo van Doesburg led to the founding of the magazine *De Stijl* and to a series of architectonic creations profoundly influenced by abstract Cubism, in contrast with the Expressionistic compositions of the imaginative Amsterdam school. Between 1918 and 1933, in his position as Rotterdam city architect, Oud made several popular city quarters distinguished by the harmonic compositions of the volumes and by the white plaster surfaces on which openings painted in the pure colors of Mondrian stand out. In 1933 he returned to private practice, and his subsequent works show a softened style along with stylistic revisions that earned him criticism from several architects of the Modern movement.

Ieoh Ming Pei

(Canton, China, 1917)
In 1935, at the age of seventeen, Pei emigrated to the United States. After studies at MIT and Harvard he went to work in 1948 for the New York builder William Zeckendorf. In 1955 he opened I.M. Pei and Associates, still ranked among the best in the United States, and achieved immediate international fame, building a large number of public and commercial buildings of great effect throughout the world. Because of the stylistic diversity among the associates and the long period of time over which the office has been active, the projects made have been very different, but they have always been distinguished by

extremely refined and skilled designs that range from rationalism to Postmodernism. Pei's best known creations include the design for the Grand Louvre of 1983–1993 with its underground entryway entered by way of an enormous glass pyramid located in the courtyard, one of the most disputed architectonic creations of its time.

Dominique Perrault

(Clermont-Ferrand, France, 1953)
In 1978 Perrault was graduated from the École Nationale Supérieure des Beaux-Arts in Paris, and in 1981 he opened his own office in that city. The competition-winning design for the university buildings for electronic engineers and technicians in Marne-la-Vallée in the 1980s earned him attention and important commissions. Among these, the best known was without doubt

his design for the Bibliothéque Nationale de France in Paris, of 1989–1997, with its four large towers marking off a natural garden. His architecture has always been distinguished by strongly abstract and minimalist technical works and volumes, enriched and embellished by the high quality of the industrial-made construction materials used in the projects.

Auguste Perret
(Brussels, Belgium, 1874–Paris, France, 1954)
Perret began studies at the École des Beaux-Arts in Paris, but quit, completing his training by joining, along with his two brothers, his father's construction firm, known from 1905 on as Perret Frères. His theoretical and business training led him to work out a synthesis between the ideals of classical harmony and the financial demands of the construction industry. He achieved this

through the use of reinforced concrete and the exploitation of its technical and expressive possibilities. These linguistic efforts reached a particular lyricism in the church of Notre Dame du Raincy, of 1923, in which the bearing structure in reinforced concrete is also the building's decoration. After

World War II Perret and his brothers made several large works, including the 1948 reconstruction of the city of Le Havre, the first official recognition of Perret's long and distinguished career as a builder, a career that puts him among the pioneers of Modern architecture.

Marcello Piacentini
(Rome, Italy, 1881–1960)
Piacentini got his training in his father's office and at the College of Fine Arts in Rome. He initially revealed his talent in a series of ephemeral works of clear eclectic inspiration and in various urbanistic designs of a

Mitteleuropean and North American style. His Roman designs of the 1920s, made for wealthy private patrons, show that he was up to date on stylistic trends in Vienna. His position against the young architects of the rationalist movement and in favor of an architecture suited to contemporary life but also respectful of tradition soon made him one of the Fascist regime's official architects. His many public commissions during the 1930s included the 1936–1942 project for the E 42 Exhibition in Rome, of which he designed the general layout with its evocation of the pomp of the ancient Roman Empire,

also visible in the Palace of Italian Civilization designed by Guerrini, La Padula, and Romano. The war brought an end to the many large worksites he was involved in, along with his professional career.

Renzo Piano
(Genoa, Italy, 1937)
Piano studied at the University of Florence and at the Milan Polytechnic, graduating from the latter in 1964. After collaborating with several of the best known contemporary architects, he founded Renzo Piano Building Workshop, in 1981, with offices in Genoa, Paris, and Houston, in which engineers, architects, and artisans from throughout the world work on the creation of design projects, civil and industrial buildings, as well as the restoration and reuse of the historical patrimony. Despite the influence of various figures, such as Kahn, Nervi, and the

Archigram group, Piano's architecture is the expression of an independent elaboration, directed at integrating a highly specialized technical culture, attentive to structural problems and to the technical and expressive potentials of materials, with a profound analysis of natural phenomena and biological demands, which enables him to elaborate a different solution, appropriate to the context, each time.

Dimitris Pikionis
(Piraeus, Greece, 1887–Athens, Greece, 1968)
After earning a degree in civil engineering at the Athens Polytechnic in 1908, Pikionis went to Munich to study painting and sculpture and then to Paris, where he studied architecture. In 1912 he returned to Athens and took part in an architectonic

movement directed at the revival of local traditions. The influence of this movement is clear in his first works, which were inspired by building models from ancient Greece. The tendency to mix modern and traditional components, supported on the theoretical plane, continued into his later works. In the 1950s his architectonic production went through a period of renewed interest, winning him commissions for public and private buildings. His master plan for the reworking of the area surrounding the Acropolis of Athens in 1951–1957 earned him international recognition.

Josef Plecnik
(Ljubljana, Slovenia, 1872–1957)
After an apprenticeship as a carpenter in his father's workshop and at the crafts school of Graz, Plecnik studied in Vienna in 1894 and was

taken into the office of Otto Wagner, whose teaching is legible in Plecnik's first works. In 1901 he joined the Secession movement and opened a studio, which remained active until 1911, when he moved to Prague to teach at the School of Applied Arts. In 1920 he was made professor in the Architecture Faculty of the just created University of Ljubljana, where he moved definitively and spent most of his professional career. In 1925 he began work on the reconstruction of his birth city, contributing to the modification of its appearance by designing many public and private buildings in which he sought to give an adequate expression of the national Slovenian culture through a language created from the synthesis of an imaginative classicism and elements from vernacular art.

Hans Poelzig
(Berlin, Germany, 1869–1936)
After studies at the Technische Hochschule in Berlin, in 1900

he moved to Breslau, where he taught at the school of art, subsequently serving as the school's director between 1903 and 1916, anticipating the reformist teachings of the early 1920s by combining craftwork and the figurative arts. His initial works were in the eclectic style, but the works he made as city architect for the city of Dresden between 1916 and 1920 anticipated the Expressionist language that he later developed in Berlin and that had its highest expression in the

transformation of the Schumann Circus building into the Grosses Schauspielhaus of 1918–1919. Poelzig then attenuated the imaginative freedom of his earlier works to progressively align himself with the conventional rationalist language, albeit with a few concessions to the monumental emphasis.

Paolo Portoghesi
(Rome, Italy, 1931)
In 1957 Portoghesi graduated from the University of Rome and began intense activity of historical research, teaching, and professional work destined to make him a key figure

within the contradictory Postmodern debate. By the end of the 1950s, his close study of the architecture of the past had led him to align himself against functionalist rationalism in favor of an historical orientation for the new architectonic culture. Joined to his theoretical works were original and unmistakable creations, generated by the synthesis of notions drawn from Oriental architecture, from the Gothic, baroque, the Jugenstil, and from eclecticism, with compositional and formal elements drawn from Modern architecture. The apex of his work was the Mosque and Islamic Culture Center in Rome, made between 1975 and 1993.

Fernand Pouillon

(Cancon, France, 1912–Rignac, France, 1986)
After his years of training at the École des Beaux-Arts in Marseilles and Paris, Pouillon graduated in architecture in 1942 and began a collaboration with Eugène Beaudouin. Between 1944 and 1953 he worked on urbanistic complexes with his associate René Egger. In 1953 he was called to Algeria to make several public-housing

complexes. The 1961 CNL construction scandal cost him a period in prison followed by flight and later amnesty from President Pompidou. The works he completed before the scandal were distinguished by a notable urban sensibility, obtained through the use of traditional building elements and schemes, such as ancient

walls, streets, and plazas. In 1965 he was welcomed back to independent Algeria and went to work on an ambitious project of modernizing the country, including the creation of public and private buildings. During the 1980s he received many official recognitions for his work, including a personal show at the Biennale of Venice in 1982 and the Legion of Honor in 1985.

Franco Purini

(Isola del Liri, Rome, Italy, 1941)
In 1966 Purini opened his own architectural studio in Rome, along with Laura Thermes; in 1971 he graduated from the

University of Rome with Ludovico Quaroni. In his projects he experimented with a severely rationalistic formal repertory that, while forced and fragmentary to the point of fantasy when presented on paper, takes on closed spatial configurations when made concrete. Among his most important projects are the series of three plazas in Gibellina Nuova, Sicily, and the residential complex in Naples-Marianella, both made in the 1980s.

Richard Rogers

(Florence, Italy, 1933)
Rogers studied at the Architectural Association of London and specialized at Yale in New Haven. His first professional experiences took place between 1963 and 1967, when he was a member of Team 4, together with his wife, Su, and the Fosters. His tendency to insert formalist and Constructivist motifs in his projects, already visible in his last works with the group, became even more marked after his separation from the group and culminated in the project with which Rogers acquired international fame, the Georges Pompidou Centre in Paris, made in 1977 in collaboration with Renzo Piano. In 1977 he opened an office in London where he continued to work out his personal language, distinguished by the overt display of the structural and operating-plant elements of buildings, negating all traditional sense of a façade,

which has made him one of the emblematic exponents of high-tech architecture.

Aldo Rossi

(Milan, Italy, 1931–1997)
The fundamental elements in Rossi's formation, aside from his studies at the Milan Polytechnic, from which he graduated in 1959, were his editing of the magazine *Casabella-continuità* between 1955 and 1964 and his studies of Adolf Loos and Etienne Louis Boullée, which influenced his first works. In the 1960s he began the series of studies on the relationship between architectonic typology and urban morphology, collected in the book *L'Architettura della Città* (1966), a text destined to have a great deal of influence on later generations of architects. His theory of the presence of primary elements in the processes of construction of the city with which he affirmed the objective and impersonal

character of architecture became a reference point for neorationalism. The methodology of his theoretical efforts found fruitful confirmation in the poetic dimension of his design practice, based on the always new combinations of traditional and autobiographical architectonic elements, earning him numerous commissions and international recognitions.

Eero Saarinen

(Kirkkonummi, Finland, 1910–Ann Arbor, Michigan, USA, 1961)
Eero Saarinen, son of the equally well known architect Eliel Saarinen, emigrated to the United States with his parents in 1923. He studied sculpture in Paris between 1929 and 1930 and then studied architecture at Yale, earning his degree in 1934. In 1937 he joined his father's studio in Ann Arbor. After initial works of architecture, furnishings, and design that were characterized by a geometric and technological purism clearly derived from Mies van der Rohe, he turned to a stylistic pluralism and a continuous search for singular plastic forms, based on his youthful preference for sculpture, that were always combined in evocative, heterogeneous, and sometimes disturbing solutions that were hard to connect to any precise linguistic category. In his last years he reached a daring structural expressionism, legible in some of his most famous works, including his last challenge, the

elegant and expressive Terminal Building at Dulles International Airport in Washington, DC, from 1959 to 1964.

Eliel Saarinen

(Rantasalmi, Finland, 1873–Bloomfield, Michigan, USA, 1950)
Eliel Saarinen studied painting and architecture in Helsinki, where he was active as an architect from 1896 to 1923, the year in which he moved to the United States. His youthful works, made in collaboration with the architects Herman Gesellius and Armas Lindgren, show signs of the National Romantic style that, influenced by English models, was presented as an alternative to the dominant classicism. The collaboration among the three architects ended in 1904 when Saarinen won the competition for the main train station of

Helsinki, built between 1904 and 1919, on the basis of a design he created personally on a rationalist base influenced by German models and destined to become a primary model for railroad architecture in that period. During those same years he became greatly interested in urban planning, which from then on was an inseparable part of his architectonic projects, as in the complex of the Cranbrook Academy of Art, from 1926–1941, a synthesis of his romantic naturalism and the American pioneering tradition. His son trained in his Ann Arbor studio and continued its activity.

Antonio Sant'Elia

(Como, Italy, 1888–Monfalcone, Italy, 1916)
After technical studies in Como and a period working as a master builder in Milan, Sant'Elia took courses at the Brera Academy and earned a degree as professor of architectonic design at the Bologna Academy of Fine Arts in 1912. He opened his own studio in Milan and in 1914 joined the Futurist movement, for which he wrote the text of the "Manifesto of Futurist Architecture." From a formal matrix still tied to models from

the Vienna Secession, as in the Elisi Villa at San Maurizio, near Como, the only work Sant'Elia made in 1911, he later developed a volumetric and spatial style at the theoretical-design level that was a precursor of the later Constructivism movement and some lines of development of the Modern movement. The more than three-hundred designs he made, most of them between 1913 and 1914, give visionary form and image to a utopian metropolis of the future, with terraced skyscrapers, large multilevel arteries for vehicular traffic, and daring monumental buildings that could never have been constructed.

Carlo Scarpa

(Venice, Italy, 1906–Sendai, Japan, 1978)
Scarpa studied at the Academy of Fine Arts in Venice, earning his degree in 1926. Beginning in 1933 he was assistant and then professor at the University of Venice. He dedicated himself primarily to the production and arrangement of exhibitions and shows, the restoration of monumental complexes, and the building of shops and private homes, genres in which he was best able to express his artistic language, distinguished by a sure sense of proportion, daring combinations of materials, refined craftwork in details, and an intensity of spatial compositions reminiscent of ideas from *De Stijl*, Wright, and the Jugenstil. He revealed his poetics in the design of glassware and furnishings with which he debuted at the end of the

1920s, and he developed it further during the postwar period in important productions at the Biennale of Venice, to which he contributed throughout his life. His style reached one of its most mature moments in the Ottolenghi House in Bardolino, from 1974–1979.

Hans Scharoun

(Bremen, Germany, 1893–Berlin, Germany, 1972)
From 1912 to 1914 Scharoun studied at the Technische Hochschule in Berlin. His idea for an organic architecture that would be an alternative to rationalism immediately put him in the ranks of the Expressionist avant-garde. He was active in the Gläserne Kette, founded by Bruno Taut, and was a member of the Der Ring association. In these early years of activity he explored the possibilities of home designs in numerous sketches, competitions, and a few actual buildings. Unpopular with the Nazi regime, he withdrew during the period from 1933 to the end of the war, limiting his production to a few single-family homes and numerous designs. In the postwar period he was involved in the plans for the reconstruction of Berlin. He had many important projects and commissions during the

1950s. Without doubt, the most important creation of his later career was the Berlin Philharmonie of 1956–1963, his attempt at a vast typological renewal in which he gave preference to an increasingly organic spatiality while at the same time deliberately ignoring the formal details.

Rudolf Schwarz
(Strasburg, France, 1897–Cologne, Germany, 1961)
Schwarz trained at the Technische Hochschule in Berlin and went on to make an important contribution to the development of religious architecture with the design of numerous Catholic churches. He made himself known between 1929 and 1930 with the church of Corpus Domini at Aachen and intensified his activity in the postwar period, to which belong the reconstruction and new design of numerous religious

buildings. The modernization he applied to these works was both formal, often making use of symbolic layouts in the form of rings or chalices, and also functional, creating a sense of continuity between the area made for the faithful and that made for the altar. He presented his ideas and theories in two texts that also came to be used as guidebooks by those working in lay undertakings; Schwarz himself served as chief city planner for Cologne in 1946 and 1951. He had a strong influence on others also through his teaching activities, first as director of the School of Applied Arts in Aachen from 1927 to 1934 and later as teacher at the Academy of Düsseldorf from 1953 to 1961.

Shreve–Lamb–Harmon
The fame of this studio, founded in the 1920s by Richard Harold Shreve (1877–1946), William Frederick Lamb (shown in the photo; 1883–1946), and

Arthur Loomis Harmon (1878–1958), is tied to the construction of the Empire State Building, completed in 1931, which with its 380 meters of height was the tallest building in the world until 1974, the year of the construction of the Sears Tower

in Chicago. The other works made by the studio include an office building on Fifth Avenue in New York, from 1931, Hunter College, made in 1940, and the building for the New York Supreme Court, from 1957.

SITE (Sculpture In The Environment)
This multidisciplinary group of designers was founded in New York in 1969 by James Wines, Alison Sky, Michelle Stone, and Emilio Sousa. Their goal was to join art to architecture while at the same time freeing architecture from orthodox functionalism. The group attracted attention during the 1970s for the imaginative series

of stores designed for the Best Products supermarket chain, in which artistic concepts that distort the construction discipline were applied to architecture. The result was a series of façades transformed by the effect of imaginary external agents, such as an element resting casually atop a building, as in the store in Towson in 1978 or an element in ruin, as in the store in Milwaukee in 1984. The surprising results of these experiments won the group a series of commissions and construction projects throughout the world.

Álvaro Siza

(Matozinhos, Portugal, 1933)
After architecture studies
at the Escola Superior de Belas
Artes in Porto and a period of
apprenticeship with Fernando
Tàvora, Siza opened his own
studio in 1958 on the occasion
of his first professional
commissions.
His very first creations made
immediately clear that his was

an esthetic-critical attitude far
too original to be fit into any
paradigm of reference.
His language employs formal
elements drawn from a wide
variety of very different
sources, all of which, however,
lead back to the period of the
flowering of Modern
architecture, combined with a
profound attention to
topography and an effort to
match architecture to
environment.
This has earned him world
fame and increasingly
important commissions, often
outside Portugal.
His most important recent
work was the Portuguese
pavilion for the 1998
Exhibition in Lisbon.
Together with this intense
professional activity Siza
is also an active critic and
theoretician and has presented
his ideas in many essays and
interviews.

Eduardo Souto de Moura

(Porto, Portugal, 1952)
Between 1974 and 1979 Souto
de Moura studied architecture at
the Escola Superior de Belas
Artes in Porto, while at the
same time working with Álvaro
Siza. He began his professional
career on his own in 1980 with
the design of the covered market
in Braga, the language of which
revealed the Brutalist teaching of
his master, Fernando Tàvora. In
later works he abandoned
Brutalism in favor of an original
purism, a synthesis of regional
building traditions with abstract
elements drawn from the works
of Mies van de Rohe and
Barragán. This language, which
he applied to various luxurious
residential buildings made in
Porto in the 1980s, helped him
win many national and
international competitions. In
addition to his activity as an
architect Souto de Moura is also
an active designer, with furniture
designs in Portugal and
elsewhere, and teacher, first at
the Escola Superior de Belas

Artes and more recently in the
architecture faculty of the
University of Porto.

Rudolf Steiner

(Kraljevec, Croatia,
1861–Dornach, Switzerland,
1925)

Steiner is known primarily as a
philosopher and is included
within the history of
architecture because of a single
work that he made at Dornach
near Basel in the 1920s: the
Goetheanum, a temple-theater
made to host the ritual
performances of the
Mysteriendrama, composed by
Steiner himself. The first
version, built entirely in wood,
was erected between 1913 and
1920 with a layout based on
intersecting circles. Destroyed
by fire in 1922, the building
was rebuilt between 1924 and
1928 with a structure in
reinforced concrete on a large
irregular base. Designed by
Steiner and built on the basis of
clay models, the Goetheanum
constituted one of the most
notable examples of
Expressionist architecture, its
monumental mass based on
allusions to human and natural
forms. This singular experience,
along with Steiner's ideas on
architecture, published in 1919,
contributed to the formation of
the "living organic architecture"
movement.

Robert A. M. Stern

(New York, USA, 1939)
After studies at Columbia
University in New York and at
Yale in New Haven he worked
with Richard Meier and later as
a city planner for New York. He

in collaboration with James Gowan on a series of buildings with an unmistakable Brutalist language. He began a period working alone in 1964, making large university buildings and taking part in several competitions with designs that reveal a receptive dialogue with the context. In 1970 he began

opened his own office in New York in 1977. Once ranked among the leading representatives of Postmodernism, he is today a supporter of "modern traditionalism" in which his works, both residential buildings and offices, are conceived as total cultural products, with constant references to other periods, regions, or personalities of architecture, always cited with great originality and skill. He shows special sensitivity when called on to perform the enlargement of an existing structure or the insertion of a new structure, as in the case with the Ohrstrom Library of the St Paul School in Concord, New Hampshire, from 1987 to 1991. His fame is also tied to his activity as an historian of architecture, a critic, and a writer .

James Stirling
(Glasgow, UK, 1926–London, UK, 1992)
After studies at the University of Liverpool and a period of apprenticeship in the London office of Lyons, Israel and Ellis, Stirling began his professional activity, which can be divided into three main periods. During the first, which covers the years from 1956 to 1963, he worked

his third period, working in collaboration with Michael Wilford, which led to the commission for the Staatsgalerie of Stuttgart of 1977. One of the architect's most important and controversial projects, it introduced the version of design, based on a strong expressive language and eclectic experimentation, that he was to apply to later projects.

Louis Henry Sullivan
(Boston, USA, 1856–Chicago, USA, 1924)
After a brief period of studies, first at MIT and then at the École des Beaux-Arts in Paris, Sullivan joined the office of Dankmar Adler in 1879, becoming a full partner in 1883. In 1886 he began work on the Auditorium Building in Chicago. Although the synthesis between structure and decoration was not completely successful, Sullivan's philosophy

was made clear, most of all his desire to make the architectonic form result from the harmonic and organic growth of its various parts. In later buildings the expressive unity that was lacking in the façade of the Auditorium Building was achieved through the rhythmic arrangement of equal stories, accentuated by vertical openings and minimal decoration. After Alder's retirement in 1895, Sullivan received fewer commissions. Even so he made the great Schlesinger and Meyer warehouse in Chicago (today Carson Pirie Scott & Co.), the work in which his style, synthesized in the famous statement "form should follow function" finds its fulfillment in the use of the support skeleton as the basis of the composition.

Kenzo Tange
(Imabari, Japan, 1913)
After earning a degree in engineering from the University of Tokyo in 1938 Tange began working in the office of Kunio Mayekawa, a former collaborator of Le Corbusier. He went out on his own in 1946, making a series of important projects destined to bring about a renewal of

Japanese architecture by freeing it from Western models. The works he made during the 1950s were distinguished by a symbolic rereading of the Japanese architectonic tradition joined to an open-minded application of the Modern language. With the increase in interest in urbanistic problems in the 1960s, Tange made several large-scale projects, including his plan for the city of Tokyo of 1960—perhaps his most important work—and buildings with strong urban impact that made clear his approach to the style of the Metabolism Group. He gained fame in 1964 for the arenas he made for the XXVIII Olympic Games in Tokyo, leading to commissions from throughout the world. The style of these later works has been less characteristic and more international.

Bruno Taut
(Königsberg, Germany, 1880–Istanbul, Turkey, 1938)
Taut trained at the construction school in Königsberg and opened his own office in Berlin in 1909. He immediately attracted great attention with his "Monument to Steel" Pavilion at the Leipzig exhibition in 1913 and with the Glashaus at the first exhibition

of the Deutscher Werkbund in Cologne in 1914. The latter work brought him into contact with the poet and utopian Paul Scheerbart, whose ideas for Glasarchitektur greatly influenced Taut, so much that they led, during World War I, to the brief but intense phase of his theoretical research,

destined to be the guiding light to the more radical avant-garde wing of German Expressionism. In 1920 he moved closer to rationalism and in later years was kept busy designing large works of public housing to which he applied his Tayloristic theories of functional and economic architecture, theories that led to the realization of some of the most interesting works of twentieth-century architecture, such as the *Siedlungen* of Britz and of Zehlendorf. He carried on intense teaching activity between 1930 and 1933, when for political reasons he emigrated first to Japan and then to Turkey.

Giuseppe Terragni
(Meda, Italy, 1904–Como, Italy, 1943)
In 1929 Terragni earned his diploma from the Milan Polytechnic and while still very young became a member of

both Gruppo 7 and MIAR (Movimento Italiano per l'Architettura Razionale), immediately adhering to rationalism and, thanks to his strongly classical bent, contributing to freeing it from the dictates of the European Modern movement. Terragni's undisputed masterpiece is the Casa del Fascio in Como, from 1932 to 1936, in which he made clear the abstract , independent style that distinguished his personal language. His highly original adhesion to classical modernity, halfway between academic classicism and orthodox rationalism, based on an astute elaboration of the best aspects of Italian twentieth-century poetics and the painting of Giorgio de Chirico, was destined in the 1960s to influence the rational architecture of Aldo Rossi and the work of the New York Five.

Heinrich Tessenow
(Rostock, Germany, 1876–Berlin, Germany, 1950)
Tessenow began his career in his father's carpentry workshop, an experience that led him, over the course of his difficult career as a teacher and architect, to commit himself to the rebirth of artisan culture, which in his opinion could be achieved by

reviving the values of humility and group effort that are typical of all the applied arts. In 1909 he became an assistant in the Dresden Polytechnic and began his professional activity, collaborating in the creation of Hellerau, the first German garden city, where he applied the essential forms that distinguished his architectonic

language. In 1910 he became a member of the Deutscher Werkbund. In 1913 he was called to teach at the Vienna art school, where he met Wagner, Hoffmann, Klimt, and Moser. In 1926 he became professor at the Technische Hoschschule in Berlin, where he made various works and took part in numerous competitions. By 1934 the advent of Nazism had isolated him both culturally and professionally.

Oswald Mathias Ungers
(Kaisersech, Eifel, Germany, 1926)
Having completed his studies at the Technische Hochschule of Karlsruhe, Ungers opened a studio in Cologne in 1950. He earned a great deal of attention with a series of buildings in the 1950s, but in the middle of the

1960s his activity underwent a sudden stop, which gave him time for a period of reflection and theoretical research. Beginning with a critical revision of rationalism and organic expressionism, he arrived at the definition of a methodology of design based on the composition of geometric volumes in heterogeneous wholes. This method was expressed in the projects he made at the end of the 1960s, anticipating similar theoretical positions taken by Aldo Rossi, Robert Venturi, Colin Rowe, and Fred Koetter. His many creations, which reveal his ongoing efforts towards urban renewal and reworking the morphology of the city, have contributing to making him the most famous international representative of rational architecture in Germany.

Jørn Utzon
(Copenhagen, Denmark, 1918)
Utzon studied at the Copenhagen Academy of Arts. Influenced by the ideas of Alvar Aalto and Gunnar Asplund, in whose offices he worked for a certain period, as well as by those of Frank Lloyd Wright, whom he met during a stay in the United States in 1949, he

was soon drawn to an organic conception of architecture. In 1950 he opened a studio in Copenhagen and put in practice his ideas for a progressive architecture that takes its teaching from nature and makes use of new materials suitable to specific demands. He applied these ideas to a series of very different projects, all

distinguished by imagination, vitality, and technical skill. In 1957 he won first prize in the competition for the Sydney Opera House, which became his unquestioned masterpiece, the work responsible for his world fame. To work on it he moved to Australia in 1962; in 1966 he returned to Denmark, leaving conclusion of the work to other architects. He has since made many works inspired by the construction methods he first applied in the Sydney theater.

Livio Vacchini
(Locarno, Switzerland, 1933)
After studies at the Technische Hochschule in Zurich and years of apprenticeship in Stockholm and Paris, Vacchini opened his own studio in Locarno in 1961 together with Luigi Snozzi,

active from 1962 to 1971. Returning to the theoretical tradition of classicism, his architecture presents an ideal continuity of the styles inaugurated by the Modern architects of classical extraction, such as Perret, Mies van der Rohe, and Kahn. The works of his first phase were distinguished by clear, simple geometric structures; he then moved to a further simplification of which his own atelier, of 1985, is a poetic manifesto. He continued to emancipate the formal typologies from established schemes and to move them towards becoming architectonic archetypes. In his most recent works he exploits the possibilities offered by reinforced and precompressed concrete to complete his efforts towards a correspondence between structure and form.

Henry van de Velde
(Antwerp, Belgium, 1863–Zurich, Switzerland, 1957)
Van de Velde studied painting at the Academy of Fine Arts in Antwerp and then in Paris, where he met Impressionist and Symbolist artists whose vision of space seemed to indicate new routes for architecture. The writings of Ruskin and Morris directed him towards a social vision of the work of art and led him to abandon painting in favor of furniture design. In 1896 he made his first work of architecture, the Bloemenwerf House in Uccle, near Brussels, in which he displayed the primary characteristics of his artistic thinking: awareness of the functions of constructions and of the value of use along with the rejection of naturalistic ornaments or stylistic elements from the past. The fluent forms and curving lines of his furnishings and his architecture, most highly appreciated in Germany, made Van de Velde one of the primary exponents of Art Nouveau.

Robert Venturi
(Philadelphia, USA, 1925)
Venturi studied at Princeton University in New Jersey and worked in the studios of Eero Saarinen and Louis I. Kahn. In 1958 he set up an office together with several associates. In 1967 his wife, Denise Scott-Brown, joined the studio, from then on working together with Venturi on many projects and on the theoretical writings to which he owes his world fame. The studio, known as Venturi, Scott-Brown and Associates since 1989, has created many very different structures over the course of the years, but all have had in common the attempt to translate motifs taken from the psychology of perception into an autonomous and deeply American architectonic language. This led to the intriguing and polemical invitation to consider commercial architecture, with its elements of advertizing and neon, as sources to draw on for the design of contemporary architecture, a notion that became a key concept within Postmodernism.

Otto Wagner
(Penzing, Vienna, Austria, 1841–Vienna, Austria, 1918)
After studies at the Technische Hochschule in Vienna and at the Bauakademie in Berlin, he completed his training at the Academy of Fine Arts in Vienna, from 1861 to 1863. He made numerous works in Vienna using a robust, restrained classical style, soon becoming one of the best-known professional architects in the city and receiving many public and academic commissions. He expressed his ideas in *Moderne Architecktur* (1896), calling for the need for a new approach to architecture and formulating the principles

of an architecture generated by functional aims and expressed by calling attention to building principles and to the materials used. He put these theories to use in the Post Office Savings Bank in Vienna in the early years of the twentieth century. With his teaching, his writing, and his buildings Wagner had a strong influence on a large part of European avant-garde architecture.

Frank Lloyd Wright

(Richland Center, Wisconsin, USA, 1867–Phoenix, Arizona, USA, 1959)
After a short period studying engineering at the University of Wisconsin, Wright entered the Adler and Sullivan studio in 1888, collaborating with them for six years. During that period he completed his training, which came to blend the individualistic ideology of the American frontier with a love of nature and notions from the shingle style as well as Japanese architecture. All this

contributed to the development of an "organic" ideal, anticlassical and anti-European, leading him to seek out a form of architectural expression with genuine American bases. The professional career he began in 1893 was destined to last more than seventy years, during which the incessant changes of forms and the development of an endless variety of ideas evoked the myth of the American pioneer forever looking for something new to conquer. Wright's individualistic language did not generate students, but he did have many imitators, and he influenced the most disparate forms of architecture. The results of his continuous experiments are, among many others, the series of Prairie Houses, the later Usonian Houses, and finally the spatial continuum he created by the union of the spiral and the circle in the Guggenheim Museum in New York.

Peter Zumthor

(Basel, Switzerland, 1943)
After apprenticeship as a carpenter–cabinetmaker, Zumthor studied interior architecture at the Schule für Gestaltung in Basel and furniture design at the Pratt Institute in New York. Back in Switzerland he worked as a consultant for the office overseeing the preservation of monuments in the Graubünden Canton. In 1979 he opened his own studio in Haldenstein. His first works showed an affinity with Italian rational architecture. With time he developed his own, thoroughly

original, style in which the controlled use of materials, building elements, light, and space permitted him to create works of high quality and sensitivity. He has attracted much interest at the international level. His more important works include the exhibition space "Topographie des Terrors" in Berlin in 1993 and the thermal baths in Vals, made between 1991 and 1996.